Rubicon

Second Edition

Hugh Holmes

MENTOR BOOKS

MENTOR BOOKS
43 Furze Road
Sandyford Industrial Estate
Dublin 18
Tel: 01-295 2112
Fax: 01-295 2114
Website: www.mentorbooks.ie
e-mail: admin@mentorbooks.ie

Edited by:
Una Whelan and Treasa O'Mahony

Cover, typesetting and design:
Kathryn O'Sullivan

© Hugh Holmes 2019

ISBN: 978-1-912514-42-7

Acknowledgements

The Publishers would like to thank the following for kind permission to reproduce material:
CartoonStock.com; Random House for an extract from *The Lost Continent* by Bill Bryson published by Secker & Warburg;
Mary Arrigan for 'Making a Fiery Impression' by Mary Arrigan; *The Sunday Times* for 'Christmas is a Conspiracy against
Women' by Marian Keyes and 'Who's Deprived Now' by India Knight; Donal Minihane for 'Thank You for Your Feedback'
by Donal Minihane; Faber & Faber for an extract from *Lord of the Flies* by William Golding; Abner Stein for *All Summer
in a Day* by Ray Bradbury; Julia Copus for 'The Back Seat of My Mother's Car' by Julia Copus; Claudine Nowlan for
'Weakness' by Alden Nowlan; Bloodaxe Books for 'For Meg' by Fluer Adcock and 'The Immortals' by Rita Ann Higgins;
The Wylie Agency for an excerpt from *The Crucible* by Arthur Miller; Paweł Kuczyński for three cartoons; Little, Brown
Book Group for an extract from *The Glass Castle* by Jeanette Walls.

Contents

For Emma, Marnie and Tilda

Chapter 1:
True Tales –
Anecdote, Autobiography, Memoir and Personal Writing

There are no limits to the fantastic worlds, people and situations that writers are free to create. Imagination is a powerful source for so much wonderful writing. However, many writers draw on their own lives for inspiration. These experiences can prove very valuable for a writer, and, when explored creatively, even the most everyday events can be rich in meaning.

This chapter shows how writers can use their own personal memories, from simple day-to-day events to incredible experiences, as a source for great writing material.

As you read and discuss the pieces in this chapter, you should reflect on your own life and experiences to inspire your writing.

The true tales in this chapter have been arranged thematically – Early Days, Family, Offbeat.

Facing Down a Bully

Pat Dargan

Family Fortunes is a regular feature of *The Irish Times* newspaper in which ordinary people contribute stories about their pasts. The article below is from that series in which the writer remembers dealing with a particularly powerful school bully.

Growing up in Limerick during the 1950s, it was commonly believed that the only way to handle a bully was to face him down. However, the bully in my life was my teacher, a Christian Brother. This gaunt, sinister-looking man was noted for his use of 'the leather', which he liberally meted out to the pupils for even the most minor failure in school lessons; not an easy threat for a small, 10-year-old schoolboy to face down. However, the solution to my difficulty materialised from an unusual direction.

One particular morning, during English class, the teacher began asking each pupil to spell a word. As spelling was not my strong point, I was apprehensive. When my turn came around I was asked to spell 'laugh'. In my panic I stuttered: 'L-A-F'. First there was total silence. Then the teacher screamed, 'L-A-F, L-A-F! You stupid boy I'll give you something to L-A-F about', as he charged down the classroom to where I was standing. His face was purple with rage as he brandished his leather about him like a person in a craze. I was terrified.

First, I could feel my vision clouding over. Then, as he drew near, I felt a sour feeling in my gut, as my partially digested breakfast began to force its way back up my throat into my mouth, from where it exploded outwards in foul-smelling spray. It hit the teacher in the chest and slowly spread down his black soutane, bringing a halt to his charge.

He was stunned and never uttered a word. He immediately left the classroom and returned some time later with a change of clothing, but made no reference to the event. As far as the rest of the class was concerned, I was a hero: the only schoolboy who had ever faced down the teacher. Throughout the remainder of the year, the brother never again asked me a question. I had effectively faced down and defeated my bully.

– From *The Irish Times*

GLOSSARY
meted: dealt / distributed
apprehensive: anxious / worried
brandished: waved something in a threatening way
soutane: a gown worn by men in religious orders

Reading for Meaning

1. Give two reasons why the author panicked when he was called on to spell.
2. Why was the author considered to be a 'hero' by his classmates?
3. When the teacher returned, why do you think he 'made no reference to the event'?
4. How does the writer create a sense of tension in this piece?
5. (a) The writer begins his story with the sentence, 'Growing up in Limerick during the 1950s, it was commonly believed that the only way to handle a bully was to face him down.' Do you think that this idea is still believed nowadays? Explain your answer.
   (b) If someone close to you was being bullied, what advice would you give on how to deal with this situation?

Style Guide

Anecdote: An anecdote is a short account of a single incident. Anecdotes are often amusing, entertaining or unusual or they may be told to illustrate a point.
Our own lives can provide interesting moments to write about. Personal anecdotes can bring colour to a piece of writing or can form the main story. *Facing Down a Bully* is a personal anecdote as it is a short account of a moment from the writer's schooldays.

Writer's Workshop

A Personal Anecdote: In *Facing Down a Bully*, Pat Dargan recalls a moment from his early schooldays. Write an anecdote about a moment you remember from primary school. This may be a humorous event, a time you were unhappy or a moment when you learned a valuable lesson.

Links

You can link *Facing Down a Bully* in terms of its subject matter and themes to other texts in this book and elsewhere:
In this book: Sylvia Plath's *Superman and Paula Brown's New Snowsuit* (page 118)
Elsewhere: Tobias Wolff's memoir, *This Boy's Life*; Margaret Atwood's novel, *Cat's Eye*

Space to Play

Paul Merton

Paul Merton is a comedian and presenter. In this adapted extract from his autobiography, Only When I Laugh, he recalls the council flat in London where he grew up.

I used to enjoy sitting inside my parents' wardrobe. At the age of five, I was small enough to squeeze into it but sufficiently strong to hold the door closed behind me. I often sat in the darkness amidst the aroma of mothballs, imagining the great adventures that could be had if only I could find a secret door that would lead to a strange and wonderful world where small shy boys were prized for their ability to sit inside large items of furniture. I enjoyed being slightly scared in the darkness. I was in another world. Invisible. An outsider inside. That fascination for hidden worlds has never left me.

In the centre of London, I'm always intrigued by those bits and pieces that only a few of us ever see. The other side of the houses and offices that you pass in the street. Rooftops and iron fire escapes leading from obscure doors down to unsuspected alleyways leading to who knows where. A landscape of air-conditioning units and air vents. I always look out the back windows whenever I find myself in Soho, or around Fulham where I spent my early childhood, and I'm seldom disappointed. Occasionally you glimpse the prize that is a rooftop garden, with dozens of green plants and a couple of deckchairs. Up high where no one at street level can see you. A patio in the sky. An ordinary part of our world, but secretly set apart from it, somewhere you can drift off to.

Just like the inside of my head.

Our council flat in Robert Owen House was a cosy affair and beautifully situated in grounds set back from the Fulham Palace Road. The flats were built in the mid-1930s to accommodate those made homeless by the slum clearance programme around the environs of Wandsworth Bridge.

Grandad's club foot guaranteed us a ground floor flat because, although the flats ran to four floors, there were no lifts. We had a living room, a small kitchen, a short hallway with a couple of bedrooms off it, and a toilet. I remember my parents' bedroom and my room, but not my grandad's. I suspect I was never allowed in there. However, one thing I do remember all too clearly is the wallpaper in my room. It's one of my earliest memories and still gives me the shudders to this day. My room was decorated on all four walls with a grotesque tableau featuring gnomes and goblins with distorted evil faces, long prominent noses and dark black eyes. Some of them were mending shoes. Others were sitting upon giant toadstools. As light seeped through cracks in the curtains, I would glimpse malignant faces grinning at me. The stuff of nightmares stuck on your wall, staring at you forever!

I've also always been afraid of balloons bursting. I see a brightly coloured balloon and I recoil at the prospect of it suddenly popping. To explode from a buoyant globe of fun, floating in slow motion, to sudden, ragged scraps of torn rubber is a traumatic event whichever way you look at it. Especially if you're a balloon.

The keen amateur psychologists amongst you will be pleased to know that this phobia can be directly traced back to an incident that I have no memory of, but which my mother told me about many years later. It's a simple story involving a twelve-month-old baby, his father, a big red shiny balloon and a pin. According to Mum, I was holding the balloon with gurgling delight and bubbling laughter when Dad stuck the pin in sharply and literally burst my world, causing me to cry uncontrollably for the best part of half an hour.

Did Dad really hate me so much to upset me so unnecessarily? Or was he in a rather unthinking way simply playing a rather stupid joke which he thought might get a laugh? I'm sure it's the latter, because he could be a fun and caring parent.

Kevin was my first real friend as opposed to the many imaginary creatures that bubbled up from my brain. (I used to play on my own with my fingers and thumbs, investing each one of them with a character. They had conversations between themselves. An only child finds games to play.) Kevin looked like an angel with his white mop of curly hair. He was a couple of years younger than me so I was generally in the position of coming up with games and ideas. Once I tore up a sheet of white paper into tiny pieces and, with Kevin by my side, I threw these scraps up into the air from the height of a third-floor balcony. We watched them flutter up and away in the wind.

'Do you see these bits of paper flying away?' I asked.

'Yes,' said Kevin, watching them with wide-eyed wonder.

'Later, those bits of paper will turn into white butterflies,' I said.

'Will they?' said Kevin, his voice full of excitement.

'Yes, I bet we see one tomorrow.'

And he believed me. I didn't feel I was playing a trick on Kevin because I half-believed it myself. Imagine the beauty of such a feat! We saw quite a few white butterflies over the next couple of days, and we were both very excited to see the paper transformed.

– From *Only When I Laugh* (adapted)

Reading for Meaning

1. Describe the type of world Paul Merton grew up in.
2. What evidence is there in this extract to show that the writer was an imaginative and creative child?
3. How does Merton capture the unique perspective of a child in this extract?
4. Do any of the memories described by the writer remind you of your own childhood? Explain in detail.

Style Guide

Writing with Colour: In writing, the ordinary can be made extraordinary. Simple details and ordinary events can be transformed if the writing is colourful.

In the extract on pages 10–11, Paul Merton's quite ordinary childhood world is made interesting by the colourful details he adds. His description of the bedroom wallpaper adds colour to his writing as we can imagine the pattern in great detail. Similarly, the anecdote about the balloon and paper butterflies are colourful notes that help to paint a picture of his childhood.

In your own personal writing, try to add colourful details that will lift the writing and keep the reader interested.

Autobiography: An autobiography is an account of a person's life written by that person. It usually aims to tell the full story of the person's life from childhood to the present day. Autobiographies are interesting because they give personal insight into the thoughts and experiences of the writer. However, it should be remembered that the writer may have an interest in presenting him/herself in a favourable way.

A biography is an account of a person's life written by someone else.

Writer's Workshop

First Impressions of the World: Paul Merton successfully offers a child's point of view of his childhood world in this extract. Cast your mind back to your early days. Write a short composition in which you focus on the world as you remember it as a child. Where did you like to go? How did you see this world? What were your fears and hopes?

Links

You can link *Space to Play* in terms of its subject matter and themes to other texts in this book and elsewhere:
In this book: Bill Bryson's *Growing Up in Des Moines* (page 16)
Elsewhere: Paul Auster's autobiography, *Report from the Interior*

Santa's Borrowed Suit

Giles Brody

The Little Book of Christmas Memories is an anthology of personal Christmas stories from some of Ireland's best-loved writers. The book was compiled in aid of the Aware charity. Giles Brody's hilarious story 'Santa's Borrowed Suit' is taken from that anthology.

Santa came to our house on Christmas Eve looking for his suit. Daddy had told me he'd borrowed the suit for his work social. I was worried that Daddy would forget to return the suit and that Santa would be forced to go around the world delivering presents to the boys and girls with only his beard to keep him warm. This worried me.

On the days before Christmas Day I kept looking in Mammy and Daddy's room and every day Santa's suit would still be there hanging in a wrinkly heap in a bag on the back of the door. What was Daddy playing at? Did he want Santa to catch a cold? Did he care about all the boys and girls in the world getting their presents? Maybe he's jealous because Santa doesn't give him presents anymore.

I remember asking Daddy when Santa stopped coming to him. He said Santa stopped when he was twelve. I asked why? Daddy said it was something to do with letting the younger children enjoy Christmas but I think it's because Daddy was bold and Santa put him on his naughty list. But then why would Santa loan him his suit for the work social?

That and a lot more questions were buzzing around my brain as I tried to go to sleep on Christmas Eve. Mammy and Daddy had gone to the pub to meet the neighbours. It was a tradition and it meant that none of the parents would disturb Santa while he was delivering presents. I didn't want to disturb Santa either, but I did want to see him, so I hid behind the sofa with a few stuffed bears for company and my blue rug in case it got cold. At midnight there was no sound of hooves but there was a tap tap tap on the window followed by a smashing sound. A minute later Santa had climbed in through our window and was standing in our living room.

I knew Daddy had his suit so Santa wouldn't look like he did in pictures. I didn't expect him to be wearing a black tracksuit and a black woolly hat. He was fat, but not Santa fat, and his beard was black with flecks of white. Aha, I thought, clearly snow from the North Pole.

Santa had a lamp on his head and was picking up our television when I walked into the living room.

'Santa, your suit isn't under the telly silly. It's in a bag in Mammy and Daddy's room.'

Santa froze, hoping I didn't see him. He looked pale and his lips were trembling. I'd realised then that I'd given him a big fright so I said sorry.

'I didn't mean to scare you, Santa.'

'Santa?' Santa said.

'You don't look like Santa but that's because Daddy has your suit in a bag. When you put it on you get fat and your beard will turn white.'

Santa shook his head slowly and smiled.

'I'll go and get your costume from Mammy and Daddy's room. While I'm gone you should eat some of the treats we left out to help fatten you up.'

Santa nodded. He wasn't jolly like the Santa in the shopping centre. He must have been tired from travelling all round the world. By the time I'd returned with his costume, Santa was trying to climb back out the window.

'Santa, don't go!'

The sash on the window came down and bumped Santa on the head. I ran over to see if he was alright.

'Santa, there's red coming from your head!'

Santa nodded and made a shhh gesture. He thought Mammy and Daddy were in the house and he mustn't have wanted to disturb them. He really was the nicest man in the world!

Santa said he'd dress himself in his suit so long as I stayed quiet. He wobbled about as he put it on over his black tracksuit. I asked him lots of questions about the North Pole. He said he'd answer them so long as I was quiet. Sometimes for fun I'd start off asking a question very quietly and then YELL AT THE END. It gave Santa such a fright.

A few minutes later, Mammy and Daddy returned from the pub. Daddy was so happy to see Santa that he gave him a big hug into the wall. Santa fell on the ground and must have hurt his head because the next thing I knew, Daddy was sitting on Santa's head and calling for help on his phone. Daddy told Mammy to bring me to bed. 'Goodnight Santa!' I said sleepily as Mammy picked me up and brought me upstairs. 'I'm glad you got your suit back!'

– From *The Little Book of Christmas Memories*

Style Guide

The Unreliable Narrator: First-person ('I') narratives can offer the reader an interesting point of view. When the narrator is a character in the story, the reader needs to be aware that they are hearing only one side of the story. A first-person narrator may have feelings and prejudices that affect the telling of the story. If the narrator is untrustworthy, he/she may be referred to as an 'unreliable narrator'. Narrators who are mentally ill, children or deceitful may often offer a skewed version of events.

Santa's Borrowed Suit is told from the perspective of a child. This means that the reader needs to 'read between the lines' in order to pick out the true events. This technique adds colour and humour to the story as we imagine ourselves in the naïve (innocent) position of the child.

Reading for Meaning

1. What do you learn about the narrator from his account of this incident?
2. The narrator of this story is unreliable. Give an account of what really happened.
3. Why do you think 'Santa' agrees to put his costume on at the boy's request?
4. How do you think 'Santa' felt throughout this ordeal?
5. Do you find this piece amusing?

Writer's Workshop

Newspaper Article: It is the following day and the media are reporting on the incident described in this story. Write a newspaper article based on the event. You may wish to include interviews with the narrator, the narrator's parents or the authorities. Alternatively, you could create a short video report to be aired on the 6 o'clock news.

Links

You can link *Santa's Borrowed Suit* in terms of its use of the unreliable narrator to other texts in this book and elsewhere:

In this book: Edgar Allan Poe's *The Tell-Tale Heart* (page 130)
Elsewhere: Morris Gleitzman's novel, *Once*

Growing Up in Des Moines

Bill Bryson

In his travel book, *The Lost Continent*, Bill Bryson describes his journey around small towns in the United States in search of the 'real America'. In this extract he describes growing up in his hometown: Des Moines, Iowa.

I come from Des Moines. Somebody had to.

When you come from Des Moines you either accept the fact without question and settle down with a local girl named Bobbi and get a job at the Firestone factory and live there for ever and ever, or you spend your adolescence moaning at length about what a dump it is and how you can't wait to get out, and then you settle down with a local girl named Bobbi and get a job at the Firestone factory and live there for ever and ever.

Hardly anyone ever leaves. This is because Des Moines is the most powerful hypnotic known to man. Outside town there is a big sign that says WELCOME TO DES MOINES. THIS IS WHAT DEATH IS LIKE. There isn't really. I just made that up. But the place does get a grip on you. People who have nothing to do with Des Moines drive in off the interstate, looking for gas or hamburgers, and stay for ever. There's a New Jersey couple up the street from my parents' house whom you see wandering around from time to time looking faintly puzzled but strangely serene. Everybody in Des Moines is strangely serene.

When I was growing up I used to think that the best thing about coming from Des Moines was that it meant you didn't come from anywhere else in Iowa. By Iowa standards, Des Moines is a Mecca of cosmopolitanism, a dynamic hub of wealth and education, where people wear three piece suits and dark socks, often simultaneously. During the annual state high school basketball tournament, when the hayseeds from out in the state would flood into the city for a week, we used to accost them downtown and snidely offer to show them how to ride an escalator or negotiate a revolving door. This wasn't always so far from reality. My friend Stan, when he was about sixteen, had to go and stay with his cousin in some remote, dusty hamlet called Dog Water or Dunceville or some such improbable spot – the kind of place where if a dog gets run over by a truck everybody goes out to have a look at it. By the second week, delirious with boredom, Stan insisted that he and his cousin drive the fifty miles into the county town, Hooterville, and find something to do. They went bowling at an alley with warped lanes and chipped balls and afterwards had a chocolate soda and looked at a *Playboy* in a drugstore, and on the way home the cousin sighed with immense satisfaction and said, 'Gee thanks, Stan. That was the best time I ever had in my whole life!' It's true.

I had to drive to Minneapolis once, and I went on a back road just to see the country. But there was nothing to see. It's just flat and hot, and full of corn and soya beans and hogs. Every once in a while you come across a farm or some dead little town where the liveliest thing is the flies. I remember one long, shimmering stretch where I could see a couple of miles down the highway and there was a brown dot beside the road. As I got closer I saw it was a man sitting on a box by his front yard, in some six-house town with a name like Spigot or Urinal, watching my approach with inordinate interest. He watched me zip past and in the rear-view mirror I could see him still watching me going on down the road until at last I disappeared into a heat haze. The whole thing must have taken about five minutes. I wouldn't be surprised if even now he thinks of me from time to time.

– From *The Lost Continent* (adapted)

Reading for Meaning

1. What do you think Bill Bryson is suggesting when he writes, 'I come from Des Moines. Somebody had to.'?
2. What is your impression of Des Moines from this extract?
3. Based on this extract, do you feel that Bryson is an amusing writer?
4. (a) Bill Bryson often exaggerates in this extract. Write down two examples.
   (b) Why do you think Bryson uses exaggeration in this extract?
5. This extract contains a number of anecdotes (see page 9). Describe one that you find interesting and explain why it interests you.

Style Guide

Hyperbole: Hyperbole is another word for exaggeration. Writers often use it to emphasise an idea or to amuse the reader. For example, the sentence 'We had to wait an eternity in the queue' is not literally true, but it stresses the idea that it was a long wait.

Bill Bryson uses hyperbole throughout this extract. He exaggerates the idea that Des Moines and parts of rural America are dull places. This communicates his impression of these places and adds colour and humour to the writing.

Writer's Workshop

Where I'm From: Write a short personal composition describing the place that you come from. You might try to use hyperbole like Bryson does to emphasise an idea. Try to make your writing colourful and interesting for the reader. Include anecdotes in your composition to help the reader form an impression of the place.

Letter from Des Moines: Imagine you are from Des Moines and you have just read this extract. Write a letter to Bill Bryson commenting on his portrayal of Des Moines.

Links

You can link *Growing Up in Des Moines* in terms of its setting to other texts in this book and elsewhere:
In this book: Bill Bryson's *The Toity Jar* (page 29)
Elsewhere: Lasse Hallström's film, *What's Eating Gilbert Grape?*

I Was on Fire

Jeanette Walls

In her memoir, The Glass Castle, Jeanette Walls remembers her extraordinary childhood in which she was raised in extreme poverty and with little parental supervision. In this extract she recounts her earliest memory.

I was on fire.

It's my earliest memory. I was three years old, and we were living in a trailer park in a southern Arizona town whose name I never knew. I was standing on a chair in front of the stove, wearing a pink dress my grandmother had bought for me. Pink was my favourite color. The dress's skirt stuck out like a tutu, and I liked to spin around in front of the mirror, thinking I looked like a ballerina. But at that moment, I was wearing the dress to cook hot dogs, watching them swell and bob in the boiling water as the late morning sunlight filtered in through the trailer's small kitchenette window.

I could hear Mom in the next room singing while she worked on one of her paintings. Juju, our black mutt, was watching me. I stabbed one of the hot dogs with a fork and bent over and offered it to him. The wiener was hot, so Juju licked at it tentatively, but when I stood up and started stirring the hot dogs again, I felt a blaze of heat on my right side. I turned to see where it was coming from and realised my dress was on fire. Frozen with fear, I watched the yellow white flames make a ragged brown line up the pink fabric of my skirt and climb my stomach. Then the flames leaped up, reaching my face.

I screamed. I smelled the burning and heard a horrible crackling as the fire singed my hair and eyelashes. Juju was barking. I screamed again.

Mom ran into the room.

'Mommy, help me!' I shrieked. I was still standing on the chair, swatting at the fire with the fork I had been using to stir the hot dogs.

Mom ran out of the room and came back with one of the army surplus blankets I hated because the wool was so scratchy. She threw the blanket around me to smother the flames. Dad had gone off in the car, so Mom grabbed me and my younger brother, Brian, and hurried over to the trailer next to ours. The woman who lived there was hanging her laundry on the clothesline. She had clothespins in her mouth. Mom, in an unnaturally calm voice, explained what had happened and asked if we could please have a ride to the hospital. The woman dropped her clothespins and laundry right there in the dirt and, without saying anything, ran for her car . . .

The doctors said I was lucky to be alive. They took patches of skin from my upper thigh and put them over the most badly burned parts of my stomach, ribs and chest. They said it was called a skin graft. When they were finished, they wrapped my entire right side in bandages.

'Look, I'm a half mummy,' I said to one of the nurses. She smiled and put my right arm in a sling and attached it to the headboard so I couldn't move it.

The nurses and doctors kept asking me questions: How did you get burned? Have your parents ever hurt you? Why do you have all these bruises and cuts? My parents never hurt me, I said. I got the cuts and bruises playing outside and the burns from cooking hot dogs. They asked what I was doing cooking hot dogs by myself at the age of three. It was easy, I said. You just put the hot dogs in the water and boil them. It wasn't like there was some complicated recipe that you had to be old enough to follow. The pan was too heavy for me to lift when it was full of water, so I'd put a chair next to the sink, climb up and fill a glass, then stand on a chair by the stove and pour the water into the pan. I did that over and over again until the pan held enough water. Then I'd turn on the stove, and when the water was boiling, I'd drop in the hot dogs. 'Mom says I'm mature for my age,' I told them, 'and she lets me cook for myself a lot.'

Two nurses looked at each other, and one of them wrote something down on a clipboard.

I asked what was wrong. Nothing, they said, nothing.

– From *The Glass Castle* (adapted)

Reading for Meaning

1. After questioning the young Jeanette, what do you think the nurse wrote on the clipboard?
2. What is your impression of Jeanette's mother from this extract?
3. 'Mom says I'm mature for my age' – do you agree with Jeanette's mother?
4. Do you agree that the writer adds lots of tension to this tale? Explain your answer.
5. Do you think that the writer is successful in bringing this experience to life for the reader?

Style Guide

Memoir: A memoir is a personal account of a period in a writer's life. The facts of a memoir are true but the author uses his/her imagination to tell the story in an interesting manner.

Whereas an autobiography provides a chronological account of the author's life from the start to the present day, a memoir may just explore a particular period in the author's life.

This extract is taken from Jeanette Walls' *The Glass Castle*. This memoir focuses primarily on her extraordinary childhood and tells us little about her adult life.

Writer's Workshop

My Earliest Memory: What is your first memory? Write about this earliest memory, bringing it to life for the reader. Include descriptive details and reflect on this experience.

Links

I Was on Fire explores childhood memories. You can link this piece to other texts in this book and elsewhere:
In this book: Gary Soto's poem, *Oranges* (page 150)
Elsewhere: Jeanette Walls's full autobiography, *The Glass Castle*

Your Father Has the Hay Fever

Tony Powell

For his American radio programme *Weekend All Things Considered*, the writer Paul Auster invited members of the public to send in true stories about their lives. He promised to read them out on air. Auster received over 4,000 submissions. Recognising how interesting some of the stories were, he chose 180 to be published in a book called *True Tales of American Life*. In one of those stories, 'Your Father Has the Hay Fever', Tony Powell describes how his father's hay fever sabotaged many family events, including family holidays.

My father is obsessed with his nose, slave to it. In his mind, he believes God created the nose as a joke around the office and forgot all about it in the rush to finish up the universe before Sunday, His day off. My father and God have a lot in common: God has the fate of all existence on his shoulders, Dad has hay fever. Dad figures it comes out about even. 'He doesn't want hay fever. Believe me.' Not a moment goes by that our household is not preoccupied with Dad's nose. How could it possibly be otherwise? It's like some kind of <u>malicious</u> presence that lives with us. Any little diversion we plan – an afternoon drive to the Dairy Queen, a game of Monopoly after supper – Dad's nose <u>vetoes</u>. And those we do manage to get underway while Old Faithful <u>slumbers</u> are invariably aborted when it awakens, like a cross wasp pinned to my father's face. We cut the picnic short or leave the movie in the middle and go home to follow Dad around the house, in search of his inhaler or nasal spray, like five ghouls patrolling their rooms, Dad leading the way with the <u>litany</u>, 'My nose, my nose, my nose,' like that is the object of our search. Anyone looking in the window would be a fool not to call the authorities.

He stands at the bathroom lavatory, both nostrils clogged beyond sanity. His arsenal is set out before him: nasal spray, nasal drops, nasal plugs, nasal cream, Vicks VapoRub, camphor oil, olive oil, motor oil, 3–in–One, Liquid–Plumr, Drano, blasting caps. He has developed combinations requiring EPA approval, industrial permits, evacuation of the neighbourhood. I stand at the door and watch as he mixes his snake oils, administers them, then waits for the miracle, absolutely still, like he's listening for faraway hoofbeats, the <u>cavalry</u>, coming to save him from his own nose. Invariably, the <u>bugle</u> never sounds, the army never arrives.

'My nose.'

Sometimes it's a statement of resignation. Lying on the couch with his handkerchief on his belly, handy you know, he groans, 'My nose.' Other times, it's a declaration of war, especially when he is trying to do something which requires concentration, like repair the lawnmower. He squats beside the machine, threading a screw the size of a flea, his eyes watering, face <u>crimson</u> and swollen. Suddenly, with no more warning than would accompany an alien invasion, he slings the screwdriver across the yard, leaps to his feet, digging in his hip pocket for his handkerchief like it's a scorpion stinging his butt. He blows. He lifts his <u>countenance</u> to the heavens. He bellows, 'My nose!'

I am six years old, Dad is trying to get the chain back on my bicycle. I am such a delinquent for allowing it to come off in the first place. Dad grumbles. I see a drop of clear liquid descend from his nostril and hang there like a <u>pendant</u>. I silently retreat a few steps. He sniffs, wipes with his sleeve, sniffs again, grumbles a curse to the creator of such an <u>inanely</u> designed <u>apparatus</u> as the human nose. He blinks his eyes rapid-fire, yanks on the chain a couple more times for show. And then the nose is in control. Dad roars like a wounded grizzly, snatches the bike over his head and heaves it down the driveway. Out comes the scorpion. He blows. Birds take flight, small mammals urge their young deeper into their burrows, folks all over town look at their watches and wonder why the noon siren's blowing at 10.25. The blast echoes off the water tower to accompany his <u>anguished</u> cry. 'MY NOSE!!!'

My mother talks to her doctor about it. She misunderstands him and tells everyone, 'Jerry has a deviant septum.' She brings home brochures, puts them in his lunch box. As if he needs reminding.

It is the summer of my ninth year, we are vacationing in Florida. Mom wants to visit Cypress Gardens. Dad is reluctant. 'What about my hay fever?' Mom opens her purse: inside is enough Contac and Triaminic to fill a beanbag chair. Interstate transport violations and border seizures flood my mind. I picture the five of us assuming the position along the side of the highway, traffic slowing to a crawl, the contents of Mom's purse strewn on the ground, photographers taking pictures of the stash.

We go on to Cypress Gardens. Before we have parked the car, Dad is well on his way to being inducted into the Hay Fever Hall of Fame.

'My nose.'

Mom breaks out the medicine. 'Here, take these.' She even has one of those plastic collapsible cups and a thermos full of orange juice. She really wants to see Cypress Gardens. 'They won't help,' Dad says, gulping them anyway. They don't.

I remember it as a day of <u>wrath</u> and embarrassment. Dad's nose was in total control of our <u>itinerary</u>. Mom and us kids wanted to see the ski show; Dad's nose wanted to go home. We wanted to eat lunch in the picnic area beneath the weeping-willow trees; Dad's nose threw a fit and asked us if we were all out of our minds.

I walk the winding paths, head down in shame, as Dad <u>heckles</u> the groundskeepers. 'Keep it up. Kill us all! You probably never had to use a vaporiser in your life!' He approaches total strangers and asks if they have a pocketknife on them. 'My nose!' he wails, to the strangers' complete horror. 'Remove my nose from my face! Just lop her right off. I'm dying here. Put me outta my misery.'

– From *True Tales of American Life*

GLOSSARY
Dairy Queen: a franchise of ice-cream restaurants in America
Liquid-Plumr and Drano: brands of chemical cleaner used for unclogging drains
blasting caps: a small primary explosive
EPA: Environmental Protection Agency
Contact and Triaminic: Medicines for colds

Reading for Meaning

1. How does the father's hay fever affect his family's plans?
2. What is your impression of the father?
3. (a) This personal composition contains a number of anecdotes (see page 9). Retell two of these in your own words.
   (b) Why do you think the writer includes these anecdotes?
4. The piece is intended as a humorous portrayal of family life. Do you find this piece to be funny?

Language Lab

1. (a) Write down two examples of hyperbole (see page 17) from *Your Father Has the Hay Fever*. These may be single phrases or a number of sentences.
   (b) What effect do these examples of hyperbole have on the reader?
2. **Improve your Word Power:** Tony Powell uses many interesting words to bring this story to life. The words (1–15) below are underlined in the extract. Match them with the correct meaning (a–o). Use a dictionary if you need to.

1.	malicious	(a)	horse-mounted soldiers
2.	vetoes	(b)	a hanging ornament
3.	slumbers	(c)	a purplish-red colour
4.	litany	(d)	a plan for a journey
5.	cavalry	(e)	distressed / suffering
6.	bugle	(f)	blocks a decision made by others
7.	crimson	(g)	sleeps
8.	countenance	(h)	harasses
9.	pendant	(i)	absurdly, lacking sense
10.	inanely	(j)	prolonged, tedious account
11.	apparatus	(k)	a brass instrument, similar to a trumpet
12.	anguished	(l)	fury
13.	wrath	(m)	face
14.	itinerary	(n)	intentionally harmful
15.	heckles	(o)	a complex device

Writer's Workshop

A Member of My Family: *Your Father Has the Hay Fever* is a colourful description of the writer's father. Choose a member of your family (immediate or extended) and write a personal composition about them. Consider using lively language and hyperbole in a similar way to Tony Powell.

Links

Your Father Has the Hay Fever offers amusing memories of family life. You can link this piece to other texts in this book and elsewhere:

In this book: Mary Arrigan's *Making a Fiery Impression* (page 34)
Elsewhere: Jonathan Dayton and Valerie Faris's film, *Little Miss Sunshine*

The Boy Soprano

Bernard Farrell

Bernard Farrell is an Irish playwright and a member of Aosdána (the National Academy for Creative Artists), most celebrated for his play *I Do Not Like Thee, Doctor Fell*. In this piece of personal writing he remembers an episode from his youth.

When I was growing up, the back garden of our house backed onto the bigger houses and bigger back gardens of Spencer Villas. In these houses lived richer people, more aloof people, people we seldom saw and, when we did, we silently and respectfully passed them by. The house at the end of our garden was owned by Mrs Brennan who, despite her Irish name, was a most aristocratic lady – 'Like the Queen of England,' my father would whisper whenever we saw her, as she promenaded down Adelaide Road with an air of majesty and entitlement. She spoke to no one, ever – but all that changed the year that my sister began to take singing lessons, the year when I turned twelve.

In our family, my sister Margaret had an exceptionally beautiful singing voice and, in her early teens, she was already taking lessons in operatic interpretation, vocal training and choral work. And every afternoon, in that last summer of my pre-teen years, she would be out in our back garden, practising her scales, rehearsing her exam pieces and occasionally, with so little effort, soaring into something by Puccini or Offenbach.

And this was the time that Mrs Brennan and I first met and spoke.

I remember I was walking up Adelaide Road when suddenly she was standing in front of me, saying loudly and firmly: 'Good morning, Bernard.' I stopped in wordless amazement but now, more like Lady Bracknell than the Queen, she was continuing, 'I was in my back garden yesterday and I heard you singing and I must say that you have the most beautiful boy-soprano voice I have ever heard.'

I looked at her, knowing that I should immediately explain that she was listening to my sister, not to me, but, at that time of my life, I was so starved of compliments that I suddenly heard myself humbly saying, 'Thank you very much, Mrs Brennan.'

And so began our relationship as, in the weeks that followed, whenever she appeared, she consistently praised me, encouraged me and assured me of how gifted I was. As I accepted these compliments, my youthful confidence continued to grow and grow, as weeks turned into months and the seasons changed, and winter drove us indoors, and spring reunited us, and then we were into a new summer. And it was at this time, with my confidence at its zenith that my voice broke.

Suddenly, I was speaking hoarser and harsher and in a tone lower than I thought possible. But as I self-consciously monitored these adolescent changes, I never once questioned the effect they would have on my relationship with Mrs Brennan – until, quite suddenly, I met her again.

She greeted me with her usual enthusiasm and it was only when I replied, 'Good morning, Mrs Brennan,' that she stopped and asked what had happened to my voice. I politely told her that, over the past few weeks, my voice had begun to break and this was now how it would be for the rest of my life.

She looked puzzled.

'But,' she said, 'I heard you singing yesterday, in your back garden.' I was trapped. I had to think quickly – and I did.

I said, 'Ah yes, Mrs Brennan – what has happened is that I have had to stop singing – but my sister, Margaret, has now started and it was probably her you heard.'

She looked at me for a moment and then said, 'Well, she does sing quite well – but she will never be as good as you.'

In the years that followed, I saw less and less of Mrs Brennan – she no longer promenaded along Adelaide Road and then I heard of her illness and, soon after, that she had passed away. By then, my sister's singing career had begun to blossom and, for many years, she revelled in the appreciation and the applause, until she relinquished it all for love, parenthood and family. And some months ago, at too young an age, she too died. At her funeral, as I remembered her, I also remembered Mrs Brennan and I wondered if they were now together, speaking to each other at long last. And I smiled at the thought of Margaret telling her who was really singing in our back garden all those years ago – and Mrs Brennan now knowing that the boy soprano never really existed, that he was just a young, insecure impostor who had once tried to live in the shadow of his much more gifted sister.

– From RTÉ's *Sunday Miscellany* (adapted)

Reading for Meaning

1. What were the people who lived in Spencer Villas like, according to Bernard Farrell?
2. Based on your reading of the whole passage, how would you describe Mrs Brennan?
3. Why did the young Bernard allow Mrs Brennan to think that he was singing?
4. At the end of the text, the writer reveals how he felt about his sister. Describe these feelings.
5. What is your impression of Bernard Farrell from this true tale?

Style Guide

Making the Ordinary Extraordinary: In *The Boy Soprano*, Bernard Farrell writes about an everyday event: a simple misunderstanding. This very ordinary incident could have been summarily described in two sentences. However, Farrell invests this simple story with meaning and uses it to describe the world he is from, the interesting character of Mrs Brennan and, most importantly, to express his feelings about his much-admired sister.

Something ordinary can be made extraordinary if written about in a certain way. As you think back on your own life, do not dismiss seemingly everyday events – everything can be meaningful.

Features of personal writing

Through personal writing, authors reflect on their lives, themselves and the world around them. A piece of personal writing will often have the features listed below. It is worth noting how these features appear in the personal writing throughout this chapter.

Autobiographical: What defines *The Boy Soprano* as personal writing is its autobiographical nature. Bernard Farrell recalls a moment that really occurred. He uses this as material to entertain, amuse and move the reader.

Personal tone: Farrell adopts a personal tone by writing in the first person ('I'). This means that the story is told directly from his point of view.

Personal emotions and thoughts: The personal quality is also achieved through the writer's expression of personal emotions and thoughts which are present throughout the piece.

Reflective quality: Personal writing often has a reflective quality. This means that the writer thinks about the significance of an event in their lives. In the last paragraph, Farrell considers the life of Mrs Brennan and reflects on his much-admired sister.

Writer's Workshop

A Misunderstanding: Bernard Farrell uses Mrs Brennan's misunderstanding as the basis of this personal story. Think about a misunderstanding from your past and use it to compose a personal composition. Consider the features of personal writing listed above and ask yourself, 'Can I make the ordinary extraordinary?'

Links

The Boy Soprano has an important sibling relationship at its centre. You can link this piece to other texts in this book and elsewhere:
In this book: Gillian Clarke's poem, *Legend* (page 152)
Elsewhere: Sean Penn's film, *Into the Wild*

Christmas Morning

Sylvia Seymour Akin

The story below featured on Paul Auster's radio programme, *Weekend All Things Considered*, in which ordinary Americans were invited to write a true story to be read on air. In this story, the writer remembers a poignant moment from her childhood in which she learned about the power of kindness.

A light drizzle was falling as my sister Jill and I ran out of the Methodist Church, eager to get home and play with the presents that Santa had left for us and our baby sister, Sharon. Across the street from the church was a Pan American gas station where the Greyhound bus stopped. It was closed for Christmas, but I noticed a family standing outside the locked door, huddled under the narrow overhang in an attempt to keep dry. I wondered briefly why they were there but then forgot about them as I raced to keep up with Jill.

Once we got home, there was barely time to enjoy our presents. We had to go off to our grandparents' house for our annual Christmas dinner. As we drove down the highway through town, I noticed that the family was still there, standing outside the closed gas station.

My father was driving very slowly down the highway. The closer we got to the turnoff for my grandparents' house, the slower the car went. Suddenly, my father U-turned in the middle of the road and said, 'I can't stand it!'

'What?' asked my mother.

'It's those people back there at the Pan Am, standing in the rain. They've got children. It's Christmas. I can't stand it.'

When my father pulled into the service station, I saw that there were five of them: the parents and three children – two girls and a small boy.

My father rolled down his window. 'Merry Christmas,' he said.

'Howdy,' the man replied. He was very tall and had to stoop slightly to peer into the car.

Jill, Sharon and I stared at the children, and they stared back at us.

'You waiting on the bus?' my father asked.

The man said that they were. They were going to Birmingham, where he had a brother and prospects of a job.

'Well, that bus isn't going to come along for several hours, and you're getting wet standing here. Winborn's just a couple miles up the road. They've got a shed with a cover there, and some benches,' my father said. 'Why don't y'all get in the car

and I'll run you up there.'

The man thought about it for a moment, and then he beckoned to his family. They climbed into the car. They had no luggage, only the clothes they were wearing.

Once they settled in, my father looked back over his shoulder and asked the children if Santa had found them yet. Three glum faces mutely gave him his answer.

'Well, I didn't think so,' my father said, winking at my mother, 'because when I saw Santa this morning, he told me that he was having trouble finding y'all, and he asked me if he could leave your toys at my house. We'll just go get them before I take you to the bus stop.'

All at once, the three children's faces lit up, and they began to bounce around in the back seat, laughing and chattering.

When we got out of the car at our house, the three children ran through the front door and straight to the toys that were spread out under our Christmas tree. One of the girls spied Jill's doll and immediately hugged it to her breast. I remember that the little boy grabbed Sharon's ball. And the other girl picked up something of mine. All this happened a long time ago, but the memory of it remains clear. That was the Christmas when my sisters and I learned the joy of making others happy.

My mother noticed that the middle child was wearing a short-sleeved dress, so she gave the girl Jill's only sweater to wear.

My father invited them to join us at our grandparents' for Christmas dinner, but the parents refused. Even when we all tried to talk them into coming, they were firm in their decision.

Back in the car, on the way to Winborn, my father asked the man if he had money for bus fare.

His brother had sent tickets, the man said.

My father reached into his pocket and pulled out two dollars, which was all he had left until his next payday. He pressed the money into the man's hand. The man tried to give it back, but my father insisted. 'It'll be late when you get to Birmingham, and these children will be hungry before then. Take it. I've been broke before, and I know what it's like when you can't feed your family.'

We left them there at the bus stop in Winborn. As we drove away, I watched out the window as long as I could, looking back at the little girl hugging her new doll.

– From *Weekend All Things Considered*

Reading for Meaning

1. The narrator's father exclaims, 'I can't stand it!' What is it that he can't stand?
2. Why do you think the narrator and her sisters do not object when their presents are given away?
3. What lesson do the narrator and her sisters learn that Christmas?
4. (a) Describe the final image from the story in your own words.
   (b) Why do you think the writer chose that image to end the story with?
5. How do you think you would have reacted if your Christmas presents were given away by your parent/guardian?

Writer's Workshop

Letter: Imagine you are a member of the family that was waiting at the bus stop. Write a letter to a member of the author's family thanking them for the kindness you received. In your letter try to express how this incident made you feel, what this act of kindness meant. Go to page 83 to learn about writing personal letters.

Speaking and Listening

Debate: As a class, debate the following motion: 'The true spirit of Christmas has been lost in the modern world.'

Pages 212-214 of this book explain how to run a debate. Also the International Debate Association's website **www.idebate.org** offers lots of useful information and may help you to prepare your arguments.

Links

Christmas Morning looks at how poverty can affect family life. You can link this piece to other texts in this book and elsewhere:

In this book: Dorothea Lange's photograph, *Migrant Mother* (page 244)
Elsewhere: Gabriele Muccino's film, *The Pursuit of Happyness*

The Toity Jar

Bill Bryson

The extract below is from Bill Bryson's hilarious memoir *The Life and Times of the Thunderbolt Kid*. Here Bryson offers the reader a snapshot of family life in 1950s America.

Like most people in Iowa in the 1950s, we were more cautious eaters in our house. On the rare occasions when we were presented with food with which we were not comfortable or familiar – on planes or trains or when invited to a meal cooked by someone who was not herself from Iowa – we tended to tilt it up carefully with a knife and examine it from every angle as if determining whether it might need to be defused. Once on a trip to San Francisco my father was taken by friends to a Chinese restaurant and he described it to us afterwards in the sombre tones of someone recounting a near-death experience.

'And they eat it with sticks, you know,' he added knowledgeably.

'Goodness!' said my mother.

'I would rather have gas gangrene than go through that again,' my father added grimly.

In our house we didn't eat:

- pasta, rice, cream cheese, sour cream, garlic, mayonnaise, onions, corned beef, pastrami, salami or foreign food of any type, except French toast;
- bread that wasn't white and at least 65 per cent air;
- spices other than salt, pepper and maple syrup;
- fish that was any shape other than rectangular and not coated in bright orange breadcrumbs, and then only on Fridays and only when my mother remembered it was Friday, which in fact was not often;
- soups not blessed by Campbell's and only a very few of those;
- anything with dubious regional names like 'pone' or 'gumbo' or foods that had at any time been an esteemed staple of slaves or peasants.

All other foods of all types – curries, enchiladas, tofu, bagels, sushi, couscous, yogurt, kale, rocket, Parma ham, any cheese that was not a vivid bright yellow and shiny enough to see your reflection in – had either not yet been invented or were still unknown to us. We really were radiantly unsophisticated. I remember being surprised to learn at quite an advanced age that a shrimp cocktail was not, as I had always imagined, a pre-dinner alcoholic drink with a shrimp in it.

All our meals consisted of leftovers. My mother had a seemingly inexhaustible supply of foods that had already been to the table, sometimes repeatedly. Apart from a few perishable dairy products, everything in the fridge was older than I was, sometimes by many years. (Her oldest food possession of all, it more or less goes without saying, was a fruit cake that was kept in a metal tin and dated from the colonial period.) I can only assume that my mother did all her cooking in the 1940s so that she could spend the rest of her life surprising herself with what she could find under cover at the back of the fridge. I never knew her to reject a food. The rule of thumb seemed to be that if you opened the lid and the stuff inside didn't make you actually recoil and take at least one staggered step backwards, it was deemed OK to eat.

Both my parents had grown up in the Great Depression and neither of them ever threw anything away if they could possibly avoid it. My mother routinely washed and dried paper plates, and smoothed out for reuse spare aluminium foil. If you left a pea on your plate, it became part of a future meal. All our sugar came in little packets spirited out of restaurants in deep coat pockets, as did our jams, jellies, crackers (oyster and saltine), tartare sauces, some of our ketchup and butter, all of our napkins, and a very occasional ashtray; anything that came with a restaurant table really. One of the happiest moments in my parents' life was when maple syrup started to be served in small disposable packets and they could add those to the household hoard.

Under the sink, my mother kept an enormous collection of jars, including one known as the toity jar. 'Toity' in our house was the term for a pee, and throughout my early years the toity jar was called into service whenever a need to leave the house inconveniently coincided with a sudden need by someone – and when I say 'someone', I mean of course the youngest child: me – to pee.

'Oh, you'll have to go in the toity jar then,' my mother would say with just a hint of exasperation and a worried glance at the kitchen clock. It took me a long time to realise that the toity jar was not always – or even often – the same jar twice. In so far as I thought about it at all, I suppose I guessed that the toity jar was routinely discarded and replaced with a fresh jar – we had hundreds after all.

So you may imagine my consternation, succeeded by varying degrees of dismay, when I went to the fridge one evening for a second helping of halved peaches and realised that we were all eating from a jar that had, only days before, held my urine. I recognised the jar at once because it had a Z-shaped strip of label adhering to it that uncannily recalled the mark of Zorro – a fact that I had cheerfully remarked upon as I had filled the jar with my precious bodily nectars, not that anyone had listened of course. Now here it was holding our dessert peaches. I couldn't have been more surprised if I had just been handed a packet of photos showing my mother in flagrante with, let's say, the guys at the gas station.

'Mom,' I said, coming to the dining-room doorway and holding up my find, 'this is the toity jar.'

'No, honey,' she replied smoothly without looking up. 'The toity jar's a special jar.'

'What's the toity jar?' asked my father with an amused air, spooning peach into his mouth.

'It's the jar I toity in,' I explained. 'And this is it.'

'Billy toities in a jar?' said my father, with very slight difficulty, as he was no longer eating the peach half he had just taken in, but resting it on his tongue pending receipt of further information concerning its recent history.

'Just occasionally,' my mother said.

My father's mystification was now nearly total, but his mouth was so full of unswallowed peach juice that he could not meaningfully speak. He asked, I believe, why I didn't just go upstairs to the bathroom like a normal person. It was a fair question in the circumstances.

'Well, sometimes we're in a hurry,' my mother went on, a touch uncomfortably. 'So I keep a jar under the sink – a special jar.'

I reappeared from the fridge, cradling more jars – as many as I could carry. 'I'm pretty sure I've used all these too,' I announced.

'That can't be right,' my mother said, but there was a kind of question mark hanging off the edge of it. Then she added, perhaps a touch self-destructively: 'Anyway, I always rinse all jars thoroughly before reuse.'

My father rose and walked to the kitchen, inclined over the waste bin and allowed the peach half to fall into it, along with about half a litre of goo. 'Perhaps a toity jar's not such a good idea,' he suggested.

So that was the end of the toity jar, though it all worked out for the best, as these things so often do. After that, all my mother had to do was mention that she had something good in a jar in the fridge and my father would get a sudden urge to take us to Bishop's, a cafeteria downtown, which was the best possible outcome, for Bishop's was the finest restaurant that ever existed.

– From *The Life and Times of the Thunderbolt Kid*

GLOSSARY

defused: to remove the fuse (from a bomb)

sombre: extremely serious

gas gangrene: a deadly disease which produces gas as bodily tissue dies

consternation: a feeling of confusion or anxiety

adhering: sticking

in flagrante: 'caught in the act', literally: 'in blazing' (Latin). In this case Bryson is using it to mean 'caught in a sexual act'.

Reading for Meaning

1. (a) How did Bryson's father react when he was taken to a Chinese restaurant for the first time?
   (b) What does this suggest about the Bryson family's eating habits?
2. The Great Depression was a time of extreme poverty and hardship in America. Bryson mentions that his parents were brought up during this time. How did this experience affect the way they treated food?
3. Having read about the Bryson family's experience of food, do you think that Bishop's cafeteria was truly 'the finest restaurant that ever existed'?
4. Did you find this extract funny? (Take a look at the Style Guide to the right.)

Language Lab

1. (a) Write down two examples of hyperbole (see page 17) from this extract. These may be single phrases or a number of sentences.
   (b) What effect does Bryson's use of hyperbole have?
2. (a) Bill Bryson makes use of lists in this piece. Offer two examples.
   (b) Why do you think he makes use of lists? What effect do they have?

Style Guide

Humour: We all like to laugh. A humorous piece of writing can be wonderfully entertaining for a reader. Writers usually amuse a reader by:

- Laughing at themselves.
- Poking fun at others. Writers have to be careful that this type of humour doesn't cause offence.
- Describing amusing situations.
- Using language in a humorous manner. For example, hyperbole (see page 17) can be amusing.

In *The Toity Jar*, Bill Bryson uses all four of these forms of humour.

Speaking and Listening

Interview: Eating habits have changed a lot over the past few decades. Interview an elderly person (perhaps a grandparent, elderly relative or neighbour) and try to learn about what they ate when they were young. Write an account of the interview which includes the questions you asked and the interviewee's responses.

Links

The Toity Jar shows how food and family life often go hand-in-hand. This piece can be linked to other texts inside this book and elsewhere.

In this book: The comedy sketch, *Four Yorkshiremen* (page 215)

Elsewhere: S.J. Clarkson's film, *Toast*

Waiting

Martina King

The Quiet Quarter was a five-minute radio programme on RTÉ that featured a daily story. The stories were often moving or thought-provoking. *Waiting* is one of these stories.

The railway station was bleak. A solitary engine revved sporadically as though about to depart, but stayed put like the rest of us. We were all in abeyance, standing about, resting on grimy benches – waiting. An icy wind kept us company. Hopping from one foot to the other, we briskly rubbed our hands together, but there was no escaping the chill. It slunk along the train tracks at one end and swung in from the bus depot at the other, slapping into startled faces with the intensity of a wet rag.

My son was disappointed. It wasn't the arctic ambience, it was that the engine had no smiling face like the ones in his favourite storybook.

'Ma'am, would you mind giving a read to that, and tell me have I the right day?'

He startled me. I hadn't noticed the elderly man approach, but there was an honesty about the blue-grey eyes that looked me straight in the face, and I took the folded page from his outstretched hand without a second thought.

'Dear Dada…,' it began.

It was a difficult letter to comprehend, most words were misspelled, and the sentences constructed in a childish manner. She had no job. Patrick was two years old last week, and there was no minding him, he was into everything. It was a terror on account of the place being so small. Himself had work beyond in Bethnal Green, she didn't see much of him now, but he gave her a few pounds the odd time. She'd like to come home, maybe she'd manage it in November, around the twenty-sixth but she didn't know. Wouldn't it be grand, she and the baby and Dada together, and Patsy only down the road? There was a park nearby. She couldn't go there a lot since they were on the ninth floor and the lifts didn't work more often than not. But it had a bit of a stream along the edge and blackberry bushes beside the path, and when she went there she thought of Mama, Lord rest her, making the blackberry jam. The page was signed, 'Your loving daughter, Bernie.'

'Is it today, Ma'am? Have I the right date?'

'Yes, today's the twenty-sixth. But wasn't there anything else since the letter? A phone call maybe?'

'Divil a call I ever get.'

I handed back the yellowing paper. It smelled of turf fires as did his heavy black coat. 'She mightn't arrive today,' I said.

'She mightn't 'tis true, but sure wouldn't it be a fright if she came all the way and there wasn't a sinner to meet her?'

'How long have you been here?'

'Since the morn. You wouldn't know what train she might be on.'

He must have left before dawn; his were the soft tones of West Clare.

The sound of an approaching train interrupted us. A voice boomed from the PA system that it was the four-thirty from Dublin, and with a rumble and hiss the great orange machine slid to a halt.

My son was delighted; it mightn't sport a happy face, but this train was long and noisy and very impressive. He dragged me forward to join the crowd milling about gate number one.

'I'm frozen!' My daughter complained, 'There was no heat on the train. And I'm starving, what's for dinner? I haven't been home for weeks; I can't wait to meet my friends. Mum, let's go! What are you doing?'

I was looking back, trying to find him. There he was, scanning the remaining stragglers alighting from the train.

He was the last to leave the platform. I watched him return to a shabby bench, and sit there, erect and dignified – waiting.

– From RTÉ's *The Quiet Quarter* (amended)

GLOSSARY
abeyance: in a state of waiting
grimy: covered with dirt
ambience: atmosphere
milling: moving with no particular purpose or reason

Reading for Meaning

1. Describe the atmosphere of the train station.
2. Why was the narrator's son disappointed as they waited on the train platform?
3. What details does the narrator learn about the man's daughter from the letter?
4. How does the writer encourage you to feel sorry for the man waiting on the platform?
5. When the writer's daughter arrives off the train, she has a number of complaints. How do you feel about these complaints in light of what you have learned about the waiting man and his daughter?

Speaking and Listening

Discussion: When we travel on public transport we often see colourful, eccentric, lonely or interesting characters. In groups, talk about interesting people you may have met while taking a bus, train or plane. Allow each person the opportunity to share a story. Choose one member of the group to tell his/her story to the class.

Style Guide

Show, Don't Tell: A subtle writer may *show* how he/she feels about something rather than simply *telling* the reader. In the story above, Martina King never *tells* us that she pities the man on the platform; instead she *shows* us by offering details and images that evoke our sympathy. This is emphasised by contrasting the man's awful situation with the petty complaints of the writer's daughter.

Skilled writers may lead us gently to a conclusion by showing us details rather than obviously telling us how they feel.

Writer's Workshop

Poem: Write a poem inspired by this personal composition.

Links

Waiting illustrates how significant personal letters can be. This piece can be linked to other texts inside this book and elsewhere.

In this book: Francis P. Church's editorial reply to a letter, *Yes, Virginia there is a Santa Claus* (page 87)

Elsewhere: Ian McEwan's novel, *Atonement*

Making a Fiery Impression

Mary Arrigan

This story first appeared on the RTÉ radio programme *Sunday Miscellany*. In it, Mary Arrigan remembers when her son's girlfriend's family came to visit – with disastrous results.

When my son's girlfriend and her parents were due to visit, we were warned to behave ourselves.

'Don't do anything weird,' we were told, 'I want for us all to make a really good impression.'

My husband promised to wear a tie and I promised not to wear any of my Oxfam stuff in case Girlfriend's mum might have been a donor.

They were due at six for dinner at seven. They arrived at four, before the impression-making leg of lamb was fully thawed and before the sitting room fire was lit. Cups of tea in the kitchen would have to fill the gap while my husband slipped away to light the fire. As I shovelled a spoonful of Earl Grey into yet another pot to give the teabags a touch of class, I noticed the heavy mist outside the front window.

'Bit of fog,' I said.

'Different weather out the other window,' commented Girlfriend's father. Sure enough, the side window showed winter sunshine.

'I think actually that's smoke,' said Girlfriend helpfully. Billows of smoke wafted into the kitchen. But, as we'd been warned against weirdness, we tried to keep a half-decent conversation going while husband and son ran back and forth with wet sacks and shovels. The bewildered visitors pretended not to notice the smuts that settled on their hair and faces and continued to sip cold tea from pale-grey cups.

Finally my son stuck his blackened face around the door.

'No good,' he said, 'you'll have to call the fire brigade.'

The phone was on a shelf beside Girlfriend's father's shoulder. As I dialled I noticed smuts on his white shirt and leaned forward to blow them away before they'd ingrained into the fabric. He turned suddenly, catching me with puckered lips close to his neck. Before I could explain, I got through to the fire brigade. The emergency service was answered by a woman who I knew had been in hospital recently. I thought it fitting that I should enquire after her health, as one does. It's good manners.

'By the way,' I said when we'd got all the pleasantries out of the way, 'my house is on fire. Do you think you could organise the brigade lads to come out?'

The tea got colder and the cups and the visitors got blacker. Still, nobody mentioned the raging chimney in the next room. Finally, my son, responding to a quiet threat from me, asked the visitors if they'd like to see the Hiberno-Romanesque arch in the ruined church across the field from our house. I hadn't known they were so passionately interested in Hiberno-Romanesque arches. Their enthusiasm brought tears to my eyes as they fought their way out the back door. It was simply grand when seven large firemen with confidence-inspiring helmets and gear finally made it into our yard.

Across the field we could see our guests at the ruined church. Funnily enough they weren't looking at the Hiberno-Romanesque arch at all.

When the last spark had been stamped out, we gratefully invited the seven firemen into the kitchen for tea. By now the visitors had arrived back and were wedged between the beefy brigade men. I caught my son's eye and wondered how we were rating on the making-an-impression scale. Then again, maybe I didn't want to know. It was only then I discovered that my electric kettle was banjaxed. That meant boiling a saucepan of water on a gas ring.

'Anyone got a match?' I asked.

Seven firemen, three esteemed guests and sundry neighbours all shook their heads. In a house recently visited by fire, we hadn't the means to light a gas ring. At this stage Girlfriend's parents made an excuse and left. Pity really. They missed the fine roast lamb dinner we had just after midnight. They'd have been really impressed.

– From RTÉ's *Sunday Miscellany*

Reading for Meaning

1. At the start of the story we learn that the narrator's son warned his family, 'Don't do anything weird'. Why do you think the reader is told this?
2. Why do you think the visitors pretend not to notice that the chimney is on fire?
3. This story contains a number of amusing incidents. Which do you think was the funniest?
4. Based on their behaviour, how do you think Girlfriend's family felt about everything that happened during their visit?
5. What is your impression of the narrator's family?

Speaking and Listening

Discussion: In small groups, share amusing stories about your family. Allow each member of the group to tell the funniest story he/she can about his/her family or a family member. Each group should choose one person to tell a story to the class.

Writer's Workshop

Laughing at Ourselves: What is the funniest or strangest thing that has happened to your family? Write an account of this incident. It may help to consider the Style Guide to humour on page 31. You might also like to talk to members of your family for ideas.

Links

Making a Fiery Impression shows the hilarious results that can happen when different families are brought together through romance. This piece can be linked to other texts such as Damien O'Donnell's film, *East is East*.

I Believe in Angels – and I Saw One Recently

Michael Harding

Michael Harding is a novelist, playwright and columnist. Now a Buddhist, he was formerly a priest, and also worked as a teacher and prison social worker. Harding is a member of Aosdána (the National Academy for Creative Artists). This article is taken from Harding's *Irish Times* column.

I was staring at witches in a shop window in Tralee last week. Vampires and zombies and green rubber devils, and a black hand reaching up from the floor with a gold cross and chain hanging on its dead fingers. And that was all just in one shop.

Farther down the street there were more cobwebs and so many windows full of orange and black plastic and grim pumpkins with nasty faces that I realised Halloween was just around the corner – that great American festival of anxiety when people celebrate the macabre possibility that evil is erotic, random and probably lurks beneath the bed.

It was all so American that I decided to slip into a burger joint for some food. I asked for chicken and chips but the boy behind the counter said he didn't accept laser cards.

'There's a cash machine round the corner,' he said, so off I went and returned later with €20.

He took my order again, but said it would take 15 minutes to fry the chicken leg. I waited among a cluster of fat teenagers, wearing what looked like pyjamas in a variety of pastel colours, their bodies stuffed to the gills and their cheeks bulging like bloated fish. Maybe they are zombies, I thought, returned from the dead, like hungry ghosts they cannot stop eating. Or maybe they are reincarnated fish, who slither around burger joints like bottom feeders at a sewage pipe. But I don't believe in zombies or witches or any other malignant creature that the unconscious mind invents.

Instead I believe in angels – and I saw one recently in a café in Warsaw. He was disguised as a homeless man in a restaurant. I ordered tomato soup. The waitress wore white trousers and top. She looked like a dentist's assistant and she made the homeless man a latte.

A woman with long grey hair had her nose stuck in a laptop near the window. The homeless man sat close to her. His hair was like a floor mop.

He had extremely long nails on his right hand and his jeans were ripped from hip to knee, exposing the white marble flesh of his thigh. But it was the fingernails that gave him away, long manicured nails as though they were blackened by life on the streets.

Pop music was pumping from speakers on the ceiling and it irritated him. He began talking to the air and waving his arm, which irritated the computer woman. She frowned over her black-rimmed glasses a few times but said nothing.

He persisted. Eventually she spoke. I don't know what she said, but it seemed both respectful and firm, as if she was talking to a kid brother. He became quiet again and sullen. The grey-haired woman returned to her laptop. Then he began again, manifesting furiously at the air. I guessed he just didn't like the pop music.

Eventually the waitress spoke into his ear and he got up and took his latte and walked out with great dignity. Nor did she charge him for his drink. His fingers surrounded the coffee cup like a claw, but not a zombie's claw, more like a broken angel's claw.

It was a beautiful hand and I could imagine the nails plucking strings on a guitar, or maybe a harp. Maybe he played in an orchestra or a jazz band long ago, and just got too fond of alcohol, or drifted away from his loved ones and then lost everything. Now he walks the streets of Warsaw, sleeps in shop doorways and gets a few free coffees from kind waitresses.

As he left though he looked at me and that's when I realised he was an angel. It's not that he was trying to teach me anything. He was just there, a beautiful creature who deserved my respect.

Angels are like that. They appear without reason. They have no message. They just open the universe to us in an accidental moment.

I spoke to the laptop woman when he was gone and she said it was a pity about him because 'many of them don't survive the winter snow. The harsh weather sweeps them away.'

I thought of him for weeks. Even in Tralee, as the fat zombie children huddled around their paper boxes of chicken bones and chips, and I wished he was there for them, that they could see beyond the plastic pumpkins and the veil of cobwebs that hung from every wall.

– From *The Irish Times*

Reading for Meaning

1. Describe the physical appearance of the 'angel' Michael Harding saw.
2. In what way could the homeless man be considered 'an angel', according to the writer?
3. Based on the evidence in this article, how do you think Harding views the modern world?
4. What point is Harding trying to make in this piece?
5. A number of readers complained that Michael Harding refers to Halloween as 'an American festival'; they made the point that it is traditionally an Irish festival (Samhain). What point do you think Harding is making by calling it 'an American festival'?
6. When articles are published online, readers are often given a space to comment and discuss the piece in the comment thread. Here are two comments that followed this article. Which point of view do you most agree with?
   - This is definitely the worst article I have ever read – what appalling writing.
   - Thank you again, Michael – more poetry in prose, deep insights and sensitivity.

Speaking and Listening

Comment Thread: As a class, pass around a large piece of paper and create a comment thread. Each comment should be relatively short and include the author's name. Once everyone has contributed, stick the comment thread on the wall and together discuss what is written.

Writer's Workshop

Homelessness Article: Homelessness continues to be a serious problem in modern Ireland. Write an article in which you discuss this issue. Express your personal opinion and make use of facts to support your ideas.

How I Became a Cat Person

Patrick Freyne

Patrick Freyne is a columnist and television critic with The Irish Times. *The article below combines humour and a sense of loss as Freyne remembers his pet cat.*

Here are some things I've learned about cats based purely on scientific observation of the only cat I've ever owned.

1. Cats are fat and white and are really bad at jumping.
2. Cats have to eat a special diet food.
3. Cats don't hunt and are confused when small birds fall out of their nests in the garden. They just stare at them. Left to their own devices I'm sure the cat and the bird would become friends, with the cat warding off predators and the bird plucking fruit from the farthest branches, and possibly working together to play 'tricks' on 'humans'. But we'll never know because my spoilsport wife intervened and put the bird back in its nest.
4. Cats make this sound: 'wack, wack, wack'. They do not say 'meow', as my toddler nephew insists. 'You're wrong,' I say firmly. 'And it's 'cat' not 'gat'.' He doesn't like that. 'Oh, here come the waterworks!' I say.
5. Cats have a complicated cosmology in which humans control the weather. If, for example, a cat wants to be let into the back garden and then sees it is raining, it will look up at you expecting you to change the weather. When you do not, it will go to the front door, where it assumes atmospheric conditions are different. Sometimes, surprisingly, they are.
6. In the wild, cats would probably be f***ed.

My cat came as part of a package with my wife. In a way, she was my 'step-cat', but soon I came to see her as my own. Her name was Princess Arjumand. She was named after a cat in a Connie Willis novel, who turns out to be the centre of the universe. The name was shortened, of course, to Ju Ju, the well-known abbreviation for Princess Arjumand. I would, of course, have preferred a tougher name, like Fang or White Thunder, but Ju Ju had already been cat-christened by the time she moved in with me. She did, I have to admit, have an aristocratic sense of entitlement that suited the name.

As someone who worked from home, I began to bond with Ju Ju. I started seeing her more as a work colleague than a pet.

'Good day, Ju Ju,' I would say every morning as I stumbled to the coffee pot.

'Wack, wack, wack,' she would quack back, looking up at me accusingly when I didn't fill her bowl straight away or because I was late with a deadline.

As I stood there in my underpants, wielding my coffee spoon like a mighty sword, I fancied we looked like He-Man and Battle Cat, although possibly He-Man and Battle Cat in later years, after they'd retired.

Ju Ju lived to be a very old cat. When my wife got her, she was a slightly traumatised rescue animal. After her first owner died, she spent a few months in a small pen in a veterinary clinic. When she arrived at my wife's house she nestled down outside the kitchen like a brooding hen and refused to move for a whole week.

Thankfully, she soon came out of herself and became a demanding little tyrant. The vet estimated that she was about five years old when she came into our lives. She was with us for a further 13 years.

Once, early on, she disappeared for a week. We were, to our surprise, distraught. It turned out she had moved in with some wealthy old ladies down the road. I suspect she had some sort of grift or long con underway. When she suddenly turned up again she glared at us with contempt. She had moved on to a better life and we were pulling her back down into the mire.

She was pretty sedentary compared to other neighbourhood cats, whom she hated. She particularly hated Bobby, the cat from next door, an energetic ginger cat who would gyrate sexily in the window at her as she glowered out.

'Oh Ju Ju, you are all woman!' I imagine him saying in a rich baritone. 'I am in luuuv with uuuu.'

'I hate you Bobby,' I imagined Ju Ju responding in her high-pitched quack, puffing her fur up and growling out the window.

Of course, I did not say these words aloud, employing special 'cat voices', because that would be weird. We did not do a special voice for our cat. That would be nuts. Seriously. Who would do that? Next you'll be saying we invented long involved narratives about her adventures – about how she was an avid balloonist who travelled the world looking for a mystical jade monkey, for example. But that would be crazy. Stop looking at me.

Ju Ju outlived all of her hated neighbour cats. She was disinclined to wander towards traffic and she liked the simple pleasures – sitting still, misanthropy and overeating. She was a medical marvel. She was prescribed a special diet food. She had cat asthma. She got skin cancer despite always being plastered with sunscreen (white cats are prone to skin cancer), so she had to have the tips of her ears removed, leaving her with little round ears, like a bear.

Once a big dog ran into the garden, picked her up by the scruff of the neck and shook her until I intervened. It was very upsetting. It had all the hallmarks of a gangland hit. 'What enemies has she made?' I wondered. I'd long realised I'd miss her if anything happened to her.

Then she survived a house move, which I barely survived myself. It's touching to watch an elderly cat trying to figure out a new environment – tentatively sniffing and padding about (she probably felt the same about me).

She had become a regal old lady. But her health started to get worse, even by her own unhealthy standards. And this is where the funny story about a funny pet turns melancholy. She could no longer manage to get on our bed. She began weeing in inappropriate places so we had to restrict her to certain rooms. 'Hello again!' was how the vet greeted us on weekly visits.

One day we realised Ju Ju's sight was failing. Shortly afterwards she went missing. ('Are you looking for a weird-looking white cat?' said a passing man. 'She's sitting up there in that garden.') We began confining her to the house. She was diagnosed with kidney disease and we were told she had only six months to live, but she lived for another year-and-a-half on a cocktail of medicines and obsessive care.

She was not in pain. But she was unkempt (we had to groom her) and confused (she didn't know the difference between day and night) and not really her proud, loud, annoying self (although she still purred happily when we stroked her under the chin). And then the vet said it was time to let her go.

We were given a final weekend with her. Then we brought her into the Anicare Veterinary Clinic for the last time. They were lovely. In an adjoining room they put a cannula in her arm. Then, with Ju Ju peacefully perched on a blanket on a silver table, they gave us time to say goodbye. We stroked her. She purred. We cried. They gave her a sedative and the drug that killed her. 'Goodbye Ju Ju,' we said. 'We love you.' She breathed a few last breaths and all life went from her skinny, no longer fat, little body.

Losing a pet is not like losing a person. The grief is not bottomless. But it does leave a sad little four-legged hole in your life. It's a bit like our house had a grumpy, fat, white, fluffy soul, and now that's gone. When I come home now my instinct is still to greet her. 'Good day, Ju Ju!' I want to say. But I don't, because I wouldn't hear her say 'wack, wack, wack'.

– From *The Irish Times*

GLOSSARY

cosmology: beliefs about the universe

He-Man: a 1980s children's cartoon character. Battle Cat was a giant cat with a saddle that He-Man would ride on

grift: swindle, scam

mire: swamp, muddy land

sedentary: spending a lot of time sitting down

gyrate: dance in a wild manner

glowered: stared angrily

Reading for Meaning

1. In this article Patrick Freyne successfully describes Ju Ju's personality. Describe what sort of cat she was.
2. Describe the relationship the writer had with his cat.
3. 'In *How I Became a Cat Person*, Patrick Freyne perfectly balances hilarity and sadness.' Do you agree with this statement?

Style Guide

Tongue-in-Cheek: When a writer is making a joke but appears serious in his/her tone, we can describe the writing as tongue-in-cheek. Patrick Freyne is often tongue-in-cheek in this article. For example: 'It turned out she had moved in with some wealthy old ladies down the road. I suspect she had some sort of grift or long con underway.'

Writer's Workshop

Pets: As Patrick Freyne shows in this article, pets can have a special place in our lives, giving us great joy but also sadness when they're gone. Write a composition about a pet you once had. If you've never had one, write about your idea of the ideal pet.

Links

How I Became a Cat Person shows how deeply connected we can be to animals. This article can be linked to other texts in this book and elsewhere:

In this book: Romesh Ranganathan's article, *Zoos are Prisons for Animals* (page 47)
Elsewhere: Barry Hines's novel, *A Kestrel for a Knave*

The Enamel Jug

Peter Jankowsky

Peter Jankowsky is a German-born writer living in Ireland. He has translated numerous poems for Irish and German publications as well as publishing a memoir, *Myself Passing By*. In this piece he recalls an incident from his childhood in post-war Berlin.

In winter, the playground of the kindergarten was reduced to a few grassy square metres rising, just about, over low-lying ground which, from autumn onwards, turned into a morass, the remnant of a number of allotments, now devastated by war action. All around the mud loomed the typical four-storey houses of Berlin, many of them now in ruins. A group of children were playing on the little patch of green, five-, six-year olds, a single boy and half a dozen girls. It wasn't peaceful play: it consisted of chases and scuffles, the girls nagging the boy, he making them scream by pulling their sleeves and their hair – all bitterly enjoyable in the dim November light of the first winter after the end of the war.

Unnoticed by the playing children, another boy had appeared on the scene; like an emanation of their grim surroundings, a tall, scraggy lad of maybe fourteen years, poorly dressed in something uniform-like that hung down from his shoulders, as did his long arms. His right hand clutched the handle of an enamel jug, the kind you would take to a field kitchen for a ladle-full of soup. He stood there motionless, watching, a pale face without expression.

The little boy had just burst into a wild dervish dance, making the girls scatter and scream, when the din was cut, as if by a knife, by the tall boy's voice.

'Look away!' he ordered the girls calmly. The children all froze and looked at him. The small boy stood in front of the tall one, looking up at him. He saw him raise his right arm slowly, the handle of the chipped enamel jug clenched in his fist, he saw him swing his arm back as far as he could. And then the stranger, with all his might, brought the pot down on the little boy's head, hitting it just above his right eyebrow and cutting down to the bone.

They all could hear the short, hard knock, as if on wood; the little boy heard it from within. Blood spurted out promptly, then after a moment of silent shock came a howl, more of horror than of pain. Fingers covering the violated face were flooded with blood and tears and saliva. He stumbled forward, calling for the kindergarten nurse, the girls fluttering all around him, now screaming with genuine terror. They completely forgot about the tall boy who had vanished, unseen, back from where he had first appeared, the ruined city. The bleeding boy was brought to a first-aid station in the neighbourhood. The wound needed a few stitches and with a big bandage, like a turban, he was delivered home into the arms of mother and grandmother.

And that's where that day ended for me – in a nest of warmth and nourishment and care. Where did the tall boy go? Where had he come from? For half a century now, his darkly looming figure, his right arm swung back, has been a regular visitor to my sleepless hours. Why had he wanted to erase me from his world? For that had been his intention, no doubt about that; had he had an axe instead of that enamel jug, he would have used it, such was his ferocity. Over the years I have brooded over every one of the few details I can remember. Those uniform bits, for instance. Had

he perhaps been one of the unfortunate teenage boys the Nazis had drafted in at the very end of the war, had taught to kill, to be heroes, to defend their mothers and sisters? Had he, in his confused mind, wanted to rescue those little girls from their tormentor? Even then I had felt that jealousy had been a motif, not so much of me being with girls, but of me not being alone.

And that pitiful enamel jug – had he no one to feed him? Were his parents dead, maybe still buried under the rubble? Was he just roaming around, homeless, gone feral, after all he had seen, all he had lost? Was he, when we met, as impregnated with death and killing as I was as yet untouched by it? I will never get the answers to these questions, but over a lifetime they have brought him ever closer to me, my would-be executioner.

– From RTÉ's *Sunday Miscellany*

GLOSSARY
morass: marshy ground

Reading for Meaning

1. What possible motivations does the writer consider that might explain his attacker's behaviour?
2. What are the writer's feelings towards the boy?
3. (a) The narration of the story changes from the third person ('he' / 'the boy') to the first person ('I'). Identify where this happens.
   (b) Why do you think the writer chose to begin the story in the third person and then change to the first person?
4. (a) There is considerable tension in this piece. Which part of the story do you feel is particularly tense?
   (b) How does the writer create this sense of tension?
5. Would you agree that this episode from his life had a serious effect on the writer? Explain your answer.

Writer's Workshop

Diary: Imagine you are the older boy in *The Enamel Jug*. Write a diary entry for the day described in the story. Try and explore your reasons for attacking the younger child.

Links

The Enamel Jug shows how war can profoundly affect individuals, leaving deep psychological scars. This piece can be linked to other texts in this book and elsewhere:
In this book: Michel Morpurgo's short story, *No Trumpets Needed* (page 112)
Elsewhere: Pat Barker's anti-war novel, *Regeneration*

Chapter 2:
Something to Say –
Opinion Pieces, Social Commentary, Travel Writing and Reviews

It can be fascinating to read about how other people view the world. Sometimes people's opinions can convince us to adopt their point of view; other times they can provoke us into argument. Either way, reading a well-written opinion piece can be a rewarding experience as it encourages us to look at life from a fresh perspective or point of view.

Modern media, whether print (e.g. a newspaper you buy in a shop), online (e.g. a newspaper website) or broadcast (e.g. a radio station or television channel), exposes us to an incredible amount of information and ideas. Understanding how opinions are expressed is an important part of engaging with mass media.

In this chapter you will read a mix of different opinion pieces, social commentary (i.e. commenting on society), travel writing and reviews. The writers featured in this chapter use different language styles. Some write opinion pieces out of a sense of anger or outrage; others use humour or personal anecdotes to make their point. The wide variety of styles shows how persuasion, argument and commentary can be best employed to get your point across.

You should feel encouraged to start expressing your own opinions and to reflect on society. By modelling your work on the texts in this chapter, you will improve your ability to write a convincing and sincere opinion piece in your own voice.

You may find yourself agreeing or disagreeing with the writers in this chapter. The texts selected are intended to be thought provoking and do not necessarily reflect the views of this book's author.

Opinion Pieces

Christmas is a Conspiracy against Women

Marian Keyes

Marian Keyes is one of the most successful Irish novelists of all time. Her work has been published in 33 languages and includes a number of bestsellers. In this article for *The Sunday Times*, she discusses her reasons for not celebrating Christmas.

Last Christmas morning, I awoke to a house devoid of tinsel. No pile of alluring presents twinkled beneath the tree. Because there was no tree. No turkey marinated in an aluminium bath in the shed, no visiting siblings slept in the spare bedroom, no holly wreath hung on the front door. If you'd just landed from another planet and called at my house, you'd have never known it was Christmas.

Because I don't do Christmas, not even a teeny, tiny bit. It's not necessarily that I hate it. In fact, when I can access those elusive memories of being a child on Christmas morning, seeing the toys under the sparkly, shiny tree, I feel I might die of magic. What I am is a conscientious objector. Not for religious reasons, but because the festive season piles unbearable burdens on people already at breaking point and I can't be part of it.

Looking back, Christmas was game over as soon as I discovered the truth about Santa. Without that enchanting patina, the grim reality of the season revealed itself, becoming ever more pronounced the older I got. By my twenties, I knew that Christmas is not the most wonderful time of the year, it's the worst: the hubbub, the hangovers, the non-stop bonhomie; battling through crowded shops to buy presents for people I didn't like with money I didn't have; scrubbing the house for the arrival of visitors whose hygiene standards were much higher than my own; drunkenly wrapping presents at two in the morning; overeating to the point of self-hatred; being knocked off-kilter by bitter squabbles that erupted from nowhere, and the desperate aching desire for half an hour alone in a cool, quiet room.

Worst of all was the misery of watching my poor mother run herself ragged trying to produce the perfect dinner – shouting and chaos in a steam-filled kitchen, only for me and my siblings to give a wide berth to the roughly hacked slices of dry turkey because we'd all been on the selection boxes since 5 a.m.

Eventually, I begged Mammy Keyes to knock off the turkey, to go with something more manageable, like, say, a chicken. For a moment, hope gleamed in her eyes, then abruptly she shut the whole idea down, as if she feared a visit from the Christmas secret police. 'Shop-bought bread sauce? No chipolatas? You are a failure as a mother, as a wife, but most of all as a woman!' Because – and I can't stress this enough – Christmas is a feminist issue. It's exhausting for everyone, but it's women who end up doing the majority of the work, and it's women who feel they must measure up to some impossible ideal.

About 10 years ago, after a truly terrible Christmas, when the pressure got too much for one person, and shouting, tears and a family rift ensued, I had an epiphany. 'That's it,' I decided. 'No more. I can't be a part of this horrible endurance test any longer.'

My husband was in full agreement. So the following year, as soon as family members began asking, 'What are we doing this Christmas?' (and Mammy Keyes's inquiries usually begin around January 2nd), I said, in a voice trembling with wonder at my own audacity, 'I'm not doing it. Not this year. Not ever again.'

Uproar ensued, but despite being a bone-deep people-pleaser, I laid out my reasoning: people were getting into debt buying reindeer onesies they would only wear for a morning; life was hard enough without having to buy potpourri – and wrap it – for distant relations they disliked intensely. Back in the days when food was scarce, a big, celebratory feast made sense – but when creeping obesity is a national concern, it seems obscene.

I honestly thought I might start a revolution. Throw down your sticky tape! Tear off your scratchy Lurex dress! Skip the office party!

Sadly, no. When I'm obliged to tell people my stance, and after they've understood that I really mean it – which takes some time, because they ask incredulously, 'Tell me you have a turkey? You must have a turkey?' And, 'No presents? Nothing?' – they behave as if I drown kittens for a hobby.

Granted, I don't have children, and if I did, my husband and I wouldn't have this choice. The only people we've ever met who think as we do are our friends Posh Kate and Posh Malcolm (which is probably one reason we're friends). For the past few years, the four of us have spent Christmas Day enjoying a forest walk by a fast-flowing river. The stony path ends at a waterfall, where we have sandwiches (not turkey – not ever). Sometimes Kate brings mini-mince pies and Christmas crackers, which I go along with. Good Lord, I'm not a total monster.

Despite this, the taunts from 'loved ones' continue – Scrooge. Killjoy. Freak. 'Smug bitch', though, that's the jibe that riles. I eschew Christmas not just as an act of self-care (dread phrase), but for altruistic reasons, too – to demonstrate to those already buckling under the burden that they can dial the whole wretched business down, even a little.

My radical position is not for everyone. But seriously, if you don't have the neighbours round for homemade mulled wine, the world won't end. Social media can survive without a fun! fun! fun! family photo of you all in Santa hats. Strawberry jam will do if you forgot to get cranberry sauce – just stick it in a bowl, who cares, everyone will be too drunk to notice. Baby steps are the start of your path to freedom. You could give it a go. After all, you have nothing to lose but a nervous breakdown.

– From *The Sunday Times*

GLOSSARY

devoid: free from

alluring: very attractive

elusive: difficult to remember

conscientious objector: a person who refuses to serve in the armed forces for reasons of conscience

patina: a thin layer / film

bonhomie: friendliness / good-natured manner

epiphany: sudden insight

jibe: a taunting remark

riles: irritates / provokes

eschew: avoid / abstain

altruistic: unselfish concern / for the good of others

Reading for Meaning

1. Marian Keyes gives a number of reasons for the fact that she doesn't 'do Christmas'. Outline the argument she makes.

2. Do you agree that 'Christmas is a feminist issue' and that 'it's women who end up doing the majority of the work'? Explain your answer.

3. 'In *Christmas is a Conspiracy against Women*, Marian Keyes expresses a strong opinion using entertaining and humorous language.' Discuss this statement making reference to Keyes's use of language.

Speaking and Listening

Debate: Hold a debate in your class on the following motion: 'Christmas is just for kids.' Go to Chapter 6, pages 212–214 to learn how to organise a debate.

Writer's Workshop

Letter: Write a letter to Marian Keyes in response to her article, in which you either agree with her viewpoint or take issue with her argument.

In your letter, try to adopt the lively style that Keyes uses in her article. You might wish to add colour to your writing by including personal anecdotes (see page 9).

Links

Christmas is a Conspiracy against Women uses a light-hearted touch to explore the position of women in society. This issue is discussed in a more serious manner in other texts in this book and elsewhere:

In this book: Kate Chopin's *The Story of an Hour* (page 140)

Elsewhere: Marjane Satrapi's graphic novel, *Persepolis*

Zoos are Prisons for Animals – No one needs to see a depressed penguin in the flesh

Romesh Ranganathan

Romesh Ranganathan is a British stand-up comic, actor and TV personality. In this article from *The Guardian* newspaper, he argues that zoos are not justifiable in the modern world.

In an age when David Attenborough can virtually take us inside an elephant's bottom, is there any value to keeping animals in captivity?

That a zoo in Cumbria is having its licence revoked as a result of nearly 500 animals dying there over a two-year period comes as no shock – but it still slightly surprises me that anybody thinks that we should have zoos at all. The animals always look miserable in captivity. If you don't believe me, visit a farm park. It's as likely as not that you will see a goat, pleading with its eyes to be euthanised, while a sign on the enclosure says: 'Gerry the goat is quite the character – he often plays a game in which he looks like he has been crying for many, many hours!'

A lot of zoos play the conservation angle, which is a rationale that has been reverse engineered. That's not really why zoos exist. Zoos exist so that we can wander round with our children and say: 'No, don't bang the glass, Timothy, he's getting agitated,' before going home to post on social media about the educational day that we have had.

The argument that zoos have educational merit might have once seemed convincing, but there is less reason to see animals in captivity than ever before. David Attenborough's *Planet Earth* shows you all the animals you could ask for in their natural habitat, with added drama and narrative arcs. We are surely only a few series away from filming inside the animals, with Attenborough using his dulcet tones to give the origin story of an elephant turd. Why, then, do we need to see them in prison?

On holiday recently, I was persuaded by my family to visit a marine theme park that bombards you with messages of preserving marine life. We spent the afternoon seeing seals and penguins that looked to be in varying stages of depression before taking in the dolphin show, which meant watching a 2-minute video about saving dolphins, and a 10-minute demonstration of how the park has managed to enslave them and get them to perform tricks. I wondered about the message behind getting the dolphins to pull some kids around in a boat almost as much as I wondered why my own children hadn't been offered that experience.

When Cecil the lion was killed, the general public were so incensed that the dentist who shot him became an international hate figure; the perfect example of the public picking and choosing when to care about animals. It's apparently really bad to shoot Cecil despite the fact he has had a much better life than the huge number of lions that we continue to keep in captivity. I am not suggesting that it is wrong to care about Cecil, but if we are in uproar about that, why aren't we as upset about the animals in tanks and cages, or the ones that we eat? I wonder if we would have been so upset if the lion didn't have a name. Or was called Piers.

There are counter-arguments, of course. After a visit to the Sea Life centre in Brighton, my eldest son took a passionate interest in marine life that has stayed with him, and I wouldn't be surprised if animal conservation went on to be one of his primary concerns. This is almost certainly as a direct result of our visit, but it's also first-world privilege in micro form: 'We must have some animals in cages for little Stephen to look at, otherwise how will he learn?'

Similarly, the idea that kids only get excited about things they can see in the flesh is ridiculous. My kids are obsessed with dinosaurs that no longer exist, and Skylanders, which have never existed. One of our sons watches endless YouTube videos of Kinder Surprise eggs being opened, so the bar is set pretty low in terms of what will get him interested. I would, however, be delighted to hear that the YouTubers responsible for these videos had been put in a series of cages for our enjoyment.

I have no doubts that the people working in zoos, safari parks and conservation centres all really care about the animals. But there is a pretty strong argument that there is a negative effect on conservation awareness, given that children take away the message that 'endangered species' are probably OK because they have seen them in the zoo. Plus, zoos and conservation spaces are impossible to effectively regulate. Have a look online and see the number of cases of animals being killed because of lack of space, horses being painted to look like zebras, animals in aquariums showing clear signs of distress.

Still, I was struck by my own hypocrisy when I was looking to get a family pet. When I found myself Googling: 'How long will a puppy cry for its mother and siblings?' it occurred to me that I probably no longer wanted to do it. The idea that I don't want animals to be imprisoned, but that I quite fancy having a prisoner of my own doesn't sit comfortably. This might sound extreme and no doubt cat owners will tell me that their cats are free to go wherever they want but always return. I live in Crawley, however, and often when I'm out I immediately want to return straight home. I could never be sure if the cat coming back was a thumbs-up for the family, or a silent protest against the lack of amenities in town. I'm also starting to consider setting my children free.

– From *The Guardian*

GLOSSARY

narrative arcs: plotline, story
dulcet tones: sweet, soothing voice
euthanised: killed to relieve pain or suffering
Cecil the lion: a lion that was legally hunted and killed for sport by an American dentist. Cecil was living in a national park in Zimbabwe where he was a tourist attraction and part of a study being conducted by the University of Oxford. Media coverage of Cecil's death fuelled significant international outrage.
Crawley: a town in West Sussex, England

Reading for Meaning

1. What effect does the opening sentence have on the reader?
2. Outline the argument made by Romesh Ranganathan against the practice of keeping animals in zoos.
3. Why do you think the author uses personal anecdotes rather than hard facts to make his case?
4. Do you agree with the point being made by Ranganathan?
5. 'Romesh Ranganathan manages to make a serious argument using lively and humorous language.' Discuss this statement making reference to the author's language use.

Writer's Workshop

Poster: Do some online research on the issue of zoos. Create a poster to support or oppose the argument presented above. Include facts in your poster, ensuring that it is pleasing to look at and clear to understand. You might consider using an online poster tool such as www.canva.com to help you.

Style Guide

Rhetorical Questions: A rhetorical question is one in which the answer is implied. It is asked not for the answer, but for the effect. Rhetorical questions influence the reader and can be used to:

• persuade readers that a particular point of view is correct
• emphasise a point
• wrap up an argument.

In *Zoos are Prisons for Animals*, rhetorical questions are used to great effect. For example, in the opening sentence, the author writes, 'is there any value to keeping animals in captivity?' Here the writer wants to draw attention to his central argument that zoos are unjustified. The statement is framed as a question to add emphasis.

Rhetorical questions imply the answer and reflect the viewpoint of the author. In the article, the author asks, 'Why, then, do we need to see them [animals] in prison?' and 'why aren't we as upset about the animals in tanks and cages, or the ones that we eat?' These rhetorical questions are intended to persuade the reader of the article's main point. The implied answer is that animals should not be held in captivity and that we should be upset about this practice.

When writing or reading an opinion piece, it is worth considering how rhetorical questions can be a powerful tool for a writer who has something to say.

Links

Zoos are Prisons for Animals looks poorly on humanity's treatment of animals. This article can be linked to other texts in this book and elsewhere:

In this book: William Stafford's poem, *At the Bomb Testing Site* (page 196)
Elsewhere: Jonathan Safran Foer's non-fiction book, *Eating Animals*

The Noble Art

In this article, the writer uses a variety of persuasive writing techniques to condemn the sport of boxing.

They call it the noble art. But what is noble about two men slugging away at each other until one of them is unconscious on the canvas while hundreds of people, safe in their seats, roar and shriek for blood, and a few others, without lifting a fist, can pour money into their bank deposits?

If you have ever seen a boxer after a bout, you would never call boxing noble. You must have seen the close-ups on television, those bleary half-shut eyes, those bruised thickened lips, that puffy battered flesh, the blood pouring from cuts around the eyes. It is degrading to think that a man has been prepared to put up with that kind of punishment in the name of sport and as a means of making a living. It is degrading to think that it was another man who inflicted that pain and punishment on him for the same reasons.

But it goes beyond a battered face and a loss of dignity. Recently [in 1986], the boxer Steve Watt died in the ring, and pressure rose again for the sport to be banned. And rightly so. What kind of sport is it that ends in a man's death? The chief medical officer for the British Boxing Board of Control has pointed out, that since 1948, there have only been twelve deaths within the game and has said, 'If only every sport could be as safe as that.'

It is true that people die in motor racing or climbing mountains. But there is a difference. In those sports, people are pitting themselves against speed or natural hazards. They are not being pounded to death by their fellow men for the entertainment of the masses. In any case, it's not simply a case of deaths. How many boxers have had to retire into a premature senile old age because of brain damage? A recent televised film on Muhammad Ali was shocking. Someone who had once been a vital quip-a-minute young man became a bewildered inarticulate zombie. Constantly being beaten around the head by men determined to knock you out is bound to have some effect.

And there is evidence to prove it. The British Medical Association Working Party on boxing has stated that x-ray brain scanning shows beyond doubt that permanent brain damage commonly occurs in men who box. Doctors may differ in their opinion, but the fact that the BMA has this kind of evidence and is campaigning to have boxing banned must carry a lot of weight.

It's not just the dangers of boxing itself that cause concern. It is also the whole atmosphere that surrounds it. That crowds of people – men and women – can cheer and get excited at the sight of two men doing their best to hurt and damage each other, is sickening. It is uncivilised. It is little better than the Roman gladiatorial fights to the death which history and society condemned long ago.

It has been argued in favour of boxing that it is one of the few ways in which 'a working-class lad' can achieve fame and fortune. But for how many is this true? One in a million? More typical is the case of Randy Turpin, once a world champion, who ended up a drunk and practically destitute, and finally committed suicide.

No, it's not the boxers who make the money, it's the promoters. With their betting and big deals, and

Mafia organisations, they're the ones who go laughing all the way to the bank. When one of their boxers is finished, his brains beaten to a pulp, they drop him without a backward glance and seize on someone else to exploit.

'What a piece of work is man!' says Shakespeare in *Hamlet*, 'How noble in reason! how infinite in faculty! in form, in moving, how express and admirable! in action how like an angel! in apprehension how like a god! the beauty of the world! the paragon of animals!'

The next time you see a boxing match on television, with two exhausted men, faces bruised and bloodied, hanging on to each other because their legs are giving way, being jeered at by the crowd and urged on to show them some action, think of that. Do boxers live up to this view of what man is or ought to be? There is more dignity in sweeping roads.

Anonymous

Reading for Meaning

1. The author makes a number of points that criticise boxing as a sport. Summarise the author's argument.
2. (a) What evidence does the author offer to support the argument against boxing?
   (b) Is the evidence well chosen? Why / why not?
3. Do you feel that the quotation from *Hamlet* helps to persuade the reader? Explain your answer.
4. The author views boxing as 'uncivilised' and compares it to 'Roman gladiatorial fights to the death'. Do you think that this is a fair position to hold? Explain your answer.

Style Guide

Persuasion: Persuasive language works by appealing to a reader's emotions, suggesting ideas and using language such as rhetorical questions. This type of language is found in newspaper articles, speeches, debating, advertising, sermons, propaganda, etc.

- **Emotive language:** Language that stirs the reader's emotions is referred to as emotive language. This type of language is clearly on display in *The Noble Art*. For example, when describing the physical dangers of boxing, the author offers a very negative image of 'bleary half-shut eyes . . . bruised thickened lips . . . puffy battered flesh, the blood pouring from cuts around the eyes.' The emotive language provokes a sense of disgust and makes an emotional plea to the reader to oppose boxing as a sport.
- **Suggestion:** An author can suggest an idea as being universally true through his/her use of language. For example, in the piece above, the author suggests that boxing spectators are uncivilised and celebrate physical pain: 'crowds of people – men and women – can cheer and get excited at the sight of two men doing their best to hurt and damage each other'. This is not necessarily a true representation of boxing spectators but adds drama and emotion to the article.

- **Comparisons:** The author of *The Noble Art* unfavourably compares boxing matches to 'Roman gladiatorial fights to the death.' In reality there is of course a lot of difference between boxing and gladiatorial combat, but through this dramatic comparison the author looks to persuade the reader.

- **Repetition:** Repeating a phrase or word can be an effective way to emphasise an idea. In this piece, the phrase 'It is degrading' is repeated in the second paragraph. This underlines the point being made and strengthens the author's voice.

- **Rhetorical questions:** A question where the answer is implied is known as a rhetorical question (see page 49). *The Noble Art* is peppered with rhetorical questions that exert a persuasive pressure on the reader. For example: 'what is noble about two men slugging away at each other . . . while a few others, without lifting a fist, can pour money into their bank deposits?' The implied answer is that there is nothing noble about this practice.

Writer's Workshop

Speech: Write a speech to be delivered to your classmates about a sport that you strongly support or criticise. In your speech present the virtues or flaws of your chosen sport. You may consider: how this sport affects those who play it, the culture of the sport, the industry around this sport (TV, media, advertising, etc.). You may wish to echo the style used in *The Noble Art*. Try to use some of the persuasive language devices listed above.

Links

The Noble Art offers a very pessimistic view of the sport of boxing. This piece can be linked to other texts such as Clint Eastwood's film, *Million Dollar Baby*.

Who's Deprived Now?

India Knight

India Knight is a journalist and author. She often comments on social issues. In this article, she explores the modern-day problem of violent crime.

In the week when the word 'yob' was banned by Scotland Yard because it might 'alienate' teenagers and injure their tender feelings (oh boo hoo), Stevens Nyembo-Ya-Muteba, 40, was murdered by a gang of 'youths' outside his flat in East London.

Stevens, a married father of two little girls, was an immigrant from the Democratic Republic of Congo to Britain, where he held down two jobs – delivering food for Tesco during the day, night portering at a restaurant in the evenings – to pay for his education. He was in the third year of a maths and finance degree at a local university having turned down a place at Cambridge so as to stay closer to home. A 17-year-old 'youth' has been charged with his murder.

Stevens lost his life because he had had the temerity to ask the gang to keep the noise down after they broke into the communal area of the council estate where he lived. It was about 10 p.m. 'Some of us have work in the morning,' he'd reportedly said which, as rebukes go, is both polite and mild. He was stabbed for his pains and left to bleed to death on a stairwell.

It has since emerged that Stevens and other residents had repeatedly urged the police and the council to do something about the appalling goings-on at the estate. 'Prostitutes, smackheads, people having sex on the stairs,' one resident said. Another mentioned gangs of youths congregating in stairwells, taking drugs, urinating and trying to start fires. 'The police and the council had been aware of it all for some time,' a relative of Stevens said last week.

I used to live in this part of London. There were needles in the local park and crack-smoking paraphernalia littered the pavements. We were once woken in the night by two dozen armed police who explained that there had been a burglary and that the burglars, who had guns, had taken refuge on our roof.

This in an area, by the way, which was last week described by a London newspaper as up-and-coming and made to sound rather charming and cosmopolitan, with bars and cafes open until 5 a.m. (I rather wonder who the paper thinks goes drinking at 5 a.m. Schoolteachers? Yummy mummies? Or – here's a thought – a feral underclass celebrating the night's pickings?) It made no mention of the gun crime, the stabbings, the drugs or the desperation.

What is especially depressing about this whole depressing story, which took place in a depressed area full of depressed people doing depressing things, is that I imagine Stevens himself knew a thing or two about deprivation; and that what he knew would put his assailants' poxy little gripes to shame. Originally from Kinshasa, which is a horrible city in a grim country, I don't expect the offer of a place at Cambridge exactly fell into his lap. 'I believed in myself and got what I wanted,' he once told his college newsletter.

There are unsettling moments when I feel myself turning very conservative, and this is one of them.

What's with the pathetic, weedy nonsense from Scotland Yard about hurting yobs' feelings, when stories such as Stevens' have, shamefully, become commonplace? Who cares about their feelings? I don't. I couldn't care less. I don't care how hard their lives are: I don't expect Stevens' life in Kinshasa was much of a picnic either but at least he was doing his best to better himself to make a new life for his family. And I am so tired of the stupid notion (held by me for decades) that gangs of hoodies are all gigantically deprived and thus need our pity, love and support, rather than our reprobation. What they need, actually, is to be locked up.

Deprivation is relative: none of them is starving, all of them are clothed and all of them have access to free education. Besides, one of the yobs arrested in connection with Stevens' murder is, if you please, the son of a social worker, which doesn't quite constitute the frontline of ghettohood.

The gangs that periodically terrorise my new extremely salubrious, picture-postcard corner of north London aren't 'deprived' in any material sense that I can understand, either – not when they are wearing several hundred pounds' worth of designer clothing. They are certainly emotionally deprived to which the only solution is first-rate education – starting with nursery and, in some cases, psychotherapy from the age of five.

That is a political point. The broader social point is that the killing in East London is the merest tip of a deformed, monstrous iceberg. We are all, wherever we live, at the mercy of marauding gangs of underclass yobs, intent on damage, and there seems to be little that anyone can do about it (which is why I'm sounding so cross. I'd have been less cross 10 years ago, and hardly cross at all 20 years ago, but the crossness escalates with every year that passes because the problem gets worse and nothing happens).

I was recently told by a representative from my local Safer Neighbourhood Team that its powers were somewhat limited: it could ask gangs of boys what they were doing lurking in residential areas at 2 a.m., but since it was not legally allowed to make physical contact with them, it could not actually remove them if vocal persuasion failed.

Besides, the representative said mournfully, they're often on bikes, which means they move too fast. As for Asbos: not terribly helpful when in some circles an Asbo is a badge of honour. I mean, really: someone's having a laugh and it's not you or me.

Being frightened in the street and even in our own homes – feeling scared to intervene when yobs are behaving badly for fear of one's own safety – has become the norm in this country. We moan about it in the same way that we moan about leaves on the line or automated telephone systems: it's just everyday life.

You have to prepare yourself for the worst before opening the local newspaper, because its tally of crimes makes you come over all agoraphobic. I used to be absolutely appalled by gated communities – the super-rich making themselves safe because they can afford to. These days I grudgingly see the point. And that feels profoundly demoralising.

– From *The Sunday Times* (adapted)

GLOSSARY

temerity: boldness / gall
rebuke: scold / reprimand
deprivation: the absence of something needed / the state of being deprived

reprobation: disapproval, condemnation
salubrious: upmarket, wealthy
marauding: plundering / raiding

Reading for Meaning

1. What is the overall point India Knight is making in this article?
2. Do you agree with the author's point of view?
3. How does India Knight encourage us to sympathise with the victim and his family?
4. This article explores the problem of criminality in London. Do you feel that the issues raised here are relevant to Ireland?

Language Lab

1. (a) Describe the tone of the opening sentence.
   (b) Why do you think India Knight adopts this tone?
2. (a) Write down an example of repetition in this article.
   (b) What effect does this use of repetition have on the reader?
3. India Knight's opinions are strongly expressed in this article. Write down two phrases from the article that you feel are powerful and explain why you find them so.
4. The writer uses rhetorical questions (see page 49) successfully in this article. Find two examples and comment on their effect.

Style Guide

Illustration / Exemplification: An illustration or exemplification is an example offered by a writer to support an idea. Writers may illustrate their points using a variety of evidence such as facts, statistics, expert opinion or personal anecdotes.

In *Who's Deprived Now?* India Knight draws on her own experiences throughout the article to support her viewpoint: 'I used to live in East London . . . We were once woken in the night by two dozen armed police who explained that there had been a burglary and that the burglars, who had guns, had taken refuge on our roof.' This example strengthens Knight's assertion that violence is common in this part of London.

She also uses the sad case of Stevens Nyembo-Ya-Muteba's murder and information from a local community worker as evidence of a violent society.

India Knight's views on the violence of modern society are strengthened by her use of illustration. The examples she gives make this a compelling piece of writing.

Writer's Workshop

Article: Write an article for a newspaper giving your views on how society should deal with the problem of violent crime. Like India Knight, try to make use of examples to illustrate your ideas.

Links

Who's Deprived Now? presents the world as a very violent place and explores the issue of social disorder. This article can be linked to other texts in this book and elsewhere:

In this book: Norman MacCaig's poem, *Hotel Room, 12th Floor* (page 188)
Elsewhere: William Shakespeare's *Macbeth*

Paddy's Day

Peter Cunningham

This article from the *Irish Daily Mail* tackles the issue of alcohol in Irish society. The writer, Peter Cunningham, strongly condemns how Ireland deals with this serious problem.

It was the expression 'drunken mob' used in media reports earlier this week to describe what occurred in Dublin that was surprisingly shocking. Last Monday, St Patrick's Day, the Garda riot squad moved into an area of Dublin that had been taken over by young thugs running amok. Cars were hijacked and torched, their occupants beaten up. Children as young as 10 years old were reported to have been intoxicated.

Loutish behaviour on St Patrick's Day, particularly in Dublin, has become pretty much standard in recent years and therefore to hear about it again shouldn't come as much of a surprise. Yet, nowadays in the wider world you don't hear much about 'drunken mobs'. Riots and political demonstrations that get out of control, yes. Crowds of rampaging dissenters where the abuse of power has provoked despair and violence, certainly. But drunken mobs? Crowds whose behaviour is fuelled by drinking so much alcohol that the riot police have to be called in? It's a modern rarity – except in Ireland.

When it comes to doing drunk, we still do it better and more consistently than anyone. Alcohol abuse is an Irish epidemic. We binge drink on an epic scale and we pay the consequences: at least half of all fatal and serious road accidents are linked to drink-driving. Drunken brawls are commonplace. Recently, two Polish men were murdered when they refused to buy drinks for local youths. Drunkenness in Ireland is not new, but the link between drink and violence is a worrying modern phenomenon.

It wasn't always like this. Drink has truly become the demon in our midst. Alcohol abuse has devastating consequences: depression, anxiety, suicide, marriage breakdown, criminal behaviour, unemployment and poverty all come after the hangover. The community too pays a high price. Alcohol misuse is estimated to cost the economy more than €2.7 billion a year in health costs and lost productivity. Many Irish adults are familiar with what is known as the drink culture, in reality a dingy subculture where alcohol is the major form of recreation; where the system of measuring alcohol in units is seen as a scorecard rather than a medical imperative.

Alcohol is Ireland's biggest public conspiracy. We are all in it and we all sustain it. We laugh knowingly at the booze-soaked fossil that is Father Jack, but the truth is, we all know a Father Jack. Drink is everywhere in Ireland and in the battle to try and weave a path through it and not be swallowed up, we have eulogised and celebrated 'the jar' for generations. We have presented ourselves to the world as the only people who truly know how to have fun and are mystified when we encounter cultures who seem to have fun without getting legless. We feel sorry for such people. They haven't discovered the magic potion, as we have.

Yet, the fact that a drunken mob can take over a residential area of Dublin in the 21st century should ring alarm bells in the heads of anybody who cares about Irish society. This image, like a throwback to that of a medieval mob, should at the very least cause us to have a long hard look at ourselves. Isn't it high time that we admitted that our freewheeling alcohol consumption is both personally ruinous and a devastating example to the younger generations? We are the inheritors of centuries of alcohol abuse, but we are not alone. In Georgian London it was estimated that a quarter of all households were used for the production or sale of gin. 'Drunk for a penny, dead drunk for twopence' was the catchy advertising slogan of the day.

By 1838, the caricature of the drunken Irishman was well established when Father Theobald Mathew went on a nationwide crusade to exhort people to take a pledge not to drink. At its height, just before the Famine, Father Mathew's temperance drive had enrolled nearly three million people. The abuse of alcohol was so widespread and destructive in the United States in the early twentieth century that a national prohibition on the manufacture and sale of alcohol was imposed from 1920 to 1933.

Today the sale of alcohol is still outlawed in many towns and communities across the United States. In Norway, Sweden, Finland and Iceland, the sale of liquor to consumers takes place only through government monopolies. Many countries of the Middle East, North Africa and Central Asia, either partially or totally, ban the sale and consumption of alcohol. Similar restrictions exist in South Asia and South-East Asia. And even parts of Australia have a tradition of alcohol prohibition. What all this is saying is that alcohol is a dangerous drug that most societies feel it necessary to legislate for. Not here. In Ireland today, where taking the pledge and Father Mathew sound like embarrassing sound bites from an era of ignorance and poverty best forgotten, alcohol roars in the ears of the nation. We all enjoy it, we are all complicit. If a home teams wins a coveted trophy, or a horse trained in the home village wins a big race, the media interview with the locals usually ends with the line: 'And I've no doubt that there'll be plenty of sore heads here tomorrow!' We take it for granted that celebration and drunkenness are natural companions. The craic, that term that seems to encompass all any of us could ever wish for, means only one thing.

The myth of drink is rooted in us as fiery, goblet-swilling Celts. Drink was long celebrated too as being synonymous with genius: Brendan Behan and Flann O'Brien, both of whom I remember as sad and paralytic, were writers whose genius was overtaken by their tragic alcohol-led destiny. This Irish drink myth gets carried forward by the likes of Shane McGowan, whose self-destruction from alcohol is worn as a badge of distinction. But when I hear about drunken mobs on the rampage, attacking innocent bystanders and 10-year-old kids throwing up because they're drunk, I have to wonder where we all went wrong.

It's as if Ireland is still in the era of Gin Lane or Oliver Twist. There's no point in complaining that we're victims of our genes or of our tragic past. There's little pride in blaming the Irish weather, or the lack of alternative activities to being in a pub in Ireland, or the wisdom found at the end of a row of pints. We need to try and think our way soberly out of this mess, which is no longer just a drunken mess but has become a murderous one as well.

'People are no closer to the acceptance of alcoholism as a disease than they were when this centre opened in 1978,' says John Donohoe, senior counsellor at the Hanly Centre. 'The focus now is all on drugs. It goes without saying that drink is the biggest drug of all but, of course, the government gets a lot of money from alcohol sales.' More than €2 billion every year, to be exact. What the government should do, but won't, is ban all advertising and sports sponsorship of alcohol. What else can kids think of but a future on the booze when whatever sport they have chosen to play or watch is intrinsically interwoven with intoxicating liquor? It comes at them from every quarter.

We have made things this bad. I wish we hadn't. But there comes a time when we shoulc as a nation and assert ourselves as more than just part of a drunken mob.

– From the *Irish Daily Mail*

GLOSSARY

eulogised: praised highly

Brendan Behan and Flann O'Brien: famous Irish writers

Shane McGowan: former lead-singer of The Pogues

Gin Lane: an 18th-century print by Hogarth depicting the damage caused by drinking g

Oliver Twist: a 19th-century novel by Charles Dickens in which alcohol is portrayed as destructive influence on some of the characters

Hanly Centre: an organisation that deals with alcohol-related harm

Reading for Meaning

1. According to the writer, how does Irish drinking culture impact on the community?
2. (a) What image of Irish society is presented in this article?
   (b) Do you believe this is a fair representation of Ireland? Why / why not?
3. (a) What solution to excessive drinking among young people does the writer offer at the end of the article?
   (b) Do you believe that this solution would help deal with the problems outlined?
4. (a) Which Irish writers and singers does the article refer to?
   (b) What point does Peter Cunningham make in relation to these artists?
5. Do you find the writer's overall argument to be convincing? Explain your answer.

Language Lab

1. (a) Find three emotive phrases (see page 51) in this article.
   (b) Why do you think Peter Cunningham uses emotive language?
2. (a) Find an example of a rhetorical question (see page 49) in this piece.
   (b) Why do you think the writer chooses to use rhetorical questions in this article?

Style Guide

Argument: In an opinion piece, a writer may try to convince the reader of his/her point of view by arguing in a logical, factual manner. Examples of this type of writing can be found in newspaper articles, legal writing, debating, philosophy, scientific journals etc. This strategy relies on solid evidence on which to base viewpoints.

The following are common features of the language of argument:

- **Facts:** Peter Cunningham uses hard facts to support his ideas. For example, he notes that 'Alcohol misuse is estimated to cost the economy more than €2.7 billion a year.'
- **Logic:** In this article, the writer offers a number of logical arguments. He states that young people are exposed to advertising for alcohol which affects the choices they make in life. Therefore, Cunningham argues, the government should 'ban all advertising and sports sponsorship of alcohol.'
- **Anticipatory arguments:** The writer anticipates some objections people may raise to his ideas. He then tries to dismiss them: 'There's no point in complaining that we're victims of our genes or of our tragic past. There's little pride in blaming the Irish weather, or the lack of alternative activities to being in a pub in Ireland'.
- **Reliable authorities:** Cunningham appeals to reliable experts to add weight to his argument. For example, he quotes a counsellor from the Hanly Centre – a centre where alcoholics can be treated for their addiction – who illustrates how serious the problem of alcohol abuse is in Ireland.

Writer's Workshop

Article: This article deals with a serious social issue. Write an article that deals with a social issue that you feel is important. Try to use some of the techniques of argument identified in the Style Guide above.

Links

In its opening, *Paddy's Day* offers a critical view of the behaviour of some young people. This article can be linked to other texts in this book and elsewhere:

In this book: Rita Ann Higgins's poem, *The Immortals* (page 180)

Elsewhere: S.E. Hinton's novel, *The Outsiders*

Are We Going Out?
I'll Get My Pyjamas

Róisín Ingle

Róisín Ingle is a journalist and social commentator, well known for her articles in *The Irish Times*. In the article below she discusses the phenomenon of people wearing pyjamas as day-wear.

A sign at a health centre in Blanchardstown asked people not to turn up for appointments in pyjamas. Is it fair to impose a dress code on welfare claimants?

On a grey Wednesday afternoon two people are queuing to see the community welfare officers based at Damastown Health Centre, in Blanchardstown, in north Dublin. For the record, neither of them is wearing pyjamas.

Damastown is one of the health centres that hit the news this week because of a sign banning claimants from wearing sleepwear when attending appointments. 'Please be advised that Pyjamas are NOT regarded as appropriate attire when attending Community Welfare Services at these offices', read the notice, which also appeared in nearby Corduff Health Centre before being photographed and posted to social-media sites.

There is no sign of the controversial notice this afternoon. 'It was taken down earlier,' says a helpful HSE porter who doesn't want to be named. 'A call came from on high to get rid of it. I don't know why, but I don't think they liked the publicity. I was happy with the sign myself. I don't think people should be going into any public buildings in their pyjamas. It's only a handful of people who do it, but it's not right, especially if you are supposed to be looking for a job.'

Standing in the queue, Hanna Zebrowska from Poland nods in agreement. Until she came to Ireland she had never seen anybody wearing pyjamas outside their homes. 'When I first saw them, I thought they must be drunk or something,' she says. 'You would never see it in Poland. Not even homeless people would do that. They try to show respect in public places. In an office like this you should show respect for the people who work here and the other people who come in.'

It is understood that the sign was put up after some clients of the service complained about fellow claimants turning up in pyjamas. Asked about the policy and whether it operated in other social-welfare offices around the country, a spokesperson for the Department of Social Protection said there was no dress code for customers accessing community welfare services. 'Generally, the manner of dress is not a contentious issue, but a local manager may act on complaints or concerns expressed by customers on an individual basis,' the spokesperson said.

The sleepwear-as-daywear trend is thought to have begun in the council estates of Liverpool about a decade ago when pyjamas took over from tracksuits as the leisurewear of choice. The young women – it's nearly always women wearing pyjamas outdoors; rarely men – even acquired an uncomplimentary acronym: Yuans stood for 'young, unwashed and no sense'.

This is not the first time pyjama-wearing in public has caused controversy. In 2007, parents of children at a primary school in Belfast were admonished by the principal, who sent them a letter pointing out that wearing pyjamas on the school run was 'slovenly and rude'. A Tesco supermarket in Wales made headlines when it put up notices asking customers not to shop in sleepwear or barefoot. An editorial in the London *Times* yesterday highlighted the growing intolerance towards people wearing PJs in public.

'What we would always say is that people will judge you very quickly based on their first impression and that judgment is generally made within the first seven seconds,' says Audrey Buckley, cofounder of the Irish Image Consultants Institute.

According to Buckley, 55 per cent of that first impression is based on how a person looks: 'If you are wearing pyjamas outside the house the impression will be that you are lazy, that you haven't bothered to get dressed. It's to do with self-respect and not letting yourself down. It sends out a lot of negative signals.'

But some people won't be deterred. In recent years chain stores such as Penneys have expanded their pyjama ranges so that many of them now include clothing that blurs the line between sleepwear and daywear.

When *The Irish Times* interviewed a selection of die-hard pyjama-wearers in Dublin's inner city in 2006, they were adamant that it simply came down to comfort.

'Where we live there isn't much to get dressed for, so I suppose that's why we don't bother,' said one. 'I think if they stopped worrying about what people think and realised how comfy it is to wear pyjamas all day, more people might do it.'

From *The Irish Times*

Reading for Meaning

1. This article refers to a number of situations where efforts have been made to prevent people wearing pyjamas in public. Outline these situations and the arguments that were made.
2. Do you agree with Hanna Zebrowska (quoted in the article) that wearing pyjamas while claiming social welfare is disrespectful to those working in the social welfare office? Explain your answer.
3. The author, Róisín Ingle, never directly states her own opinion. Do you think that the article is fair to all sides, or is there a bias towards one point of view?
4. 'What you wear is nobody's business but your own.' Discuss this statement making reference to the article above and to society in general.

Style Guide

Appeals to Experts and Witnesses: To add credibility to a piece, writers often make reference to witnesses or experts. This helps to deepen the reader's understanding and may also provide important information or viewpoints.

In the article above, Róisín Ingle refers to a HSE porter, a woman in the queue, a Department spokesperson and a cofounder of an image consultancy. This brings colour to the article and adds new perspectives to the article.

A Doctor's Dilemma

James Dillard

James Dillard is a doctor in New York who practises rehabilitation medicine. In this article he describes a difficult situation he faced as a young doctor. The article was originally published in *Newsweek*.

It was a bright, clear February afternoon in Gettysburg. A strong sun and layers of down did little to ease the biting cold. Our climb to the crest of Little Round Top wound past sombre monuments, barren trees and polished cannon. From the top, we peered down on the wheat field where men had fallen so close together that one could not see the ground. Rifle balls had whined as thick as bee swarms through the trees, and cannon shots had torn limbs from the young men fighting there. A frozen wind whipped tears from our eyes. My friend Amy huddled close, using me as a wind breaker. Despite the cold, it was hard to leave this place.

Driving east out of Gettysburg on a country blacktop, the grey Bronco ahead of us passed through a rural crossroad just as a small pickup truck tried to take a left turn. The Bronco swerved, but slammed into the pickup on the passenger side. We immediately slowed to a crawl as we passed the scene. The Bronco's driver looked fine, but we couldn't see the driver of the pickup. I pulled over on the shoulder and got out to investigate.

The right side of the truck was smashed in, and the side window was shattered. The driver was partly out of the truck. His head hung forward over the edge of the passenger-side window, the front of his neck crushed on the shattered windowsill. He was unconscious and starting to turn a dusky blue. His chest slowly heaved against a blocked windpipe.

A young man ran out of a house at the crossroad. 'Get an ambulance out here,' I shouted against the wind. 'Tell them a man is dying.'

I looked down again at the driver hanging from the windowsill. There were six empty beer bottles on the floor of the truck. I could smell the beer through the window. I knew I had to move him, to open his airway. I had no idea what neck injuries he had sustained. He could easily end up a quadriplegic. But I thought: he'll be dead by the time the ambulance gets here if I don't move him and try to do something to help him.

An image flashed before my mind. I could see the courtroom and the driver of the truck sitting in a wheelchair. I could see his attorney pointing at me and thundering at the jury: 'This young doctor, with still a year left in his residency training, took it upon himself to play God. He took it upon himself to move this gravely injured man, condemning him forever to this wheelchair…' I imagined the millions of dollars in award money. And all the years of hard work lost. I'd be paying him off for the rest of my life. Amy touched my shoulder. 'What are you going to do?'

The automatic response from long hours in the emergency room kicked in. I pulled off my overcoat and rolled up my sleeves. The trick would be to keep enough traction straight up on his head while I moved his torso, so that his probable broken neck and spinal-cord injury wouldn't be made worse. Amy came around the driver's side, climbed half in and grabbed his belt and shirt collar. Together we lifted him off the windowsill.

He was still out cold, limp as a rag doll. His throat was crushed and blood from the jugular vein was running down my arms. He still couldn't breathe. He was deep blue-magenta now, his pulse was rapid and thready. The stench of alcohol turned my stomach, but I positioned his jaw and tried to blow air down into his lungs. It wouldn't go.

Amy had brought some supplies from my car. I opened an oversized intravenous needle and groped on the man's neck. My hands were numb, covered with freezing blood and bits of broken glass. Hyoid bone – God, I can't even feel the thyroid cartilage, it's gone…OK, the thyroid gland is about there, cricoid rings are here…we'll go in right here…

It was a lucky first shot. Pink air sprayed through the IV needle. I placed a second needle next to the first. The air began whistling through it. Almost immediately, the driver's face turned bright red. After a minute, his pulse slowed down and his eyes moved slightly. I stood up, took a step back and looked down. He was going to make it. He was going to live. A siren wailed in the distance. I turned and saw Amy holding my overcoat. I was shivering and my arms were turning white with cold.

The ambulance captain looked around and bellowed, 'What the hell…who did this?' as his team scurried over to the man lying in the truck.

'I did,' I replied. He took down my name and address for his reports. I had just destroyed my career. I would never be able to finish my residency with a massive lawsuit pending. My life was over.

The truck driver was strapped onto a backboard, his neck in a stiff collar. The ambulance crew had controlled the bleeding and started intravenous fluid. He was slowly waking up. As they loaded him into the ambulance, I saw him move his feet. Maybe my future wasn't lost.

A police sergeant called me from Pennsylvania three weeks later. Six days after successful throat-reconstruction surgery, the driver had signed out, against medical advice, from the hospital because he couldn't get a drink on the ward. He was being arraigned on drunk-driving charges.

A few days later, I went into the office of one of my senior professors, to tell the story. He peered over his half glasses and his eyes narrowed. 'Well, you did the right thing medically of course. But, James, do you know what you put at risk by doing that?' he said sternly.

'What was I supposed to do?' I asked.

'Drive on,' he replied. 'There is an army of lawyers out there who would stand in line to get a case like that. If that driver had turned out to be a quadriplegic, you might never have practised medicine again. You were a very lucky young man.'

The day I graduated from medical school, I took an oath to serve the sick and the injured. I remember truly believing I would be able to do just that. But I have found out it isn't so simple. I understand now what a foolish thing I did that day. Despite my oath, I know what I would do on that cold roadside near Gettysburg today. I would drive on.   – From *Newsweek*

GLOSSARY

Gettysburg: site of a well-known battle fought during the American Civil War

layers of down: layers of material made with duck feathers for warmth

Little Round Top: a hill close to Gettysburg

sombre: serious, solemn

blacktop: a road with a bitumen surface

Bronco: Ford Bronco (a brand of SUV)

quadriplegic: person whose four limbs are paralysed

traction: grip

arraigned: to be brought to court to face a charge

Reading for Meaning

1. Do you feel that the writer is successful in bringing the scene of the accident to life?
2. What comment does this article make about the modern world and the challenges facing the medical profession?
3. Comment on the article's final paragraph. Did you find yourself shocked by, or understanding of, the conclusion reached by Dr James Dillard?

Speaking and Listening

Class Discussion: As a class, discuss the doctor's conclusion that if he faced a similar situation today he 'would drive on'. Is he justified in this position?

Writer's Workshop

Short Story: Taking inspiration from *A Doctor's Dilemma*, write a short story in which a character has to face a difficult moral dilemma.

Style Guide

Suspense: Suspense can be a very compelling part of a piece of writing. It creates the sense that something important is about to happen; this keeps the reader excited and interested in the story.

By drawing out the moment in this article, James Dillard keeps the reader intrigued. The writer lays out his hesitation to provide medical help as he imagines being sued by the injured man. As readers, we wonder will the victim survive? And if he does, will he walk again? Will the doctor be sued for trying to help? All of these uncertainties keep the reader wondering as the writer momentarily suspends the action and draws out the answers to these questions.

Suspense encourages us to keep on reading. It creates tension in a piece of writing and adds emotional excitement. In your writing, try to build a sense of expectancy to create suspense so that the reader feels compelled, excited and entertained.

Links

At the heart of *A Doctor's Dilemma* is a moral choice. Other texts, in this book and elsewhere, also explore difficult moral decisions:

In this book: Alden Nowlan's poem, *Weakness* (page 168)

Elsewhere: Bernard MacLaverty's novel, *Lamb*; John Steinbeck's novel, *Of Mice and Men*

Testing the Bomb

Lansing Lamont

Lansing Lamont was a journalist for Time *magazine. The extract below is from his best-selling book* Day of Trinity *(1965) in which he described the development of the atomic bomb in America during World War II. In this extract, he describes the moment before the first test explosion in the New Mexico desert.*

The bomb rested in its cradle.

It slept upon a steel-supported oakwood platform, inside a sheet metal shack 103 feet above the ground: a bloated black squid girdled with cables and leechlike detonators, each tamped with enough explosive to spark simultaneously, within a millionth of a second, the final conflagration. Tentacles emerged from the squid in a harness of wires connecting the detonators to a shiny aluminium tank, the firing unit.

Stripped of its coils, the bomb weighed 10,000 pounds. Its teardrop dimensions were 4½ feet wide by 10½ feet long. Its guts contained two layers of wedge-shaped high-explosive blocks surrounding an inner core of precisely machined nuclear ingots that lay, as one scientist described them, like diamonds in an immense wad of cotton. These ingots were made from a metal called plutonium.

At the heart of the bomb, buried inside the layers of explosive and plutonium, lay the ultimate key to its success or failure, a metallic sphere no bigger than a ping-pong ball that even twenty years later would still be regarded a state secret: the initiator.

Within five seconds the initiator would trigger the sequence that hundreds of shadows had gathered to watch that dawn. The bomb would either fizzle to a premature death or shatteringly christen a new era on earth.

Weeks, months, years of toil had gone into it.

The nation's finest brains and leadership, the cream of its scientific and engineering force, plus two billion dollars from the taxpayers had built the squat monster on the tower for this very moment. Yet it had been no labour of love. There was not the mildest affection for it.

Other instruments of war bore dashing or maidenly names: Britain's 'Spitfires'; the 'Flying Tigers'; the 'Gravel Gerties' and 'Gypsy Rose Lees' that clanked across North Africa or blitzed bridgeheads on the Rhine; even the German's 'Big Bertha' of World War I; and, soon, the Superfortress 'Enola Gay' of Hiroshima, deliverer of an atomic bundle called 'Little Boy'.

The test bomb had no colourful nickname. One day its spawn would be known as 'Fat Man' (after Churchill). But now its identity was cloaked in a welter of impersonal terms: 'the thing', 'the beast', 'the device' and its Washington pseudonym, 'S-1'. The scientists, most of whom called it simply 'the gadget', had handled it gently and daintily, like the baby it was – but out of respect, not fondness. One wrong jolt of the volatile melon inside its Duralumin frame could precipitate the collision of radioactive masses and a slow, agonising death from radiation. Or instant vaporisation.

The monster engendered the sort of fear that had caused one young scientist to break down the evening before and be escorted promptly from the site to a psychiatric ward; and another, far older and wiser, a Nobel Prize winner, to murmur, as he waited in his trench, 'I'm scared witless, absolutely witless.'

– From *Day of Trinity*

GLOSSARY
girdled: circled by
tamped: drilled and filled with explosive
conflagration: a destructive fire
ingots: pieces of cast or shaped metal
toil: hard work
Hiroshima: a port in Japan and the site of the first atomic bomb attack
Little Boy; Fat Man: the codenames for the atomic bombs dropped by the US on Hiroshima and Nagasaki, Japan during World War II
welter: a jumble, a confused mass
pseudonym: a fictitious name used to conceal an identity
volatile: explosive
precipitate: to bring about hastily
engendered: produced, created

Reading for Meaning

1. The writer begins the piece describing how the bomb 'rested in its cradle' and finishes describing it as 'like the baby it was'. What point is being made here?
2. What impression of the bomb does Lansing Lamont give in the final two paragraphs?
3. How do the scientists featured in the extract feel about the bomb?
4. Although the writer never directly says how he feels about the bomb, what does his writing suggest about his views of the atomic bomb?

Language Lab

1. (a) Make a list of the words that compare the bomb to an animal.
   (b) Why do you think the writer uses this kind of animal imagery?
2. In this piece, the writer presents his impression of the bomb through his descriptive language. However, he also makes use of hard facts in his description.
   (a) Make a list of hard facts included in this piece.
   (b) Why do you think the writer includes these hard facts in the piece?
3. Explain how the writer develops suspense and tension in this piece.

Style Guide

Descriptive Writing: A well-written descriptive piece of writing can be captivating as the reader feels transported to a different place or scene. There are a number of descriptive writing techniques used by writers to achieve this effect. These include:

• Adjectives	• Simile	• Personification
• Adverbs	• Metaphor	• Verb choices
• Appeals to the senses	• Extended metaphor	• Attention to detail

Go to the descriptive writing techniques listed in Chapter 4, page 95 for a full explanation of these techniques. You will also find examples peppered throughout the anthologised texts.

In *Testing the Bomb*, Lansing Lamont makes use of a number of descriptive devices to bring the scene to life and to add drama around the existence of the atomic bomb.

Writer's Workshop

Description: Taking inspiration from *Testing the Bomb*, write a description of an object that you are familiar with. Lansing Lamont compares the atomic bomb to an animal, a monster and a baby. Try to make use of dramatic comparisons in your description.

Links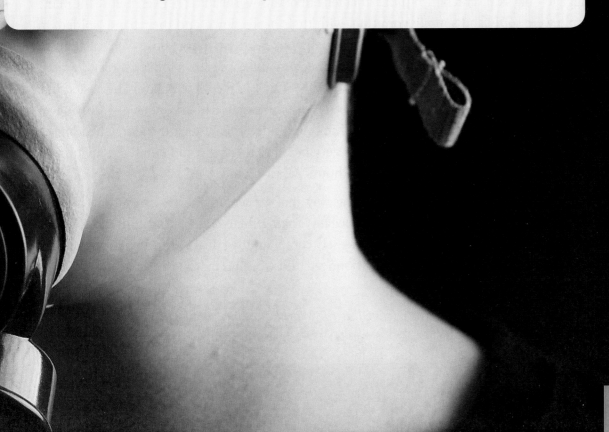

In *Testing the Bomb*, Lansing Lamont looks at the incredible destructive power human beings are capable of. This extract can be linked to other texts in this book and elsewhere:
In this book: Wisława Szymborska's poem, *The One Twenty Pub* (page 184); William Stafford's poem, *At the Bomb Testing Site* (page 196)
Elsewhere: Kurt Vonnegut's novel, *Slaughterhouse-Five*

Travel Writing

Writing about travel

Travel writing is a personal account of a writer's experience of a place and offers readers an opinion of what a particular place is like. Travel writers use their imaginations to bring locations to life for the reader. Not only does this type of writing give the reader information about places away from home, but it also encourages the reader to imagine and share in the experience of being there.

Fear of Flying

Paul Theroux

Paul Theroux is a well-known travel writer and novelist. In this short extract, *Fear of Flying*, he describes his experience of air travel in China in the 1980s.

Chinese trains could be bad. In twelve months of travelling – almost forty trains – I never saw one with a toilet that wasn't piggy. The loudspeakers plonked and nagged for eighteen hours a day. The conductors could be tyrants, and the feeding frenzy in the dining-car was often not worth the trouble. But there were compensations: the kindly conductors, the occasional good meal, the comfortable berth, the luck of the draw; and, when all else failed, there was always a chubby thermos of hot water for making tea.

Yet whatever objections I could devise against the trains they were nothing compared to the horrors of air travel in China. I had a small dose of it when I left Urumchi for Lanzhou. I was told to be at the airport three hours early – that is, 7.00 in the morning; and the plane left five hours late, at 3.00 in the afternoon. It was an old Russian jet, and its metal covering was wrinkled and cracked like the tinfoil in a used cigarette pack. The seats were jammed so closely together that my knees hurt and the circulation to my feet was cut off. Every seat was taken, and every person was heavily laden with carry-on baggage – big skull-cracking bundles that fell out of the overhead rack. Even before the plane took off people were softly and soupily vomiting, with their heads down and their hands folded, in the solemn and prayerful way that the Chinese habitually puke. After two hours we were each given an envelope that contained three caramel candies, some gum and three sticky boiled sweets; a piece of cellophane almost concealed a black strand of dried beef that looked like oakum and tasted like decayed rope; and (because Chinese can be optimistic) a toothpick. Two hours later a girl wearing an old postman's uniform went around with a tray. Thinking it might be better food I snatched one of the little parcels – it was a key-ring. The plane was very hot, and then so cold I could see my breath. It creaked like a schooner under sail. Another two hours passed. I said: I am out of my mind.

An announcement was made, saying in a gargling way that we would shortly be landing. At this point everyone except the pukers stood up and began yanking their bundles out of the racks; and they remained standing, pushing, tottering and vaguely complaining – deaf to the demands that they sit down and strap themselves in – as the plane bounced, did wheelies on the runway and limped to Lanzhou terminal. Never again.

– From *Travelling the World: the Illustrated Travels of Paul Theroux*

GLOSSARY

tyrants: oppressive rulers

berth: a sleeping space

devise: plan

laden: loaded down

oakum: loose fibre from old rope

schooner: a sailing ship

tottering: swaying as if about to fall

Reading for Meaning

1. Outline all of the negative aspects of Paul Theroux's flight.
2. Is the writer successful in capturing the atmosphere and experience of his flight in China? Explain your answer.
3. Which aspects of this piece did you find entertaining or amusing?

Language Lab

Comparison: Comparisons are a highly effective descriptive tool. You will remember from your Junior Cycle course how similes (comparisons using 'like' or 'as') and metaphors (comparisons that do not use 'like' or 'as') are often used to imaginatively bring a piece of writing to life. Personification is a particular type of metaphor in which a non-human thing is compared to a person.

Paul Theroux includes many imaginative comparisons in this extract. For each of the examples below:

1. State whether simile, metaphor or personification is being used.
2. Explain what is being compared.
3. Comment on the effect the comparison has.
   (a) its metal covering was wrinkled and cracked like the tinfoil in a used cigarette pack
   (b) a black strand of dried beef that looked like oakum and tasted like decayed rope
   (c) it creaked like a schooner under sail
   (d) the plane bounced, did wheelies on the runway and limped to Lanzhou terminal

   Appeals to the Senses: When writing descriptively, writers often appeal to the senses to transport the reader to the world of the text. For example, a writer may explain how something sounds, tastes, feels or smells to bring it to life for the reader.

4. List all of the times that Paul Theroux appeals to the senses in this piece.
5. Do you feel that this is an effective way of describing the atmosphere of the plane journey?

Speaking and Listening

Discussion: Paul Theroux writes about his fearful flying experience in the extract on the previous page. In groups, talk about the issue of phobias (things that deeply scare us). Discuss how phobias may affect people's lives and how they try to cope with them.

Writer's Workshop

Letter: Imagine you were travelling on the same plane as Paul Theroux. Write a letter of complaint to the airline about your journey. In your letter you should describe your experience and offer suggestions as to how the service could be improved. Go to page 89 to learn about letters of complaint.

Diary: Imagine you are a member of the cabin crew. Write three diary entries about your experiences. Include anecdotes about incidents on board the plane.

Anxious about Africa

Manchán Magan

Manchán Magan is a writer, travel journalist and documentary maker. In *Anxious about Africa* he describes returning to Africa after a number of years and, in particular, his experience of travelling in Ghana.

This day last month I was speeding around the rough roads of Ghana, visiting community-based tourism projects from the humid southern coast to the lush eastern highlands and arid northern semi-desert. The aim was to find places where Irish people could holiday cheaply, while benefiting locals.

I have to admit that before I left I was anxious about travelling in Africa again: the thought of clattering around on old buses, staying in pokey guesthouses and risking the Russian-roulette of street food wearied me for the first time ever. I feared I may have lost my love of travel. Would I have to begin shielding myself from my surroundings – staying in air-conditioned hotels, eating Western food, taking private taxis?

The question still loomed as I left Accra airport and had to decide whether to turn right towards the taxi rank or continue walking out to the highway where battered old Mercedes vans called tro-tros rattle along towards the city, picking up people until they are bursting at the seams and dropping them off wherever they happen to end up. A taxi costs €8 compared to 20 cent for a tro-tro, and while I would always take a taxi at night or in a risky area, Ghana is safe.

So I walked to the road and shouted, 'Downtown, downtown' at every passing van until one stopped and the passengers scooched up to allow me cram in. I was just fishing out some Ghanaian coins when a man behind me shouted up, 'No need, I've paid for you.' I turned to thank him, but the minibus was already slowing and he was heaving his way out. 'Welcome to Ghana,' he said, and I was smitten with Africa once again.

The next three weeks played out more or less the same. Though I encountered some surly, sour people, mostly I was cocooned in a network of caring Ghanaians who passed me from one to another. I'd bungle out into the sweltering 40-degree heat, knowing that whatever I needed could be found by just asking the person next to me. If they couldn't help, someone else would, and unlike elsewhere in Africa, no one expected money. I would tumble into a tro-tro mumbling about where I wanted to go and people around me would decide how best to get there, pushing me back out again and into another tro-tro if necessary, or else haranguing the driver to go out of his way to get me to my destination.

That feeling of being embraced by an entire country is a phenomenal sensation and yet it is the norm for Western travellers in most of the world.

One day I tripped on the road and instantly had a dozen people helping me up, carrying my bag, steering me towards a clinic lest I needed a bandage. That's the world I know, the world I've been travelling through for a quarter of a century without ever being robbed or harmed, except one time on my first ever trip.

– from *The Irish Times*

GLOSSARY
arid: dry
surly: bad-tempered, rude
haranguing: speaking in a forceful way

Reading for Meaning

1. What was the purpose of Manchán Magan's trip to Ghana and why was he 'anxious' about it?
2. In your view, is the writer successful in capturing the atmosphere of Ghana and giving a sense of its people? Explain your answer.
3. From what the writer describes in his article, do you think you would enjoy Ghana as a holiday destination? Why / why not?
4. Manchán Magan and Paul Theroux (pages 68 – 69) are two travel writers with very different experiences of using transport abroad. Which extract did you enjoy reading the most? Refer to the texts in your answer.

Language Lab

Synonym: Writers often work hard to find just the right word for a piece of writing. There are many words that have similar meanings to choose from: these are known as synonyms. For example, a writer may consider using the word 'happy' but there are many synonyms for 'happy' that could be used instead: joyful, elated, cheerful, merry, blithe.

1. The following words are all taken from the article *Anxious about Africa*. Write down a synonym for each. You may use a dictionary.
   (a) humid
   (b) pokey
   (c) loomed
   (d) smitten
   (e) phenomenal
2. The writer uses a number of interesting verbs in this extract to bring Ghana to life.
   (a) Write down five interesting verbs he uses.
   (b) Beside each verb write a synonym. You may use a dictionary if you wish.
3. The following phrases are underlined in the passage. Explain their meaning:
   (a) risking the Russian-roulette of street food
   (b) mostly I was cocooned in a network of caring Ghanaians
   (c) That feeling of being embraced by an entire country is a phenomenal sensation

Speaking and Listening

Presentation: Give a presentation to the class about your experiences of other cultures. You may wish to talk about a time when you were abroad, but you may also base your presentation on experiences you have had at home. Consider including an anecdote or using visual images in your presentation.

Writer's Workshop

1. **Holiday Brochure:** Design a holiday brochure for a destination of your choice. You may wish to use the internet for research or to download images. Try to use pleasing words and phrases to promote your destination.

2. **Travel Article:** *Anxious about Africa* is a travel article from *The Irish Times*. Write your own newspaper article about a holiday experience (at home or abroad). Try to include at least one anecdote in your article.

Links

At its core, *Anxious about Africa* is about how human kindness can be found amongst complete strangers. This travel article can be linked to other texts in this book and elsewhere:

In this book: Sylvia Seymour Akin's tale, *Christmas Morning* (page 26)

Elsewhere: Tim Burton's film, *Edward Scissorhands*

Reviews

Writing a Review

A review is a personal response to a film, performance, book or game. The reviewer offers his/her opinion and can often influence whether a work is a success or not. Reviews can be found in magazines, newspaper supplements and blogs.

There are three basic elements to a review:

1. **Opening**
   - In the opening paragraph(s), the reviewer will offer basic information about what is being reviewed such as: title, author/creator/director, release date, actors, etc.
   - Often the reviewer will try to grab the reader's attention with a catchy opening sentence.

2. **Overview**
   - Without spoiling the story, the reviewer will provide an outline of the plot/setting/situation.
   - He/she might mention genre and style here.

3. **Evaluation**
   - Here the reviewer offers an opinion of the work. A review may be positive, negative, lukewarm, mocking, enthusiastic, disgusted etc.
   - Depending on what the review is about, the reviewer might comment on a book's style, characters, themes, story; a film's actors, soundtrack, themes, style, characters, cinematography; a game's playability, soundtrack, graphics; a play's themes, actors, stage set, characters; an album's lyrics, song writing, listenability, genre.

War Horse: a Testament to Human Bravery

After much anticipation, *War Horse* has now leapt the fence of literary genres, galloping from the pages of Michael Morpurgo's much-loved book and onto the stage at the Bord Gáis Energy Theatre. Superbly adapted for stage by Nick Stafford, *War Horse*'s eight record-breaking years at London's West End, as well as performances to over seven million people around the world, ensures this production will be one of the highlights of the Irish stage this year.

The audience cannot help but be captivated as we witness the warhorse of the title, Joey, grow from foal to magisterial stallion. This transformation is made all the more spectacular by the puppet wizardry of this production.

Joey's story takes a dark turn when he is shipped to France to serve alongside the British army. Through his eyes, we are given fascinating insight into the horrors of World War I. After being captured, a wounded Joey finds himself wandering alone and lost in no-man's land.

Throughout Joey's ordeals, he is pursued by his 16-year-old master, Albert. So strong is Albert's devotion, that he runs away from home and enlists in the army. The love between master and horse is all the more moving when set against the backdrop of bloody trench warfare.

The story is brilliantly brought to life by the inspiring puppetry of the Handspring Puppet Company. The horse puppets appear no less real than the human actors on stage, with each puppet seeming to have a unique identity and depth of emotion.

This visual spectacle complements Nick Stafford's powerful writing and the captivating performance of Lee Armstrong as Albert.

War Horse does not shy away from presenting the worst side of humanity, but this is balanced by the recognition of our capacity for bravery, endurance and love.

–Anonymous

GLOSSARY
anticipation: expectation
magisterial: commanding, authoritative

Reading for Meaning

Considering the three elements of a review (Opening, Overview and Evaluation), think about the theatre review above.

1. The first paragraph of this review can be considered the opening. What basic information do you learn about the play here?
2. Is the writer successful in giving you a sense of the play in the overview without giving away too much of the story?
3. The review's final three paragraphs evaluate the play. Would this evaluation encourage you to see the play?

So, Walter O'Brien is one of the five smartest people alive. Who are the other four?

Patrick Freyne

The theatre review on the previous page is a positive one. In contrast, Patrick Freyne's review here pokes fun at a TV drama shown on RTÉ, *Scorpion*. The writer leaves us with a negative, yet amusing, impression of the programme.

In the opening scenes of *Scorpion* (Thursday, RTÉ 2), child hacker Walter O'Brien is arrested by Robert Patrick from *Terminator* and extradited to America, from what I assumed, based on his accent, was a Scottish-speaking region of Latvia. It was actually Kilkenny.

Walter O'Brien is based on a real-life Irish computer whiz who solves computer crime for the US government. In the world of modern television drama, you can write about anything as long as it's crime. Many TV pitches are simply: 'a [random professional] solves crime'. There have been crime-fighting mathematicians, doctors, writers, psychologists and archaeologists. Many young people have been lured into staid careers in the belief that there would be sexy explosions.

Well, Walter becomes a computer science person who solves crime. Yeah, he computer sciences the hell out of crime. He is so goddamn computer sciencey, if you were to give Walter any computer he could science it.

We meet hunky, grown-up, American-accented Walter (Elyes Gabel) as he installs a broadband router in a diner while simultaneously breaking up with his girlfriend for whom he has made an 'emotional spreadsheet'. Then he deftly patronises the sexy waitress mother of an autistic child. At this point, we're meant to think: 'Oh, Walter, you can decode any computer and yet you cannot decode the most complex programme of all, your own heart. How ironic!'

Walter takes his confounding love-organ back to the failing business he runs with fellow 'super-geniuses' – a 'human calculator' who utters statistics like a malfunctioning Satnav ('we're down to a 17% chance of success!'), a 'world-class shrink' in a fedora, and a no-nonsense 'mechanical prodigy' who likes sitting in an informal manner and whose dramatic arc will certainly lead to her straddling a chair backwards like Michelle Pfeiffer in *Dangerous Minds*.

The business is called Scorpion presumably because Walter is a predatory arthropod with a mineral-based exoskeleton (editor's note: you're confusing him with the species 'scorpion').

Then agent Robert Patrick from *Terminator*, with whom Walter has quarrelled, arrives to ask him to stop a computer virus that's causing planes to crash. Oh no! They rush to the diner with the sexy waitress/child combo because it's the only broadband connection Walter trusts, including, inexplicably, the one in his office.

Also, he wants to be rude to Paige the waitress some more. Luckily there's also sexual tension between them, seemingly because of Walter's implied similarities to Paige's son. Stop it. It's not weird. It's lovely. Stop it.

Walter is very clever. We know this because he repeatedly says so. When told by Robert Patrick to 'move on', for example, he tantrums: 'Moving on is not an option for people with photographic memories.' Earlier for no good reason he says: 'Einstein had a 160 IQ. Mine is 197.' Of course, Einstein, the fool, squandered his talent on the Theory of Relativity and never once used his book-smarts to fight crime or engage in an exciting car chase.

Walter's friends actually encourage his monstrous boasting. 'Walter O'Brien is one of the five smartest people alive,' says Robert Patrick, when someone questions Walter's credentials (the other four? At a guess: Carol Vorderman, Stephen Fry, Kanye and Bunson from *The Muppets*).

The main problem with *Scorpion*, apart from the writer's belief that anyone clever is a magic robot-wizard, is that coding is a boringly stationary activity. Presumably Walter will eventually dispense with it entirely and start using his laptop to hit baddies while shouting 'Science!' but in the meantime the writers must fabricate reasons for action. Walter and Paige go on a death-defying car chase, purely, it seems, to get a better broadband connection. And later Walter drives a convertible down a runway, while a passenger plane, which can't land because it can't contact air traffic control, flies directly overhead and lowers a DSL cable to his laptop. No one says: 'Sure, while you're 10 feet from the runway, you might as well land' or 'for f***s sake'.

While this all may sound a bit loopy, I've been told by an *Irish Times* IT person that programmers do this sort of thing all the time. Anyway, I must go. He's just abseiled past my window firing a machine-gun. My laptop must be ready.

– From *The Irish Times*

GLOSSARY
extradited: deported, handed over
staid: respectable, steady
deftly: skilfully, neatly
patronises: treats someone as inferior
dramatic arc: dramatic plotline

Reading for Meaning

1. How does Patrick Freyne grab the reader's attention in the opening of this review?
2. Is the writer successful in providing an overview of the programme *Scorpion*?
3. In his evaluation, what flaws does the reviewer see in the TV programme?
4. Do you agree that Patrick Freyne's review of *Scorpion* is a critical yet highly entertaining review?

Writer's Workshop

Review: Choose a TV programme, film or play that you have seen recently. Write a review ensuring that you pay attention to the three elements of a review: Opening, Overview and Evaluation (see page 73)

Chapter 3:
Dear World . . . –
Written Correspondence

Whether it is a comment thread, a letter or an email, written correspondence is still a major part of modern communication. It allows us to have a conversation with individuals, institutions or the whole world. This chapter explores a number of interesting forms of written correspondence and is arranged into three sections: Protest, Personal, Complaint.

As a vehicle for protest, written correspondence can be a powerful tool for the protestor, for the ones who want to challenge the status quo and offer a new way of being.

Personal correspondence offers us the chance to connect meaningfully with others when we take the time to reach out to somebody else. The rise of digital media such as blogs, comments threads and email show the importance of written correspondence. Alongside these new innovations, personal letters remain a valuable way of exploring the issues of the human heart.

A complaint can have a far greater impact when delivered in writing as it allows the complainer to measure and weigh the words that are used.

In a world of information, where different voices clamber to be heard, it is vital that we appreciate the importance of written correspondence.

Protest

There are a number of ways that we can raise an objection, make a political point or voice our disagreement. A well-crafted letter, particularly if it's publicly available, can be a powerful protest tool. The two letters of protest in this section are keen examples of this.

My Muse is Not a Horse

Nick Cave

Nick Cave is an Australian singer, songwriter, musician, author and composer. He is well known as the frontman for the bands *Nick Cave and the Bad Seeds* and *The Birthday Party*.

In 1996, Nick Cave's ninth album *Murder Ballads* became hugely popular, reaching a wider audience than any of his previous records. Nick Cave describes being 'catapulted into the role of superstardom'. Following his new popularity, MTV nominated him for the award of Best Male Artist. This is the letter Nick Cave wrote in response.

To All Those at MTV,

I would like to start by thanking you all for the support you have given me over recent years and I am both grateful and flattered by the nominations that I have received for Best Male Artist. The air play given to both the Kylie Minogue and P.J. Harvey duets from my latest album Murder Ballads has not gone unnoticed and has been greatly appreciated. So again my sincere thanks.

Having said that, I feel that it's necessary for me to request that my nomination for best male artist be withdrawn and furthermore any awards or nominations for such awards that may arise in later years be presented to those who feel more comfortable with the competitive nature of these award ceremonies. I myself, do not. I have always been of the opinion that my music is unique and individual and exists beyond the realms inhabited by those who would reduce things to mere measuring. I am in competition with no-one.

My relationship with my muse is a delicate one at the best of times and I feel that it is my duty to protect her from influences that may offend her fragile nature.

She comes to me with the gift of song and in return I treat her with the respect I feel she deserves – in this case this means not subjecting her to the indignities of judgement and competition. My muse is not a horse and I am in no horse race and if indeed she was, still I would not harness her to this tumbrel – this bloody cart of severed heads and glittering prizes. My muse may spook! May bolt! May abandon me completely!

So once again, to the people at MTV, I appreciate the zeal and energy that was put behind my last record, I truly do and say thank you and again I say thank you but no...no thank you.

Yours sincerely,

Nick Cave

GLOSSARY

muse: the source of artistic inspiration / the artist's or poet's power

tumbrel: a cart used to transport those condemned to death to the guillotine during the French Revolution

Reading for Meaning

1. Using your own words, explain why Nick Cave declined the MTV nomination.
2. Do you agree with this stance Cave has taken?
3. Explain the phrase, 'My muse is not a horse and I am in no horse race.'
4. How do you imagine the organisers of the awards at MTV felt about this letter of rejection?

Language Lab

1. Do you agree that Nick Cave's letter is full of rich, poetic imagery? You may wish to explore his use of metaphor and personification.
2. (a) Giving examples from the letter, describe the tone Cave adopts in this letter.
   (b) Why do you think he adopts this kind of tone?

Writer's Workshop

Letter of Reply: Imagine you work for MTV. Your job is to draft a response to Nick Cave's letter. Write the letter that you would send.

Links

Nick Cave's letter to MTV is ultimately about not 'selling out' or compromising your values. This letter can be linked to other texts in this book and elsewhere:

In this book: Michael Harding's article, *I Believe in Angels* (page 36)

Elsewhere: J.D. Salinger's novel, *The Catcher in the Rye*

'Daft Fatty' . . .
the Casual Cruelty of Email

Róisín Ingle

Róisín Ingle is a journalist and social commentator, well known for her column in *The Irish Times*. Her letter below is a response to a remark she received via email from a reader.

A letter to the man who called me a 'daft fatty' by email because I spelt Pocahontas wrong:

Dear Peter,

Happy New Year! How was the year for you? I hope it brought lots of opportunities for emailing pithy put-downs to people as that is an activity you obviously enjoy. There's nothing like a bit of gratuitous rudeness to make you feel better about yourself is there? Time was when people like you had to get out the Basildon Bond notepaper and the pen with green ink to scratch that particular itch. How much easier it is now to give people who spell the names of Disney princess characters wrong a piece of your mind. And thank goodness for that I'm sure you'll agree.

I'm intrigued to know if you saw me walking (waddling more like, eh Peter?) along the street whether you would tap me on the shoulder and say, 'You daft fatty!' Or would you be too embarrassed to do that? Yes, I think perhaps you would.

Because on balance it's definitely trickier to call someone a 'daft fatty' in the real world. In the real world I might answer back and you might have to explain yourself, and other people might overhear and think you are a bit of an eejit. Awkward.com eh, Peter? Hurray then for technology which allows us to tap into the meanest aspects of our nature without having to deal with any of the consequences.

Look, Peter, I am sorry I spelt Pocahontas as Pocahauntus. When people (usually my mother) point out typos in my columns I cringe. It's not ideal. But you didn't just point it out did you? You wrote:

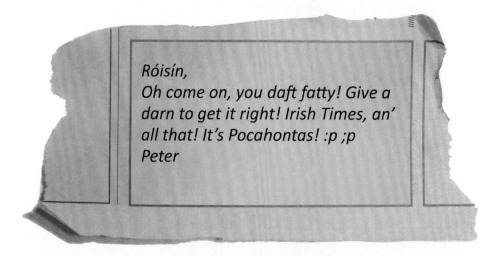

Róisín,
Oh come on, you daft fatty! Give a darn to get it right! Irish Times, an' all that! It's Pocahontas! :p ;p
Peter

Oh, Peter! You old flirt! You charmer! You wit! All those exclamation marks and those jaunty emoticons. All those attempts to intimate that you are only joshing, flourishes that just make your email even more slimy.

At *The Irish Times* (an' all that!) we do indeed strive to ensure our products are spelling-mistake free but here's the thing: sometimes people make mistakes. I know, I know. Those intolerable people should be shot at dawn, rolled in batter, deep fried and fed to the lions in Dublin Zoo. At the very least they should be emailed with remarks about their generous girth and their sadly lacking mental prowess. Especially if they are women. Especially if they are overweight women. At the very least they should be made to give a darn.

You might not be interested but just in case you are, there is an alternative tack to the email you sent me. I've even written a draft for you. I've attempted to address the issue at hand (the misspelling of Pochontas) while remaining civilised, which I believe is important in all communication. You could have written something like this:

> *Róisín,*
> *There was a spelling mistake in your last column. It's Pocahontas*
> *not Pocahauntus.*
> *Sincerely,*
> *Peter*

But where's the 'fun' in that?

Some people might think I'm giving you too much attention by devoting an entire column to your 'daft fatty' missive. But I was giving a talk to Transition Year students and you came up in conversation. One young woman asked whether I get criticism of this column and how I handle it. I told her I welcomed anything constructive, that people often have valid criticisms and that as long as people are polite, I try to respond.

But then I told her about you, and your 'daft fatty' comment and those teenagers were shocked. They couldn't believe a grown adult would sit down and write those words, as innocuous as they might seem to you. Then I talked for a bit about the online world where people like you think it's fine to be rude and sexist and racist and ignorant and mean. Where people hide behind made-up email addresses and names. Where people say things they'd never dream of saying to people's faces.

It's a world that's proving increasingly difficult for teenagers and can have depressingly tragic consequences. So it would be nice if us adults could show them a better way forward in our emails, our online comments and our general communication instead of contributing to the problem. We should give a darn to get it right.

Shouldn't we Peter?

Sincerely,

Róisín

From *The Irish Times* (amended)

GLOSSARY
Basildon Bond: a brand of writing paper
pithy: meaningful, a comment of substance
gratuitous: unjustified, uncalled for
mental prowess: mental skills
missive: letter, written correspondence
innocuous: harmless, innocent

Reading for Meaning

1. Róisín Ingle mentions that during a talk she gave to Transition Year students, the students were 'shocked' by the 'daft fatty' comment. Are you shocked?
2. (a) Describe the tone used by Róisín Ingle in this piece.
   (b) Why do you think she used this tone to tackle this issue?
3. Ingle mentions that some people might criticise her for giving so much attention to the offensive comment. Do you think Ingle was right to deal with Peter's 'daft fatty' comment in the way that she did?
4. Do you agree with the writer that the online world is 'proving increasingly difficult for teenagers and can have depressingly tragic consequences'?

Writer's Workshop

Code of Conduct: Ingle makes the point that online commentators are often anonymous and may 'say things they'd never dream of saying to people's faces.'

- In small groups, discuss this issue considering the positives and negatives of being anonymous online.
- In small groups, write a code of conduct for online commentators which sets out what is appropriate and inappropriate for users.
- As a class, discuss this issue and the different codes of conduct written by the class.

Links

In her letter responding to the 'daft fatty' comment, Róisín Ingle raises the topic of how some men comment on women's physical appearance. This letter can be linked to other texts in this book and elsewhere:

In this book: 'And That Was That Night' (extract from Brian Friel's *Philadelphia, Here I Come!* – page 222)

Elsewhere: Search online for Chimamanda Ngozi Adichie's TED Talk, *We Should All Be Feminists*

Personal

Before the advent of the internet, personal letters were a vital method of human communication. It would not be unusual for an individual to regularly send and receive a number of letters in a week. Incredibly, during World War I, 12,000,000 letters were sent per week to British soldiers. The postal system kept millions of people in contact. Letter writing was an art in which people reflected and discussed their lives.

In today's world personal letters are written less frequently. With email, video calls, social media and texting, the need for personal letters has diminished. However, there is something special and significant about taking the time to put pen to paper, enclose the letter, stamp it and send it. Perhaps it is sad that the thought and care that goes into a personal letter has been replaced by the speed of modern communication. However, the skills used to craft letters are still used in emails, social media posts and blogging.

There are a number of ways of formatting a personal letter. The template below offers a typical layout for a personal letter.

SENDER'S ADDRESS

DATE

SALUTATION

E.G. Dear ..., Hi ..., To...

MAIN BODY OF LETTER

SIGN OFF

E.G. Yours..., Sincerely..., Take care...,
Or: No sign off, just the sender's name

Send Them a Letter

The advertisement to the right was part of Australia Post's campaign to promote personal letter writing as an important mode of human communication.

If you really want to touch someone, send them a letter. **AUSTRALIA POST**

Reading for Meaning

1. What is the message of this advertisement? Refer to both the words and picture in your answer.
2. Do you think this is an effective advertisement?
3. Some people feel that it is a shame that digital communication is replacing the traditional post. Do you agree? Give your reasons.

Writer's Workshop

Speech: This advertisement deals with the changes in how we communicate nowadays. Write a speech about changes in the modern world. In your speech you may celebrate these changes or argue that society has changed for the worse.

Personal Letter: Write a genuine personal letter to somebody you know who lives in a foreign country or another county. In your letter, describe anything of interest in your life at the moment. Enquire about the other person.

Links

This advertisement shows how personal letters can inspire real human connection. This idea is echoed in other texts in this book and elsewhere:

In this book: The editorial, *Yes, Virginia there is a Santa Claus* (page 87)

Elsewhere: Search online for Arcade Fire's song, *We Used to Wait*

People Simply Empty Out

Charles Bukowski

Charles Bukowski was an American poet, novelist and short-story writer. His work focused on the lives of the poor, alcoholism and the drudgery of work.

In 1969, the publisher John Martin offered to pay Bukowski $100 a month for the rest of his life if he would give up work and devote his time to writing. Bukowski gladly accepted. Bukowski's semi-autobiographical novels centred around his alter-ego Hank Chinaski; the letter below to John Martin explores Bukowski's joy at having escaped working life and is signed 'Hank'.

Hello John:

Thanks for the good letter. I don't think it hurts, sometimes, to remember where you came from. You know the places where I came from. Even the people who try to write about that or make films about it, they don't get it right. They call it '9 to 5.' It's never 9 to 5, there's no free lunch break at those places, in fact, at many of them in order to keep your job you don't take lunch. Then there's OVERTIME and the books never seem to get the overtime right and if you complain about that, there's another sucker to take your place.

You know my old saying, 'Slavery was never abolished, it was only extended to include all the colours.'

And what hurts is the steadily diminishing humanity of those fighting to hold jobs they don't want but fear the alternative worse. People simply empty out. They are bodies with fearful and obedient minds. The colour leaves the eye. The voice becomes ugly. And the body. The hair. The fingernails. The shoes. Everything does.

As a young man I could not believe that people could give their lives over to those conditions. As an old man, I still can't believe it. What do they do it for? Sex? TV? An automobile on monthly payments? Or children? Children who are just going to do the same things that they did?

Early on, when I was quite young and going from job to job, I was foolish enough to sometimes speak to my fellow workers: 'Hey, the boss can come in here at any moment and lay all of us off, just like that, don't you realise that?' They would just look at me. I was posing something that they didn't want to enter their minds.

Now in industry, there are vast layoffs (steel mills dead, technical changes in other factors of the work place). They are layed off by the hundreds of thousands and their faces are stunned:

'I put in 35 years...'

'It ain't right...'

'I don't know what to do...'

They never pay the slaves enough so they can get free, just enough so they can stay alive and come back to work. I could see all this. Why couldn't they? I figured the park bench was just as good or being a barfly was just as good. Why not get there first before they put me there? Why wait?

I just wrote in disgust against it all, it was a relief to get the shit out of my system. And now that I'm here, a so-called professional writer, after giving the first 50 years away, I've found out that there are other disgusts beyond the system.

I remember once, working as a packer in this lighting fixture company, one of the packers suddenly said: 'I'll never be free!' One of the bosses was walking by (his name was Morrie) and he let out this delicious cackle of a laugh, enjoying the fact that this fellow was trapped for life.

So, the luck I finally had in getting out of those places, no matter how long it took, has given me a kind of joy, the jolly joy of the miracle. I now write from an old mind and an old body, long beyond the time when most men would ever think of continuing such a thing, but since I started so late I owe it to myself to continue, and when the words begin to falter and I must be helped up stairways and I can no longer tell a bluebird from a paperclip, I still feel that something in me is going to remember (no matter how far I'm gone) how I've come through the murder and the mess and the moil, to at least a generous way to die.

To not to have entirely wasted one's life seems to be a worthy accomplishment, if only for myself.

yr boy,

Hank

Reading for Meaning

1. This is a personal letter from Charles Bukowski (Hank) to a friend. Explain how the phrases and tone used are suitable for a personal letter.

2. Basing your answer on this letter alone, what is your impression of the writer?

3. (a) What point is Charles Bukowski (Hank) making about work?

   (b) Do you agree with him?

4. Which of the following words best describes this letter for you: *depressing, entertaining, insightful, cynical, joyful, interesting*? Explain your choice.

Writer's Workshop

Poem: Write a poem on the theme of work and career. Your poem may echo the ideas in Bukowski's letter or offer a new angle on the idea of work.

Links

Bukowski's letter offers a very pessimistic view of working life in the modern world. This letter can be linked to other texts in this book and elsewhere:

In this book: *Coketown* (extract from Charles Dickens's *Hard Times*, page 96)

Elsewhere: Search online for Philip Larkin's poem, *Toads*

Yes, Virginia, there is a Santa Claus

Francis P. Church

In 1897, Virginia O'Hanlon wrote to the editor of *The New York Sun* newspaper: 'Dear Editor, I am eight years old. Some of my little friends say there is no Santa Claus. Papa says, "If you see it in the Sun it's so." Please tell me the truth, is there a Santa Claus?'

A reply from *The Sun's* editor, Francis P. Church, was printed in the newspaper as an editorial (an article reflecting the editor's opinion). This is the most reprinted editorial in the English language.

Virginia grew up to be a schoolteacher. Francis P. Church died nine years after his famous editorial. He had no children.

Virginia, your little friends are wrong. They have been affected by the scepticism of a sceptical age. They do not believe except they see. They think that nothing can be which is not comprehensible by their little minds. All minds, Virginia, whether they be men's or children's, are little. In this great universe of ours, man is a mere insect, an ant, in his intellect as compared with the boundless world about him, as measured by the intelligence capable of grasping the whole of truth and knowledge.

Yes, Virginia, there is a Santa Claus. He exists as certainly as love and generosity and devotion exist, and you know that they abound and give to your life its highest beauty and joy. Alas! how dreary would be the world if there were no Santa Claus! It would be as dreary as if there were no Virginias. There would be no childlike faith then, no poetry, no romance to make tolerable this existence. We should have no enjoyment, except in sense and sight. The external light with which childhood fills the world would be extinguished.

Not believe in Santa Claus! You might as well not believe in fairies! You might get your papa to hire men to watch in all the chimneys on Christmas Eve to catch Santa Claus, but even if you did not see Santa Claus coming down, what would that prove? Nobody sees Santa Claus, but that is no sign that there is no Santa Claus. The most real things in the world are those that neither children nor men can see. Did you ever see fairies dancing on the lawn? Of course not, but that's no proof that they are not there. Nobody can conceive or imagine all the wonders there are unseen and unseeable in the world.

You tear apart the baby's rattle and see what makes the noise inside, but there is a veil covering the unseen world which not the strongest man, nor even the united strength of all the strongest men that ever lived could tear apart. Only faith, poetry, love, romance, can push aside that curtain and view and picture the supernal beauty and glory beyond. Is it all real? Ah, Virginia, in all this world there is nothing else real and abiding.

No Santa Claus! Thank God! he lives and he lives forever. A thousand years from now, Virginia, nay ten times ten thousand years from now, he will continue to make glad the heart of childhood.

GLOSSARY
supernal: exceptional
abiding: enduring, lasting a long time

Reading for Meaning

1. In an interview in later life, Virginia O'Hanlon said that the editorial changed her life adding, 'the older I grow, the more I realise what a perfect philosophy it is for life.' In your own words, summarise the positive philosophy offered in this editorial.
2. Good writing may move you emotionally or prompt you to think. What effect did this editorial have on you?
3. 'Francis P. Church's response to eight-year-old Virginia is full of generosity and wisdom.' Do you agree with this statement?

Speaking and Listening

Short Drama: Virginia O'Hanlon was inspired to write to *The New York Sun* by her father. Imagine it is the morning that the editorial has been printed. The paper has been delivered to eight-year-old Virginia's house. In pairs or small groups, write and perform the scene that takes place.

Links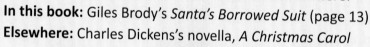

Church's editorial refers to the magic and innocence of Christmas. This editorial can be linked to other texts in this book and elsewhere:
In this book: Giles Brody's *Santa's Borrowed Suit* (page 13)
Elsewhere: Charles Dickens's novella, *A Christmas Carol*

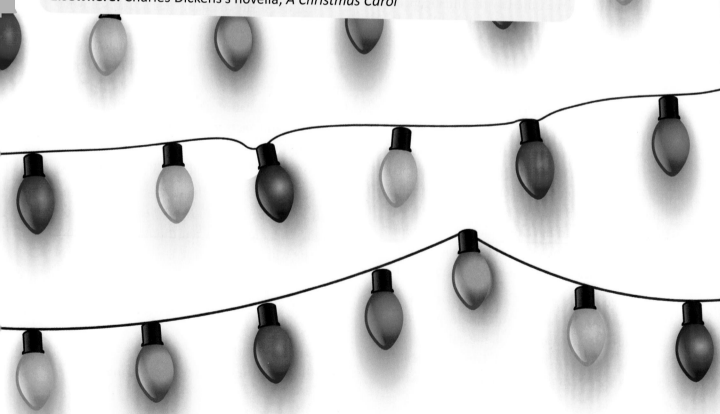

Complaint

Written correspondence is a common and often effective way to register a complaint. Individuals may choose to write to companies if they are unhappy with a product or service. Complaints can also be made in more public forums such as the 'Letters to the Editor' section of newspapers or in online forums.

Letters or emails of complaint are generally written using a formal tone. This means avoiding conversational language.

When writing a letter of complaint to a company, a formal structure should be used. There are different layouts that may be used. However, the layout below is typical.

SENDER'S ADDRESS

DATE

RECEIVER'S ADDRESS

SALUTATION

E.G. Dear…

MAIN BODY OF LETTER

SIGN OFF

E.G. Yours sincerely (if the name is known), Yours faithfully (if 'Dear Sir/Madam' is used

Private Business in Public Transport

Grace Egan

Many newspapers include a 'Letters to the Editor' page. This is a space where the editor publishes letters written by the public. Usually these letters are short and discuss issues of the day. The letter below was published in the 'Letters to the Editor' page of *The Irish Times*. The writer expresses her annoyance with the way members of the public behave on public transport.

Sir,

Having recently become a Dublin Dart and bus commuter, I am at best slack-jawed, at worst appalled, at what I am faced with daily on my commute.

One morning recently I sat beside a young man who persistently sniffed loudly and swallowed the contents of his nasal passages. I have observed fellow passengers picking their noses and after examining their finds, either wipe it on the seat or swallow it. Is there a national collective aversion to the use of tissues? Why do people who clearly need them not use them? The cacophony of coughing with mouths wide open, as well as snorting and sniffing, is nauseating.

One is better off standing on public transport. If you're unfortunate to sit at the window and want to exit your seat this manoeuvre needs to be planned at least three stops in advance as the likelihood of the person sitting next to you noticing you want to leave the bus is negligible. Your neighbour will be hooked up to a personal stereo system, or engaged in a telephone call to the exclusion of the outside world, or they will be frantically texting, Facebooking or Tweeting, or they will be asleep.

Parents using their children's buggies like weapons of mass destruction are another irritation. They simply barge on to the bus or Dart, indiscriminately injuring or disrupting any unfortunate fellow passenger in their way.

Another phenomenon is the application by women of their full make-up on public transport. I find sitting next to a woman applying a full face of make-up embarrassing.

Since when did public transport become alternative eateries? Recently I sat beside a man on the Dart who devoured two apples, munching, crunching and dribbling while doing so. What was most offensive, however, was the fact he placed the two apple cores on the seat opposite him. I looked at him doing this and I can only surmise that a faint embarrassment at being 'caught in the act' in a rare moment of consciousness forced him to retrieve them and put them in his jacket pocket.

I think it's time to take my bicycle out of storage.

Yours, etc,

Grace Egan

GLOSSARY

aversion: strong dislike
cacophony: noise, racket
indiscriminately: randomly
surmise: suspect, guess

Reading for Meaning

1. Do you feel that the author effectively describes her experiences on public transport? You may wish to look at the descriptive techniques listed in Chapter 4, page 95.
2. Describe the author's use of hyperbole (see Chapter 1, page 17) in this letter.
3. Do you agree with the point being made by the author in this letter?

Writer's Workshop

Letter to the Editor: Write a letter to the editor of a national newspaper about an issue that you feel needs attention. Try to keep your letter focused and relatively short.

Thank You for Your Feedback
Donal Minihane (General Manager of the Hotel Doolin)

The correspondence below was written in response to a harsh review received on tripadvisor.ie. The original review gave the Hotel Doolin in County Clare a one-star rating, referencing the lying staff, 'worst wifi ever' and the 'bunch of grumpy old men' who worked in the restaurant.

Thank you for staying with us at Hotel Doolin on your recent trip to Ireland and for posting your feedback. We were very disappointed with the content of your review. However, after investigating the particulars of your stay in detail with all team members I was even more disappointed to learn that the content of the review was not an accurate reflection of what actually happened. From the title of your review, other readers would think that you inadvertently stumbled into Hitchcock's Jamaica Inn and that Hotel Doolin was full of brigands and cutthroats, that our staff wear eye patches and pantaloons and are hiding behind the pillars in the lobby, cutlass clenched between our teeth, waiting to jump out and pillage passers-by.

You say the hotel is deceitful and dishonest and that one of our staff members, Emma, is a liar when, in fact, it is your good self that is being liberal with the truth. Emma did make a mistake on check-in with the rate, this was spotted the following morning by one of our more senior receptionists and was rectified before you checked out so that you never paid €240 as you stated above. Also, the duty manager met you the following morning, apologised for the mistake and gave you a further reduction on your rate.

We are 100% certain that Emma made a genuine mistake, as sometimes people do, and we feel it is very unfair and irresponsible of you to call her a liar and dishonest on a public forum.

I'm sensing a lot of anger in the review above and I know that you probably didn't mean to let loose all that anger on us. Hey, sometimes people just need to vent. Sometimes at night when I come home from a long day's work at the hotel, I check to see if everyone is in bed and then I go out into the field at the back of my house and scream into the darkness. I let it all out, like a wolf on a moonlit mountain. I feel better after that and nobody gets hurt. I'm not saying howling into the night like a wolf will work for you, I don't know your circumstances, you may have neighbours that'll think it is weird, but there are other ways of channelling rage that don't have to involve Hotel Doolin and slandering Emma.

With regards the Wi-Fi, yes, the Wi-Fi in the west of Ireland is the worst in Europe, there is nothing we can do about this for the moment, although I think we are getting high-speed broadband in the area pretty soon. In the meantime, to anybody else reading this review. DO NOT COME TO DOOLIN IF WI-FI IS MORE IMPORTANT TO YOU THAN HUMAN INTERACTION; YOU WILL BE DISAPPOINTED.

There are three men over the age of forty working in the hotel. Only one of them was working on the night you stayed, so we didn't know how to deal with the 'grumpy old men' in your review, until my assistant manager came up with the only viable solution. We've decided to execute all three of these men to ensure that no other guests will have to endure the horrific ordeal you went through that evening in the bar. Paul, Martin and Luis will be blindfolded and shot in the back of the head at Fitz's cross after mass this Sunday. There will be trad music, cocktail sausages and face-painting for the kids and I can organise a pair of complimentary tickets for you if you wish to attend. I know this will not make up for what happened to you, but we hope it will go some way towards showing you that we take your feedback seriously.

You see, even though you hurt us deeply with your review, we'd still like to be friends, we'd love if you afforded us the opportunity to change your opinion of us and hope that you will return to Doolin someday. In fact, each year on the 30th February we have a party for our valued past customers who think we are liars, we all hold hands and dance around a campfire and sing songs that help us forget about the past and look with hope towards the future.

We'd love if you could make it (that lying cheating ruffian Emma won't be there, we promise).

GLOSSARY

Jamaica Inn: a film directed by Alfred Hitchcock. The inn in question is a place filled with ship wreckers and unsavoury criminals.

brigands: bandits

cutlasses: curved swords traditionally used by sailors and pirates

Reading for Meaning

1. (a) Describe the tone used in this piece above.
    (b) Why do you think the author used this type of tone?
2. Explain how the humour used in this correspondence could be described as 'tongue-in-cheek' (see Chapter 1, page 40).
3. Do you think this was an effective way for the hotel to deal with the negative review?
4. Websites often give members of the public the opportunity to publish unedited reviews of products and services. In your view, what are the positives and negatives of this?

Writer's Workshop

Review: Donal Minihane's letter was written in response to a negative review. Write a positive review, to be published online, of something you have purchased or a place you have visited.

Chapter 4:
Fiction: The Truth that Didn't Happen –
Extracts and Short Stories

'The truth that didn't happen'? How can fiction offer us any truth at all? Although fictional stories do not recount a true event, they may offer us a deeper truth about what it means to be human. Storytelling is a tradition that predates writing and is essential to the human experience. Written fiction, like all storytelling traditions, prompts us to think about ourselves, society and life itself.

Because there is no limit to fiction, writers are free to dream up fantastic places, fascinating people and thought-provoking situations. Central to this project is a quest to understand a personal truth.

The authors collected in this chapter represent a broad range of nationalities, time periods and writing styles. Amidst this variety, they are united in their ability to move us and encourage us to think beyond the confines of our own personal realities.

Descriptive writing techniques

When writers want to bring a scene to life or portray an image vividly, they can make use of a number of descriptive writing techniques.

Adjectives – Adjectives are describing words that qualify a noun as they give more information about an object. For example, the sentence, *The door swung open to reveal a hallway*, can be made much more descriptive by introducing adjectives: *The ancient door swung open to reveal a damp, gloomy hallway*.

Adverbs – Adverbs can tell a reader more about a verb. They show *how* something is done. For example, the sentence, *The fox walked across the field*, can be made more descriptive by introducing adverbs such as *quickly, warily, recklessly* to show how the fox walked: *The fox walked cautiously across the field*.

Simile – A simile is a comparison that uses the words *like* or *as*. An effective simile can help the reader to imagine what is being described. In the following example, a volcano is compared to a sleeping giant using the word 'like': *The volcano loomed above them like a sleeping giant*.

Metaphor – Like simile, metaphor is also a type of comparison. The difference is that the words *like* and *as* are not used. In the following example a bedroom is compared to a bombsite: *My bedroom was a real mess; it was a bombsite*.

Personification – This is a particular type of metaphor, where a non-human thing is given human qualities. For example, a writer may describe how the sun shined by giving the sun human qualities: *The sun smiled down on the children*. The sun can't literally smile, but the use of personification is a more interesting way of explaining that the sun was shining.

Extended metaphor – This is when a writer continues a metaphor over a number of sentences. Read *Fire on the Mountain* by William Golding on page 96 for an excellent example of this.

Appeals to the senses – Writers often describe an item by referring to the senses other than vision. For example, a reader may learn how something tastes, sounds, smells or feels. This can help to transport the reader to another place.

Attention to detail – By providing lots of detail, a writer can build an image in a reader's mind. However, too much detail can become dull after a while, so a writer needs to be careful how they use this device by choosing to focus on significant details.

Verb choices – Writers can agonise over their work, looking for just the right verb or noun to express their ideas. The words *walked, strolled, ambled, sauntered, wandered, rambled, promenaded* all mean roughly the same thing, but each one has its own resonance. Writers should be careful to choose the best word to help them describe a scene or an event.

The following three extracts show how these writing devices can be put to use.

1. Fire on the Mountain
from *Lord of the Flies*, William Golding

Smoke was rising here and there among the creepers that festooned the dead or dying trees. As they watched, a flash of fire appeared at the root of one wisp, and then the smoke thickened. Small flames stirred at the bole of a tree and crawled away through leaves and brushwood, dividing and increasing. One patch touched a tree trunk and scrambled up like a bright squirrel. The smoke increased, sifted, rolled outwards. The squirrel leapt on the wings of the wind and clung to another standing tree, eating downwards. Beneath the dark canopy of leaves and smoke the fire laid hold on the forest and began to gnaw. Acres of black and yellow smoke rolled steadily towards the sea. At the sight of the flames and the irresistible course of the fire, the boys broke into shrill, excited cheering. The flames as though they were a kind of wild life, crept as a jaguar creeps on its belly towards a line of birch-like saplings that fledged an outcrop of the pink rock. They flapped at the first of the trees, and the branches grew a brief foliage of fire. The heart of flame leapt nimbly across the gap between the trees and then went swinging and flaring along the whole row of them. Beneath the capering boys a quarter of a mile square of forest was savage with smoke and flame. The separate noises of the fire merged into a drum-roll that seemed to shake the mountain.

2. Coketown
from *Hard Times*, Charles Dickens

It was a town of red brick, or of brick that would have been red if the smoke and ashes had allowed it; but, as matters stood it was a town of unnatural red and black like the painted face of a savage. It was a town of machinery and tall chimneys, out of which interminable serpents of smoke trailed themselves for ever and ever, and never got uncoiled. It had a black canal in it, and a river that ran purple with ill-smelling dye, and vast piles of building full of windows where there was a rattling and a trembling all day long, and where the piston of the steam-engine worked monotonously up and down, like the head of an elephant in a state of melancholy madness. It contained several large streets all very like one another, and many small streets still more like one another, inhabited by people equally like one another, who all went in and out at the same hours, with the same sound upon the same pavements, to do the same work, and to whom every day was the same as yesterday and tomorrow, and every year the counterpart of the last and the next.

GLOSSARY
coke: a solid fuel made by heating coal

3. The Wave

from *The Wave*, Liam O'Flaherty

The wave advanced, slowly at first, with a rumbling sound. That awful mass of water advanced simultaneously from end to end of its length without breaking a ripple on its ice-smooth breast. But from its summit a shower of driven foam arose, from east to west, and fell backwards on to the shoulders of the sea that came behind the wave in mountains pushing it to the cliff. The giant cliff looked small in front of that moving wall of blue and green and white water.

Then there was a roar. The wave sprang upwards to its full height. Its crest broke and points of water stuck out, curving downwards like fangs. It seemed to bend its head as it hurtled forward to ram the cliff. In a moment the wave and the cliff had disappeared in a tumbling mass of white water that yawned and hissed and roared. The whole semi-circle of the cliff vanished in the white water and the foam mist that rose above it blotting out the sky. Just for one moment it was thus. In another moment the broken wave had fallen, flying to the sea in a thousand rushing fragments. The cliff appeared again.

But a great black mouth had opened in its face, at the centre, above the cavern. The cliff's face stood ajar, as if it yawned, tired of battle. The mouth was vertical in the cliff, like a ten-foot wedge stuck upwards from the edge of the cavern. Then the cliff tried to close the mouth. It pressed in on it from either side. But it did not close. The sides fell inwards and the mouth grew wider. The whole centre of the cliff broke loose at the top and swayed forward like a tree being felled. There was a noise like rising thunder. Black dust rose from the tottering cliff through the falling foam of the wave. Then with a soft splash the whole centre of the cliff collapsed into the cavern. The sides caved in with another splash. A wall of grey dust arose shutting out everything. The rumbling of moving rocks came through the cloud of dust. Then the cloud rose and went inland.

The cliff had disappeared. The land sloped down to the edge of the cove. Huge rocks stood awkwardly on the very brink of the flat rock, with the rim of the sea playing between them. Smoke was rising from the fallen cliff. And the wave had disappeared. Already another one was gathering in the cove.

Language Lab

Use the list of descriptive devices on page 95 to help you explore each of the three extracts.

1. **Extract 1: *Fire on the Mountain*** Is the author, William Golding, successful in bringing the fire to life for the reader? You should refer to the use of simile, adverbs, extended metaphor and choice of verbs in your answer.

2. **Extract 2: *Coketown*** Does the author, Charles Dickens, do a good job of creating a sense of place in this extract? You should refer to his appeals to the senses, use of adjectives and simile.

3. **Extract 3: *The Wave*** Upon reading this extract, did you find it easy to imagine the wave? In your answer, you should refer to Liam O'Flaherty's use of personification, choice of verbs, simile, attention to detail and appeals to the senses.

4. All three of these descriptive passages are extracts. Which of the three full-length texts would you be most interested in reading? Explain why.

Writer's Workshop

Descriptive Composition: Taking inspiration from the three extracts on the previous pages, write a description of one of these images. Try to make use of the descriptive writing techniques listed on page 95.

Harrison Bergeron

Kurt Vonnegut

Kurt Vonnegut (1922-2007) was an American novelist, short story writer and playwright. His highly imaginative writing asks thought-provoking questions about society and tries to make sense of what it means to be alive. Vonnegut's uniquely playful and humorous style made him first a cult figure before achieving widespread critical success.

The short story below uses humour and a unique subject matter to ask serious questions about life and society.

The year was 2081, and everybody was finally equal. They weren't only equal before God and the law. They were equal every which way. Nobody was smarter than anybody else. Nobody was better looking than anybody else. Nobody was stronger or quicker than anybody else. All this equality was due to the 211th, 212th and 213th Amendments to the Constitution, and to the unceasing vigilance of agents of the United States Handicapper General.

Some things about living still weren't quite right, though. April, for instance, still drove people crazy by not being springtime. And it was in that clammy month that the H-G men took George and Hazel Bergeron's fourteen-year-old son, Harrison, away.

It was tragic, all right, but George and Hazel couldn't think about it very hard. Hazel had a perfectly average intelligence, which meant she couldn't think about anything except in short bursts. And George, while his intelligence was way above normal, had a little mental handicap radio in his ear. He was required by law to wear it at all times. It was tuned to a government transmitter. Every twenty seconds or so, the transmitter would send out some sharp noise to keep people like George from taking unfair advantage of their brains.

George and Hazel were watching television. There were tears on Hazel's cheeks, but she'd forgotten for the moment what they were about.

On the television screen were ballerinas.

A buzzer sounded in George's head. His thoughts fled in panic, like bandits from a burglar alarm.

'That was a real pretty dance, that dance they just did,' said Hazel.

'Huh?' said George.

'That dance – it was nice,' said Hazel.

'Yup,' said George. He tried to think a little about the ballerinas. They weren't really very good – no better than anybody else would have been, anyway. They were burdened with sashweights and bags of birdshot, and their faces were masked, so that no one, seeing a free and graceful gesture or a pretty face, would feel like something the cat drug in. George was toying with the vague notion that maybe dancers shouldn't be handicapped. But he didn't get very far with it before another noise in his ear radio scattered his thoughts.

George winced. So did two out of the eight ballerinas.

Hazel saw him wince. Having no mental handicap herself she had to ask George what the latest sound had been.

'Sounded like somebody hitting a milk bottle with a ball peen hammer,' said George.

'I'd think it would be real interesting, hearing all the different sounds,' said Hazel, a little envious. 'All the things they think up.'

'Um,' said George.

'Only, if I was Handicapper General, you know what I would do?' said Hazel. Hazel, as a matter of fact, bore a strong resemblance to the Handicapper General, a woman named Diana Moon Glampers. 'If I was Diana Moon Glampers,' said Hazel, 'I'd have chimes on Sunday – just chimes. Kind of in honour of religion.'

'I could think, if it was just chimes,' said George.

'Well – maybe make 'em real loud,' said Hazel. 'I think I'd make a good Handicapper General.'

'Good as anybody else,' said George.

'Who knows better'n I do what normal is?' said Hazel.

'Right,' said George. He began to think glimmeringly about his abnormal son who was now in jail, about Harrison, but a twenty-one-gun salute in his head stopped that.

'Boy!' said Hazel, 'that was a doozy, wasn't it?'

It was such a doozy that George was white and trembling and tears stood on the rims of his red eyes. Two of the eight ballerinas had collapsed to the studio floor, were holding their temples.

'All of a sudden you look so tired,' said Hazel. 'Why don't you stretch out on the sofa, so's you can rest your handicap bag on the pillows, honeybunch.' She was referring to the forty-seven pounds of birdshot in canvas bag, which was padlocked around George's neck. 'Go on and rest the bag for a little while,' she said. 'I don't care if you're not equal to me for a while.'

George weighed the bag with his hands. 'I don't mind it,' he said. 'I don't notice it any more. It's just a part of me.'

'You been so tired lately – kind of wore out,' said Hazel. 'If there was just some way we could make a little hole in the bottom of the bag, and just take out a few of them lead balls. Just a few.'

'Two years in prison and two thousand dollars fine for every ball I took out,' said George. 'I don't call that a bargain.'

'If you could just take a few out when you came home from work,' said Hazel. 'I mean – you don't compete with anybody around here. You just set around.'

'If I tried to get away with it,' said George, 'then other people'd get away with it and pretty soon we'd be right back to the dark ages again, with everybody competing against everybody else. You wouldn't like that, would you?'

'I'd hate it,' said Hazel.

'There you are,' said George. 'The minute people start cheating on laws, what do you think happens to society?'

If Hazel hadn't been able to come up with an answer to this question, George couldn't have supplied one. A siren was going off in his head.

'Reckon it'd fall all apart,' said Hazel.

'What would?' said George blankly.

'Society,' said Hazel uncertainly. 'Wasn't that what you just said?'

'Who knows?' said George.

The television programme was suddenly interrupted for a news bulletin. It wasn't clear at first as to what the bulletin was about, since the announcer, like all announcers, had a serious speech impediment. For about half a minute, and in a state of high excitement, the announcer tried to say, 'Ladies and gentlemen –'

He finally gave up, handed the bulletin to a ballerina to read.

'That's all right –' Hazel said of the announcer, 'he tried. That's the big thing. He tried to do the best he could with what God gave him. He should get a nice raise for trying so hard.'

'Ladies and gentlemen,' said the ballerina, reading the bulletin. She must have been extraordinarily beautiful, because the mask she wore was hideous. And it was easy to see that she was the strongest and most graceful of all the dancers, for her handicap bags were as big as those worn by two-hundred-pound men.

And she had to apologise at once for her voice, which was a very unfair voice for a woman to use. Her voice was a warm, luminous, timeless melody. 'Excuse me –' she said, and she began again, making her voice absolutely uncompetitive.

'Harrison Bergeron, age fourteen,' she said in a grackle squawk, 'has just escaped from jail, where he was held on suspicion of plotting to overthrow the government. He is a genius and an athlete, is under-handicapped, and should be regarded as extremely dangerous.'

A police photograph of Harrison Bergeron was flashed on the screen – upside down, then sideways, upside down again, then right side up. The picture showed the full length of Harrison against a background calibrated in feet and inches. He was exactly seven feet tall.

The rest of Harrison's appearance was Halloween and hardware. Nobody had ever worn heavier handicaps. He had outgrown hindrances faster than the H–G men could think them up. Instead of a little ear radio for a mental handicap, he wore a tremendous pair of earphones, and spectacles with thick wavy lenses. The spectacles were intended to make him not only half blind, but to give him whanging headaches besides.

Scrap metal was hung all over him. Ordinarily, there was a certain symmetry, a military neatness to the handicaps issued to strong people, but Harrison looked like a walking junkyard. In the race of life, Harrison carried three hundred pounds.

And to offset his good looks, the H–G men required that he wear at all times a red rubber ball for a nose, keep his eyebrows shaved off, and cover his even white teeth with black caps at snaggle–tooth random.

'If you see this boy,' said the ballerina, 'do not – I repeat, do not – try to reason with him.'

There was the shriek of a door being torn from its hinges.

Screams and barking cries of consternation came from the television set. The photograph of Harrison Bergeron on the screen jumped again and again, as though dancing to the tune of an earthquake.

George Bergeron correctly identified the earthquake, and well he might have – for many was the time his own home had danced to the same crashing tune. 'My God –' said George, 'that must be Harrison!'

The realisation was blasted from his mind instantly by the sound of an automobile collision in his head.

When George could open his eyes again, the photograph of Harrison was gone. A living, breathing Harrison filled the screen.

Clanking, clownish, and huge, Harrison stood in the centre of the studio. The knob of the uprooted studio door was still in his hand. Ballerinas, technicians, musicians, and announcers cowered on their knees before him, expecting to die.

'I am the Emperor!' cried Harrison. 'Do you hear? I am the Emperor! Everybody must do what I say at once!' He stamped his foot and the studio shook.

'Even as I stand here–' he bellowed, 'crippled, hobbled, sickened– I am a greater ruler than any man who ever lived! Now watch me become what I *can* become!'

Harrison tore the straps of his handicap harness like wet tissue paper, tore straps guaranteed to support five thousand pounds.

Harrison's scrap-iron handicaps crashed to the floor.

Harrison thrust his thumbs under the bar of the padlock that secured his head harness. The bar snapped like celery. Harrison smashed his headphones and spectacles against the wall.

He flung away his rubber-ball nose, revealed a man that would have awed Thor, the god of thunder.

'I shall now select my Empress!' he said, looking down on the cowering people. 'Let the first woman who dares rise to her feet claim her mate and her throne!'

A moment passed, and then a ballerina arose, swaying like a willow.

Harrison plucked the mental handicap from her ear, snapped off her physical handicaps with marvellous delicacy. Last of all, he removed her mask.

She was blindingly beautiful.

'Now' said Harrison, taking her hand, 'shall we show the people the meaning of the word dance? Music!' he commanded.

The musicians scrambled back into their chairs, and Harrison stripped them of their handicaps, too. 'Play your best,' he told them, 'and I'll make you barons and dukes and earls.'

The music began. It was normal at first – cheap, silly, false. But Harrison snatched two musicians from their chairs, waved them like batons as he sang the music as he wanted it played. He slammed them back into their chairs.

The music began again and was much improved.

Harrison and his Empress merely listened to the music for a while – listened gravely, as though synchronising their heartbeats with it.

They shifted their weights to their toes.

Harrison placed his big hands on the girl's tiny waist, letting her sense the weightlessness that would soon be hers.

And then, in an explosion of joy and grace, into the air they sprang!

Not only were the laws of the land abandoned, but the law of gravity and the laws of motion as well.

They reeled, whirled, swivelled, flounced, capered, gambolled and spun.

They leaped like deer on the moon.

The studio ceiling was thirty feet high, but each leap brought the dancers nearer to it. It became their obvious intention to kiss the ceiling. They kissed it.

And then, neutralising gravity with love and pure will, they remained suspended in air inches below the ceiling, and they kissed each other for a long, long time.

It was then that Diana Moon Glampers, the Handicapper General, came into the studio with a double-barrelled ten-gauge shotgun. She fired twice, and the Emperor and the Empress were dead before they hit the floor.

Diana Moon Glampers loaded the gun again. She aimed it at the musicians and told them they had ten seconds to get their handicaps back on.

It was then that the Bergerons' television tube burned out.

Hazel turned to comment about the blackout to George. But George had gone out into the kitchen for a can of beer.

George came back in with the beer, paused while a handicap signal shook him up. And then he sat down again. 'You been crying?' he said to Hazel.

'Yup,' she said.

'What about?' he said.

'I forget,' she said. 'Something real sad on television.'

'What was it?' he said. 'It's all kind of mixed up in my mind,' said Hazel.

'Forget sad things,' said George.

'I always do,' said Hazel.

'That's my girl,' said George. He winced. There was the sound of a riveting gun in his head.

'Gee – I could tell that one was a doozy,' said Hazel.

'You can say that again,' said George.

'Gee –' said Hazel, 'I could tell that one was a doozy.'

GLOSSARY

ball peen hammer: a hammer used for beating metal

birdshot: small pellets used for shooting birds

luminous: easily understood, radiating, enlightening

calibrated: measured

hindrances: obstacles, handicaps

consternation: a feeling of dread or confusion

gambolled: skipped about

riveting gun: machine used to fix metal rivets

Reading for Meaning

1. Explain how the society in Kurt Vonnegut's story has tried to make the world a fair and equal place.

2. (a) 'Although exceptional and talented, Harrison Bergeron is an unlikable character.' Do you agree with this statement?

   (b) Why do you think Vonnegut presented him in this way?

3. (a) Which of the following words best describes Hazel and George Bergeron: pathetic, vulnerable, weak, manipulated, foolish?

   (b) Why do you think Vonnegut presented them in this way?

4. Which of the following sentences best describes the point this story is making?

   - No matter what type of society we live in, powerful people will always exploit those who are less powerful.
   - If equality is taken to extremes, individuals are denied the possibility of experiencing freedom and beauty.
   - Without equality, those who are most gifted become obnoxious and oppressive.
   - It is very difficult to balance the rights to both equality and freedom in a society.

5. This story explores important social issues using humour. Do you find the story amusing and entertaining?

Writer's Workshop

Short Story: Harrison Bergeron is a highly imaginative tale that presents a world completely different to our own. Taking inspiration from this, write your own short story set in a society that is utterly different from your own.

Speaking and Listening

Debate: Conduct a class debate on the following motion: 'The most important goal for any society is to achieve true equality.' Go to Chapter 6, pages 212–214 to learn about running a debate.

Links

Harrison Bergeron presents us with a society with a strict social order, and encourages the reader to think about the rights of the individual. This story can be linked to other texts in this book and elsewhere:

In this book: 'They're Speakin' of Witchcraft' (extract from Arthur Miller's play *The Crucible*, page 218)

Elsewhere: Peter Weir's film, *The Truman Show*

Creative Writing 101

Kurt Vonnegut

American writer Kurt Vonnegut (see his story on pages 99–103) famously composed a set of eight rules for creative writing. These are a helpful guide as you analyse fiction but also come to write your own short stories. However, Vonnegut also casts a shadow of doubt over his own rules in the note at the end!

1. Use the time of a total stranger in such a way that he or she will not feel the time was wasted.
2. Give the reader at least one character he or she can root for.
3. Every character should want something, even if it is only a glass of water.
4. Every sentence must do one of two things – reveal character or advance the action.
5. Start as close to the end as possible.
6. Be a sadist. No matter how sweet and innocent your leading characters, make awful things happen to them – in order that the reader may see what they are made of.
7. Write to please just one person. If you open a window and make love to the world, so to speak, your story will get pneumonia.
8. Give your readers as much information as possible as soon as possible. To heck with suspense. Readers should have such complete understanding of what is going on, where and why, that they could finish the story themselves, should cockroaches eat the last few pages.

> The greatest American short story writer of my generation was Flannery O'Connor (1925–1964). She broke practically every one of my rules but the first. Great writers tend to do that.

From the Introduction to Bagombo Snuff Box

Reading for Meaning

1. Why do you think Kurt Vonnegut includes the note about the writer Flannery O'Connor?
2. Read *Harrison Bergeron* on pages 99–103. In your view, has Kurt Vonnegut kept to his own eight rules?
3. Read another short story in this chapter. In your opinion, does this story obey Kurt Vonnegut's eight rules for creative writing?
4. Which of the eight rules (if any) do you feel could be cut from the list?
5. If you were to add a ninth rule, what would it be?

Writer's Workshop

Short Story: Following Kurt Vonnegut's eight rules as closely as possible, write a short story on any theme of your choice. When you are finished, write a short paragraph explaining whether you found the eight rules helpful or not.

All Summer in a Day

Ray Bradbury

Ray Bradbury (1920 - 2012) was an American writer. His works are often categorised as science fiction but Bradbury himself did not like that description. Bradbury's fertile imagination allows him to use fantastical subject matter to explore a wide set of themes.

The story below is set on a planet far from home, but the themes of childhood innocence, bullying, guilt and disappointment will be very familiar to all people who live on planet Earth.

'Ready?'

'Ready.'

'Now?'

'Soon.'

'Do the scientists really know? Will it happen today, will it?'

'Look, look; see for yourself!'

The children pressed to each other like so many roses, so many weeds, intermixed, peering out for a look at the hidden sun.

It rained.

It had been raining for seven years; thousands upon thousands of days compounded and filled from one end to the other with rain, with the drum and gush of water, with the sweet crystal fall of showers and the concussion of storms so heavy they were tidal waves come over the islands. A thousand forests had been crushed under the rain and grown up a thousand times to be crushed again. And this was the way life was forever on the planet Venus, and this was the schoolroom of the children of the rocket men and women who had come to a raining world to set up civilisation and live out their lives.

'It's stopping, it's stopping!'

'Yes, yes!'

Margot stood apart from them, from these children who could never remember a time when there wasn't rain and rain and rain. They were all nine years old, and if there had been a day, seven years ago, when the sun came out for an hour and showed its face to the stunned world, they could not recall. Sometimes, at night, she heard them stir, in remembrance, and she knew they were dreaming and remembering gold or a yellow crayon or a coin large enough to buy the world with. She knew they thought they remembered a warmness, like a blushing in the face, in the body, in the arms and legs and trembling hands. But then they always awoke to the tatting drum, the endless shaking down of clear bead necklaces upon the roof, the walk, the gardens, the forests, and their dreams were gone.

All day yesterday they had read in class about the sun. About how like a lemon it was, and how hot. And they had written small stories or essays or poems about it:

I think the sun is a flower,

That blooms for just one hour.

That was Margot's poem, read in a quiet voice in the still classroom while the rain was falling outside.

'Aw, you didn't write that!' protested one of the boys.

'I did,' said Margot. 'I *did*.'

'William!' said the teacher.

But that was yesterday. Now the rain was slackening, and the children were crushed in the great thick windows.

'Where's teacher?'

'She'll be back.'

'She'd better hurry; we'll miss it!'

They turned on themselves, like a feverish wheel, all tumbling spokes. Margot stood alone. She was a very frail girl who looked as if she had been lost in the rain for years and the rain had washed out the blue from her eyes and the red from her mouth and the yellow from her hair. She was an old photograph dusted from an album, whitened away, and if she spoke at all her voice would be a ghost. Now she stood, separate, staring at the rain and the loud wet world beyond the huge glass.

'What're *you* looking at?' said William.

Margot said nothing.

'Speak when you're spoken to.' He gave her a shove. But she did not move; rather she let herself be moved only by him and nothing else.

They edged away from her; they would not look at her. She felt them go away. And this was because she would play no games with them in the echoing tunnels of the underground city. If they tagged her and ran, she stood blinking after them and did not follow. When the class sang songs about happiness and life and games her lips barely moved. Only when they sang about the sun and the summer did her lips move as she watched the drenched windows.

And then, of course, the biggest crime of all was that she had come here only five years ago from Earth, and she remembered the sun and the way the sun was and the sky was when she was four in Ohio. And they, they had been on Venus all their lives, and they had been only two years old when last the sun came out and had long since forgotten the colour and heat of it and the way it really was. But Margot remembered.

'It's like a penny,' she said once, eyes closed.

'No, it's not!' the children cried.

'It's like a fire,' she said, 'in the stove.'

'You're lying, you don't remember!' cried the children.

But she remembered and stood quietly apart from all of them and watched the patterning windows. And once, a month ago, she had refused to shower in the school shower rooms, had clutched her hands to her ears and over her head, screaming the water mustn't touch her head. So after that, dimly, dimly, she sensed it, she was different and they knew her difference and kept away.

There was talk that her father and mother were taking her back to Earth next year; it seemed vital to her that they do so, though it would mean the loss of thousands of dollars to her family. And so, the children hated her for all these reasons of big and little consequence. They hated her pale snow face, her waiting silence, her thinness, and her possible future.

'Get away!' The boy gave her another push. 'What're you waiting for?'

Then, for the first time, she turned and looked at him. And what she was waiting for was in her eyes.

'Well, don't wait around here!' cried the boy savagely. 'You won't see nothing!'

Her lips moved.

'Nothing!' he cried. 'It was all a joke, wasn't it?' He turned to the other children. 'Nothing's happening today. *Is* it?'

They all blinked at him and then, understanding, laughed and shook their heads. 'Nothing, nothing!'

'Oh, but,' Margot whispered, her eyes helpless. 'But this is the day, the scientists predict, they say, they *know*, the sun…'

'All a joke!' said the boy, and seized her roughly. 'Hey, everyone, let's put her in a closet before the teacher comes!'

'No,' said Margot, falling back.

They surged about her, caught her up and bore her, protesting, and then pleading, and then crying, back into a tunnel, a room, a closet, where they slammed and locked the door. They stood looking at the door and saw it tremble from her beating and throwing herself against it. They heard her muffled cries. Then, smiling, they turned and went out and back down the tunnel, just as the teacher arrived.

'Ready, children?' She glanced at her watch.

'Yes!' said everyone.

'Are we all here?'

'Yes!'

The rain slacked still more.

They crowded to the huge door.

The rain stopped.

It was as if, in the midst of a film concerning an avalanche, a tornado, a hurricane, a volcanic eruption, something had, first, gone wrong with the sound apparatus, thus muffling and finally cutting off all noise, all of the blasts and repercussions and thunders, and then, second, ripped the film from the projector and inserted in its place a peaceful tropical slide which did not move or tremor. The world ground to a standstill. The silence was so immense and unbelievable that you felt your ears had been stuffed or you had lost your hearing altogether. The children put their hands to their ears. They stood apart. The door slid back and the smell of the silent, waiting world came in to them.

The sun came out.

It was the colour of flaming bronze and it was very large. And the sky around it was a blazing blue tile colour. And the jungle burned with sunlight as the children, released from their spell, rushed out, yelling into the springtime.

'Now, don't go too far,' called the teacher after them. 'You've only two hours, you know. You wouldn't want to get caught out!'

But they were running and turning their faces up to the sky and feeling the sun on their cheeks like a warm iron; they were taking off their jackets and letting the sun burn their arms.

'Oh, it's better than the sun lamps, isn't it?'

'Much, much better!'

They stopped running and stood in the great jungle that covered Venus, that grew and never stopped growing, tumultuously, even as you watched it. It was a nest of octopuses, clustering up great arms of fleshlike weed, wavering, flowering in this brief spring. It was the colour of rubber and ash, this jungle, from the many years without sun. It was the colour of stones and white cheeses and ink, and it was the colour of the moon.

The children lay out, laughing, on the jungle mattress, and heard it sigh and squeak under them, resilient and alive. They ran among the trees, they slipped and fell, they pushed each other, they played hide-and-seek and tag, but most of all they squinted at the sun until the tears ran down their faces; they put their hands up to that yellowness and that amazing blueness and they breathed of the fresh, fresh air and listened and listened to the silence which suspended them in a blessed sea of no sound and no motion. They looked at everything and savoured everything. Then, wildly, like animals escaped from their caves, they ran and ran in shouting circles. They ran for an hour and did not stop running.

And then –

In the midst of their running one of the girls wailed.

Everyone stopped.

The girl, standing in the open, held out her hand.

'Oh, look, look,' she said, trembling.

They came slowly to look at her opened palm.

In the centre of it, cupped and huge, was a single raindrop.

She began to cry, looking at it.

They glanced quietly at the sky.

'Oh. Oh.'

A few cold drops fell on their noses and their cheeks and their mouths. The sun faded behind a stir of mist. A wind blew cold around them. They turned and started to walk back toward the underground house, their hands at their sides, their smiles vanishing away.

A boom of thunder startled them and like leaves before a new hurricane, they tumbled upon each other and ran. Lightning struck ten miles away, five miles away, a mile, a half-mile. The sky darkened into midnight in a flash.

They stood in the doorway of the underground for a moment until it was raining hard. Then they closed the door and heard the gigantic sound of the rain falling in tons and avalanches, everywhere and forever.

'Will it be seven more years?'

'Yes. Seven.'

Then one of them gave a little cry.

'Margot!'

'What?'

'She's still in the closet where we locked her.'

'Margot.'

They stood as if someone had driven them, like so many stakes, into the floor. They looked at each other and then looked away. They glanced out at the world that was raining now and raining and raining steadily. They could not meet each other's glances. Their faces were solemn and pale. They looked at their hands and feet, their faces down.

'Margot.'

One of the girls said, 'Well…?'

No one moved.

'Go on,' whispered the girl.

They walked slowly down the hall in the sound of cold rain. They turned through the doorway to the room in the sound of the storm and thunder, lightning on their faces, blue and terrible. They walked over to the closet door slowly and stood by it.

Behind the closet door was only silence.

They unlocked the door, even more slowly, and let Margot out.

Reading for Meaning

1. Do you feel that Ray Bradbury does a good job of showing how wonderful the experience of the rainless, sunny hours are for the children?
2. (a) How do the children feel when they remember that Margot is locked in the closet?
   (b) How does the writer show this?
3. Why do you think the writer chose not to describe what Margot's experience inside the closet was like nor how she reacted when she was released?
4. This story is rich in descriptive language (see page 95). Choose two descriptive phrases that you feel are particularly effective and explain why you found them so.
5. 'All Summer in One Day captures all of the joy and heartbreak to be found in early childhood.' Do you agree with this statement?

Writer's Workshop

Comic Strip: Create a comic strip version of this story. In groups, design and script the panels. Choose a member of the group to create the artwork. Try to capture the story's essential scenes, mood and themes.

Speaking and Listening

Watch and Discuss: A short film adaptation of this story, directed by Ed Kaplan, offers an interesting interpretation of Ray Bradbury's story. Watch this short film (27 minutes) as a class.

- In small groups, discuss the film.
- How do the film and the short story differ?
- Was the director successful in bringing this story to the screen?
- Did you find the film or the story more powerful?
- After you have discussed the film in your groups, discuss the film as a class.

To watch this video, go to **www.mentorbooks.ie/resources** and look in the TY English section. Alternatively, you may find this film on YouTube.

Links

All Summer in a Day simultaneously presents us with all of the joy and pain of childhood. This story can be linked to other texts in this book and elsewhere:
In this book: Sylvia Plath's story, *Superman and Paula Brown's New Snowsuit* (page 118)
Elsewhere: Albert Lamorisse's classic short film, *Le Ballon Rouge* (The Red Balloon)

No Trumpets Needed

Michael Morpurgo

Michael Morpurgo (born 1943) is an English writer who has written over 130 books. He is a much loved and acclaimed writer.

No Trumpets Needed is set in the West Bank, part of the occupied Palestinian territories. Since the foundation of the state of Israel in 1948, there has been tension and conflict between Israelis and Palestinians in this area.

In this story, Michael Morpurgo explores the issues of war and peace. The actions of the character Saïd offer the reader a vision for how humanity as a whole may reconcile differences.

I am a cameraman. I work freelance, working on my own. It's how I like it. I was on the West Bank a few weeks ago, my first job in the bitter cauldron of contention that is the Middle East. Of course I had seen on television, like most of us, the anguish of the grieving, the burnt-out buses, the ritual humiliation at checkpoints, the tanks in the streets, the stone-throwing crowds, the olive groves and the hill-top settlements, children playing in open sewers in the refugee camps – and now, the wall. I knew the place in images, I was there to make more of them, I suppose. But I had a more personal reason for being there too. I saw it on television, watched in disbelief as the Berlin Wall came tumbling down. It was the most hopeful, most momentous event of my young life. Now another wall had been built, and I wanted to find out about the lives of the people who lived close to it – on both sides. I began my travels on the Palestinian side.

I had been there only a couple of days when I first came across a shepherd boy. He was sitting alone on a hillside under an olive tree with his sheep grazing all around him. I had seen nothing remotely picturesque in this land until that moment, nothing until now that reminded me in any way of its biblical past. The shepherd boy was making a kite, so intent upon it that he had not noticed my approach. He was whistling softly, not to make a tune, I felt, but simply to reassure his sheep. When he did look up he showed no surprise or alarm. His smile was openhearted and engaging. I could not bring myself to pass by with a mere greeting or paltry nod of the head.

So I sat down and offered him a drink out of my rucksack. He drank gratefully, eagerly, but said nothing. I patted my camera, told him who I was, shook his hand. I tried to communicate in English, then in the very few words of Arabic I had picked up. His smile was the only reply I got. Clearly he liked me to speak, wanted me to stay, but I knew he didn't understand a word I was saying. So, after a while I lapsed into silence and watched him at work on his kite, the sheep shifting all around us under the shade of the tree, their smell pungent and heavy in the warm air.

When I began to film him he seemed unconcerned, disinterested even. We shared what food we had. He took a great fancy to some Scottish shortbread I'd brought with me from back home in Dundee, and he gave me some of his pine nuts. And we shared our silence too, both of us knowing instinctively that this was fine, as good a way as any to get to know one another.

When evening came and he stood up and began to whistle his sheep home, I knew he expected me to go with him, like one of his sheep. Later, I found myself sitting in his house, surrounded by his huge extended family, all talking amongst each other and watching me, not with hostility, but certainly with some suspicion. It was an unsettling experience. But the boy, I noticed, still said nothing. He was showing everyone the progress he had made with his kite. I could see that he was a much treasured child. We ate lamb, and the most succulent broad beans I had ever tasted, then sweet spiced cake dripping with honey. When the boy came and sat himself down beside me, I knew he was showing me off. I was his guest, and I felt suddenly honoured by that, and moved by his affection.

Then, much to my surprise one of the men spoke to me directly, and in good English. 'I am Saïd's uncle,' he began. 'You are most welcome in our home. Saïd would want to say this himself, but he does not speak. Not anymore. There was a time when you could not stop him.' He would pause from time to time to explain to everyone what he was telling me. 'It happened two years ago,' he went on. 'Mahmoud was flying his kite on the hill. It was before they built the wall. Mahmoud was Saïd's elder brother. He loved to make kites. He loved to fly kites. Saïd was with him. He was always with him. That day, a settler's car had been ambushed down in the valley. Three of them were killed. One was a little girl. Afterwards the soldiers came, and the helicopters. There was some shooting. Maybe it was a revenge killing. Maybe it was a stray bullet. Who knows? Who cares? Mahmoud was shot dead, and Saïd saw it all. In front of his eyes he saw it. Since this day he does not speak. Since this day he does not grow. God willing he will, God willing. Maybe he is small, maybe he cannot speak, but he is the best shepherd in all Palestine. And you make the best kites too, don't you Saïd? And Saïd's kites are not ordinary kites.'

'What do you mean?' I asked.

'Maybe he will show you that himself. Maybe he will fly this kite for you tomorrow. This one is ready to fly, I think. But the wind must always be from the east, or Saïd will not fly his kites.'

I spent the night under the stars, on the roof of the house. I was tired but far too troubled to sleep. I was up at dawn and went down into the valley. I wanted to film the sun rising over the wall. Once I'd done that I climbed back up the hill so that I could get a long shot of the wall, tracking it as it sliced obscenely through the olive groves and across the hillside beyond. Dogs barked, and cocks crowed at one another from both sides of the wall.

After breakfast I went off with Saïd and his sheep, Saïd carrying his kite, now with its string attached. I doubted he'd be flying it that day because there was very little wind. But an hour or so later, sitting on the highest hill above the village, with the sheep browsing in amongst the rocks, their bells sounding softly, I felt a sudden breeze spring up. Saïd was on his feet at once, eagerly offering me his kite. I noticed then for the first time that there was writing on one side of the kite, and a drawing too, of a dove.

He was urging me to run now, racing ahead of me to show me how to do it. <u>I felt the wind taking it, felt the kite suddenly air-borne, wind-whipped and tugging to be free. Saïd clapped his hands in wild delight as it swooped and soared above us. I had done this on Hampstead Heath with my father when I was a boy, but had forgotten the sheer exhilaration of it. The kite was alive at the end of the string, loving it as much as I was. Saïd tapped my arm and took the string from me. Very reluctantly I handed it over.</u>

Saïd was an expert. With a tweak of his wrist the kite turned and twirled, with a flick of his fingers he dived it and danced it. My professional instinct kicked in. I needed boy and kite in the same shot, so I had to put some distance between them and me. I backed away over the hillside, pausing to film as I went, fearful of missing these fleeting moments of innocent rapture in this war-ravaged land. I closed on the fluttering kite, then zoomed in on the wall below, following it up over the hillside, and focusing on the settlement beyond, on the flag flying there, and then on some children playing football in the street below. I watched them through my lens, witnessed the celebratory hugging as one of them scored.

I turned my camera on Saïd again. There was, I noticed, a look of intense concentration on his face. That was the moment he let the kite go. It was quite deliberate. He simply gave it to the wind, holding his arms aloft as if he'd just released a trapped bird, and was giving it its freedom. It soared up high, seeming to float there for a while on the thermals, before the wind discovered it and took it away over the olive grove, over the wall and up towards the hilltop settlement.

Saïd was tugging at my arm again. He wanted to look through my lens. I saw then what he was looking at, a young girl in a headscarf gazing up at the kite as it came floating down. Now she was running over to where it had landed. She picked it up and stood looking at us for a few moments, before the footballers came racing down the hill towards her. They all stood there then, gazing across at us. But when Saïd waved, only the girl in the headscarf waved back. They didn't fly the kite. They just took it away and disappeared.

On the way home with the sheep later that day, we came across Saïd's uncle harvesting his broad beans. 'It's a poor crop, but what can you do?' he said. 'There is never enough water. They take all our best land, all our water. They leave us only the dust to farm in.' I stayed to talk while Saïd walked on up into the village with his sheep. 'So the wind was right,' Saïd's uncle went on. 'Saïd never keeps his kites you know, not one. He just makes them, waits for the east wind, and sends them off. Did you see what he draws on each one? A dove of peace. Did you see what he writes? Salaam. Shalom. And he signs every one of them: Mahmoud and Saïd.'

'How many has he sent?' I asked.

'A hundred maybe. About one a week since they killed Mahmoud. He wrote it down for his mother once, telling her why he does it. For Saïd, every kite that lands over there, is like a seed of friendship. He believes that one day they'll send the kites back, and everything will be right, friendships with grow, and peace will come and the killing will stop. Let him have his dreams. It's all he has. He'll find out soon enough what they're like over there.'

'There was a girl who found the kite,' I told him. 'She waved back. I saw her. It's a beginning.'

'It costs nothing to wave,' he replied bitterly.

I stayed one more night. So I was there to see the embryo of the next kite taking shape, Saïd kneeling on the carpet, his whole family watching intently as he constructed the frame with infinite care, ignoring all their advice, and the food and drink they constantly offered him. 'Maybe it is good,' Saïd's uncle said to me, when Saïd had gone up to bed, 'maybe it helps him to forget. Maybe if he forgets, he will find his voice again. Maybe he will grow again. God willing. God willing.'

I said my goodbyes early the next morning and left with Saïd and the sheep. Saïd held my hand all the way. There was between us, I felt, the same unspoken thought: that we were friends and did not want to part, and that when we did we would probably never see each other again. The sheep were in clambering mood, their bells jangling loud in the morning air. We sat down on the hillside where we'd flown the kite the day before. Saïd had brought the frame of his new kite with him, but he was not in the mood for working on it. Like me he was gazing out over the valley, over the wall, towards the settlement. The flag still fluttered there. A donkey brayed balefully nearby, winding itself into a frenzy of misery. I felt it was time for me to go. I put my hand on Saïd's shoulder, let it rest there a few moments, then left him.

When I looked back a while later he was busy with his kite. I stopped to film him. It would be the perfect closing shot. I had just about got myself ready to film when Saïd sprang to his feet. The sheep were suddenly bounding away from him, scattering across the hillside.

Then I saw the kites. They were all colours of the rainbow, hundreds of them, like dancing butterflies they were, rising into the air from the hillside below the settlement. I could hear the shrieks of joy, saw the crowd of children gathered there, every one of them flying a kite. A few snagged each other and plunged to earth, but most sailed up triumphantly heavenwards. The settlers were pouring out of their houses to watch. One after the other, the kites were released, took wind and flew out over the wall towards us. And from behind me, from Saïd's village, the people came running too, as the kites landed in amongst us, and amongst the terrified sheep too. On every kite I saw the same message, in Hebrew and in Arabic: 'Shalom and Salaam'. And on every kite too there was a drawing of an olive branch. Everywhere on both sides of the wall the children were cheering and laughing and dancing about. I could see the girl in the scarf waving at us, and leaping up and down.

Around me, some of the mothers and fathers, grandmothers and grandfathers began to clap too, hesitantly at first. But others soon joined in, Saïd's uncle amongst them. But the cheering, I noticed, and the laughter and the dancing they left to the children. The hillsides rang with their jubilation, with their exultation. It seemed to me like a joyous symphony of hope.

As I raced over the hillside towards Saïd, I could hear him laughing and shouting out loud along with all the others. I realised then – idiot that I was – that I had quite forgotten to film this miracle. And almost simultaneously I understood that it didn't matter anyway, that it was the laughter that mattered. It was laughter that would one day resonate so loud that this wall would come tumbling down. No trumpets needed, as they had been at Jericho, only the laughter of children.

GLOSSARY

West Bank: an area of disputed land considered by many as Palestinian territory under Israeli occupation

Berlin Wall: a barrier that divided East (Communist) and West (Capitalist) Berlin in Germany. The wall came down in 1989

settler: in this context, 'settler' refers to somebody from Israel who has been given land in the West Bank

Hampstead Heath: a large park in London

Shalom: Peace/Hello (Hebrew)

Salaam: Peace (Arabic)

balefully: threateningly

Jericho: according to the Book of Joshua in the Bible, Jericho was conquered by the Israelite army after they surrounded the city and used their trumpets to blow the walls down

Reading for Meaning

1. How does Michael Morpurgo encourage sympathy for Saïd and his family?
2. What evidence is there in this story to show that the conflict between the Israelis and the Palestinians is a bitter one?
3. In the story's last paragraph, the narrator says, 'I realised...that I had quite forgotten to film this miracle. And almost simultaneously I understood that it didn't matter anyway.' Why do you think the narrator feels he does not need to film what is happening?
4. 'No Trumpets Needed combines the reality of violent conflict with an uplifting sense of hope.' In your view, is this statement an accurate description of the story?
5. (a) Take a look at the glossary note for 'Jericho'. With this in mind, why do you think Morpurgo named his story, *No Trumpets Needed*?
   (b) Suggest an alternative title for the story, explaining why you chose this title.

Style Guide

Allegory: An allegory is a story that has a deeper, more complex meaning. An allegory often contains symbols that enrich the story's meaning. In his modern allegory, *No Trumpets Needed*, Michael Morpurgo explores ideas of peace, hope and healing. The story offers the reader an uplifting message about the possibility of resolving conflict.

Language Lab

1. Look at the two underlined sections of the story where Saïd's kite is described. How does Michael Morpurgo bring the kite to life in these paragraphs? You should comment on the writer's use of descriptive language (see page 95).
2. To explore complex ideas, Morpurgo uses a number of symbols in his allegory (see Style Guide above). What do you think each of the following from the story represent?
   (a) Saïd's drawings of a dove
   (b) the wall
   (c) the kite
   (d) the drawings of olive branches

Writer's Workshop

Visual Poetry Display: *No Trumpets Needed* offers the reader an anti-war theme. Create a visual poetry display with a similar theme:

- **Individually:** search online for an anti-war poem or a poem that promotes peace. The following poetry websites may help you:
  www.poetryarchive.org
  www.poetryfoundation.org
  www.poetryireland.ie
- **As a class:** create a wall poster with all of your poems collected together.

Speaking and Listening

Research and Discuss:

- Find a copy of the Universal Declaration of Human Rights. This can be found online on the UN's website (www.un.org) or in any quality CSPE book.
- Think about the characters in Morpurgo's story. In groups, discuss which articles of the declaration are threatened in the story.
- Discuss what individuals and the international community could do to help people in similar situations.

Walking debate

'Fiction, poetry and film have the power to transform the world into a more peaceful place.'

- At one end of the classroom place a sign saying, 'I strongly agree'.
- At the opposite end place a sign saying, 'I strongly disagree'.
- When the teacher reads the motion, each member of the class should place themselves somewhere between the two signs to represent the strength of his/her views. For example, students with neutral viewpoints may place themselves in the centre of the room.
- The teacher will then call on different members of the class to explain why they have placed themselves in a particular place.
- Throughout the exercise, students may move if their viewpoints change.
- As a follow-up exercise, students may have a class discussion about literature and films that oppose war and conflict.

Links

No Trumpets Needed shows how moral courage and creativity can survive even the horrors of war and political violence. This story can be linked to other texts in this book and elsewhere:

In this book: Malala Yousafzai's speech, *One Pen Can Change the World* (page 201)
Elsewhere: Michael Morpurgo's novels, *War Horse* and *Private Peaceful*

Superman and Paula Brown's New Snowsuit

Sylvia Plath

Sylvia Plath (1932 - 1963) was an American writer. She struggled with depression for much of her life and was treated using Electroconvulsive Therapy. Sadly, she took her own life at the young age of 30. Her marriage to the poet Ted Hughes has received a lot of attention, often negative.

Although she died at a young age, Plath's literary legacy is hugely important and influential. The story below presents the dark moment when its narrator leaves the innocence of childhood behind her, and comes to learn uncomfortable truths about the world.

The year the war began I was in the fifth grade at the Annie F. Warren Grammar School in Winthrop, and that was the winter I won the prize for drawing the best Civil Defense signs. That was also the winter of Paula Brown's new snowsuit, and even now, thirteen years later, I can recall the changing colors of those days, clear and definite patterns seen through a kaleidoscope.

I lived on the bay side of town, on Johnson Avenue, opposite the Logan Airport, and before I went to bed each night, I used to kneel by the west window of my room and look over to the lights of Boston that blazed and blinked far off across the darkening water. The sunset flaunted its pink flag above the airport, and the sound of waves was lost in the perpetual droning of the planes. I marveled at the moving beacons on the runway and watched, until it grew completely dark, the flashing red and green lights that rose and set in the sky like shooting stars. The airport was my Mecca, my Jerusalem. All night I dreamed of flying.

Those were the days of my technicolor dreams. Mother believed that I should have an enormous amount of sleep, and so I was never really tired when I went to bed. This was the best time of the day, when I could lie in the vague twilight, drifting off to sleep, making up dreams inside my head the way they should go. My flying dreams were believable as a landscape by Dalí, so real that I would awake with a sudden shock, a breathless sense of having tumbled like Icarus from the sky and caught myself on the soft bed just in time.

These nightly adventures in space began when Superman started invading my dreams and teaching me how to fly. He used to come roaring by in his shining blue suit with his cape whistling in the wind, looking remarkably like my Uncle Frank, who was living with Mother and me. In the magic whirring of his cape I could hear the wings of a hundred seagulls, the motors of a thousand planes.

I was not the only worshiper of Superman in our block. David Sterling, a pale, bookish boy who lived down the street, shared my love for the sheer poetry of flight. Before supper every night, we listened to Superman together on the radio, and during the day we made up our own adventures on the way to school.

The Annie F. Warren Grammar School was a red brick building, set back from the main highway on a black tar street, surrounded by barren gravel playgrounds. Out by the parking lot David and I found a perfect alcove for our Superman dramas. The dingy back entrance to the school was deep set in a long passageway which was an excellent place for surprise captures and sudden rescues.

During recess, David and I came into our own. We ignored the boys playing baseball on the gravel court and the girls giggling at dodge-ball in the dell. Our Superman games made us outlaws, yet gave us a sense of windy superiority. We even found a stand-in for a villain in Sheldon Fein, the sallow mamma's boy on our block who was left out of the boys' games because he cried whenever anybody tagged him and always managed to fall down and skin his fat knees.

At this time my Uncle Frank was living with us while waiting to be drafted, and I was sure that he bore an extraordinary resemblance to Superman incognito. David couldn't see his likeness as clearly as I did, but he admitted that Uncle Frank was the strongest man he had ever known, and could do lots of tricks like making caramels disappear under napkins and walking on his hands.

That same winter, war was declared, and I remember sitting by the radio with Mother and Uncle Frank and feeling a queer foreboding in the air. Their voices were low and serious, and their talk was of planes and German bombs. Uncle Frank said something about Germans in America being put in prison for the duration, and Mother kept saying over and over again about Daddy: 'I'm only glad Otto didn't live to see this; I'm only glad Otto didn't live to see it come to this.'

In school we began to draw Civil Defense signs, and that was when I beat Jimmy Lane in our block for the fifth-grade prize. Every now and then we would practice an air raid. The fire bell would ring and we would take up our coats and pencils and file down the creaking stairs to the basement, where we sat in special corners according to our color tags, and put the pencils between our teeth so the bombs wouldn't make us bite our tongues by mistake. Some of the little children in the lower grades would cry because it was dark in the cellar, with only the bare ceiling lights on the cold black stone.

The threat of war was seeping in everywhere. At recess, Sheldon became a Nazi and borrowed a goose step from the movies, but his Uncle Macy was really over in Germany, and Mrs. Fein began to grow thin and pale because she heard that Macy was a prisoner and then nothing more.

The winter dragged on, with a wet east wind coming always from the ocean, and the snow melting before there was enough for coasting. One Friday afternoon, just before Christmas, Paula Brown gave her annual birthday party, and I was invited because it was for all the children on our block. Paula lived across from Jimmy Lane on Somerset Terrace, and nobody on our block really liked her, because she was bossy and stuck up, with pale skin and long red pigtails and watery blue eyes.

She met us at the door of her house in a white organdy dress, her red hair tied up in sausage curls with a satin bow. Before we could sit down at the table for birthday cake and ice cream, she had to show us all her presents. There were a great many because it was both her birthday and Christmas time too.

Paula's favorite present was a new snowsuit, and she tried it on for us. The snowsuit was powder blue and came in a silver box from Sweden, she said. The front of the jacket was all embroidered with pink and white roses and bluebirds, and the leggings had embroidered straps. She even had a little white angora beret and angora mittens to go with it.

After dessert we were all driven to the movies by Jimmy Lane's father to see the late afternoon show as a special treat. Mother had found out that the main feature was Snow White before she would let me go, but she hadn't realized that there was a war picture playing with it.

After I went to bed that night, as soon as I closed my eyes, the prison camp sprang to life in my mind. No matter how hard I thought of Superman before I went to sleep, no crusading blue figure came roaring down in heavenly anger to smash the yellow men who invaded my dreams. When I woke up in the morning, my sheets were damp with sweat.

Saturday was bitterly cold, and the skies were gray and blurred with the threat of snow. I was dallying home from the store that afternoon, curling up my chilled fingers in my mittens, when I saw a couple of kids playing Chinese tag out in front of Paula Brown's house. Paula stopped in the middle of the game to eye me coldly. 'We need someone else,' she said. 'Want to play?' She tagged me on the ankle then, and I hopped around and finally caught Sheldon Fein as he was bending down to fasten one of his furlined overshoes. An early thaw had melted away the snow in the street, and the tarred pavement was gritted with sand left from the snow trucks. In front of Paula's house somebody's car had left a glittering black stain of oil slick.

We went running about in the street, retreating to the hard, brown lawns when the one who was 'It' came too close. Jimmy Lane came out of his house and stood watching us for a short while, and then joined in. Every time he was 'It,' he chased Paula in her powder blue snowsuit, and she screamed shrilly and looked around at him with her wide, watery eyes, and he always managed to catch her.

Only one time she forgot to look where she was going, and as Jimmy reached out to tag her, she slid into the oil slick. We all froze when she went down on her side as if we were playing statues. No one said a word, and for a minute there was only the sound of the plane across the bay. The dull, green light of later afternoon came closing down on us, cold and final as a window blind.

Paula's snowsuit was smeared wet and black with oil along the side. Her angora mittens were dripping like black cat's fur. Slowly, she sat up and looked at us standing around her, as if searching for something. Then, suddenly, her eyes fixed on me.

'You,' she said deliberately, pointing at me, 'you pushed me.'

There was another second of silence, and then Jimmy Lane turned on me. 'You did it,' he taunted. 'You did it.'

Sheldon and Paula and Jimmy and the rest of them faced me with a strange joy flickering in the back of their eyes. 'You did it, you pushed her,' they said.

And even when I shouted 'I did not!' they were all moving in on me, chanting in a chorus, 'Yes, you did, yes, you did, we saw you.' In the well of faces moving toward me I saw no help, and I began to wonder if Jimmy had pushed Paula, or if she had fallen by herself, and I was not sure. I wasn't sure at all. I started walking past them, walking home, determined not to run, but when I had left them behind me, I felt the sharp thud of a snowball on my left shoulder, and another. I picked up a faster stride and rounded the corner by Kellys'. There was my dark brown shingled house ahead of me, and inside, Mother and Uncle Frank, home on furlough. I began to run in the cold, raw evening toward the bright squares of light in the windows that were home.

Uncle Frank met me at the door. 'How's my favourite trooper?' he asked, and he swung me so high in the air that my head grazed the ceiling. There was a big love in his voice that drowned out the shouting which still echoed in my ears.

'I'm fine,' I lied, and he taught me some jujitsu in the living room until Mother called us for supper. Candles were set on the white linen tablecloth, and miniature flames flickered in the silver and the glasses. I could see another room reflected beyond the dark dining-room window where the people laughed and talked in a secure web of light, held together by its indestructible brilliance.

All at once the doorbell rang, and Mother rose to answer it. I could hear David Sterling's high, clear voice in the hall. There was a cold draft from the open doorway, but he and Mother kept on talking, and he did not come in. When Mother came back to the table, her face was sad. 'Why didn't you tell me?' she said. 'Why didn't you tell me that you pushed Paula in the mud and spoiled her new snowsuit?'

A mouthful of chocolate pudding blocked my throat, thick and bitter. I had to wash it down with milk. Finally, I said, 'I didn't do it.' But the words came out like hard, dry little seeds, hollow and insincere. I tried again. 'I didn't do it. Jimmy Lane did it.'

'Of course we'll believe you,' Mother said slowly, 'but the whole neighborhood is talking about it. Mrs. Sterling heard the story from Mrs. Fein and sent David over to say we should buy Paula a new snowsuit. I can't understand it.'

'I didn't do it,' I repeated, and the blood beat in my ears like a slack drum. I pushed my chair away from the table, not looking at Uncle Frank or Mother sitting there, solemn and sorrowful in the candlelight. The staircase to the second floor was dark, but I went down the long hall to my room without turning on the light switch and shut the door. A small unripe moon was shafting squares of greenish light along the floor and the windowpanes were fringed with frost.

I threw myself fiercely down on my bed and lay there, dry-eyed and burning. After a while I heard Uncle Frank coming up the stairs and knocking on my door. When I didn't answer, he walked in and sat down on my bed. I could see his strong shoulders bulk against the moonlight, but in the shadows his face was featureless.

'Tell me, honey,' he said very softly, 'tell me. You don't have to be afraid. We'll understand. Only tell me what really happened. You have never had to hide anything from me, you know that. Only tell me how it really happened.'

'I told you,' I said. 'I told you what happened, and I can't make it any different. Not even for you I can't make it any different.' He sighed then and got up to go away. 'Okay, honey,' he said at the door. 'Okay, but we'll pay for another snowsuit anyway just to make everybody happy, and ten years from now no one will ever know the difference.'

The door shut behind him and I could hear his footsteps growing fainter as he walked off down the hall. I lay there alone in bed, feeling the black shadow creeping up the underside of the world like a flood tide. The silver airplanes and the blue capes all dissolved and vanished, wiped away like the crude drawings of a child in colored chalk from the colossal blackboard of the dark. That was the year the war began, and the real world, and the difference.

GLOSSARY

Icarus: a boy from Greek mythology who escaped a labyrinth using wings of wax and feathers. Despite his father's warnings, Icarus flew too close to the sun. His wings melted, and he drowned in the sea.
furlough: leave from military service

Reading for Meaning

1. Do you feel that the narrator's mother and uncle handled the problem of Paula Brown's snowsuit well?
2. Describe the narrator's attitude towards her Uncle Frank. How does she feel about him at the start of the story, and how do you think this changes?
3. Do you think it is significant that the story is set against the backdrop of World War II?
4. Do you agree that *Superman and Paula Brown's New Snowsuit* is a story full of tension and hidden conflict?
5. Re-read the final two paragraphs again.
   (a) What point do you think the narrator is making when she says: 'The silver airplanes and the blue capes all dissolved and vanished, wiped away like the crude drawings of a child in coloured chalk from the colossal blackboard of the dark'?
   (b) In the final sentence, what does the narrator mean by 'the difference'?

Language Lab

1. (a) The narrator refers to colour and light a number of times in this story. Find five examples of this.
   (b) How do the references to colour and light change in the second half of the story?
   (c) Why do you think Sylvia Plath chose to refer to colour and light in this way?
2. Re-read the moment when the narrator tries to explain that she is innocent to her mother and uncle. How does Sylvia Plath use descriptive language to express the narrator's frustration?

Writer's Workshop

Dialogue: The narrator refers to the conversation between her mother and Mr Sterling at the front door. Write the dialogue of this conversation as you imagine it.

Diary: Imagine you are Paula Brown. Write a diary entry for the day your snowsuit was ruined. Try to give an honest account of what really happened and how you felt about it.

Comparative Analysis: Read Doris Lessing's story, *Flight* (pages 124–127). Lessing's and Plath's stories both deal with female characters who are growing up. Write a comparative analysis of the two stories. Discuss:

- how the female characters are moving beyond the innocence of childhood
- how these characters interact with adults in their lives
- the conclusions reached by the two stories. Are they similar or different?

Style Guide

First-Person Narrative: A first-person narrative is a story told from the perspective of one of the characters. This encourages the reader to feel very close to the narrator and to consider the character's point of view. In this story, Sylvia Plath writes in the first-person: 'The year the war began I was in the fifth grade'; 'I lay there alone in bed, feeling the black shadow creeping up the underside of the world'; 'I lied.'

In a first-person narrative, the reader will often empathise with the character, feeling sorry for him/her if something bad happens and celebrating if the character overcomes an obstacle. In Plath's story, the reader feels concern for the narrator when Paula Brown accuses her of ruining the snowsuit, and just like the narrator, the reader feels frustrated when the mother and uncle decide to buy Paula a new one.

Links

This short story explores the difficult transition from childhood, when individuals come to understand some of the darker realities of life. This story can be linked to other texts in this book and elsewhere:

In this book: Doris Lessing's story, *Flight* (page 124); Julia Copus's poem, *The Back Seat of My Mother's Car* (page 162)

Elsewhere: Search online for Seán Ó Faoláin's short story, *The Trout*; Gabriele Salvatores's film, *I'm Not Scared*

Flight

Doris Lessing

Doris Lessing (1919–2013) was a British-Zimbabwean writer and winner of the Nobel Prize for Literature.

In the short story below, Lessing explores the ideas of growing up and letting go. The final sentences offer the reader a unique insight into the characters' world and into human relationships in general.

Above the old man's head was the dovecote, a tall wire-netted shelf on stilts, full of strutting, <u>preening</u> birds. The sunlight broke on their grey breasts into small rainbows. His ears were <u>lulled</u> by their crooning, his hands stretched up towards the favourite, a homing pigeon, a young plump-bodied bird which stood still when it saw him and cocked a <u>shrewd</u> bright eye.

'Pretty, pretty, pretty,' he said, as he grasped the bird and drew it down, feeling the cold coral claws tighten around his finger. Content, he rested the bird lightly on his chest, and leaned against a tree, gazing out beyond the dovecote into the landscape of a late afternoon. In folds and hollows of sunlight and shade, the dark red soil, which was broken into great dusty clods, stretched wide to a tall horizon. Trees marked the course of the valley; a stream of rich green grass the road.

His eyes travelled homewards along this road until he saw his granddaughter swinging on the gate underneath a frangipani tree. Her hair fell down her back in a wave of sunlight, and her long bare legs repeated the angles of the frangipani stems, bare, shining-brown stems among patterns of pale blossoms.

She was gazing past the pink flowers, past the railway cottage where they lived, along the road to the village.

His mood shifted. He deliberately held out his wrist for the bird to take flight, and caught it again at the moment it spread its wings. He felt the plump shape <u>strive</u> and strain under his fingers; and, in a sudden access of troubled spite, shut the bird into a small box and fastened the bolt. 'Now you stay there,' he muttered; and turned his back on the shelf of birds. He moved warily along the hedge, stalking his granddaughter, who was now looped over the gate, her head loose on her arms, singing. The light happy sound mingled with the crooning of the birds, and his anger mounted.

'Hey!' he shouted; saw her jump, look back, and abandon the gate. Her eyes veiled themselves, and she said in a <u>pert</u> neutral voice: 'Hullo, Grandad.' Politely she moved towards him, after a lingering backward glance at the road.

'Waiting for Steven, hey?' he said, his fingers curling like claws into his palm.

'Any objection?' she asked lightly, refusing to look at him.

He confronted her, his eyes narrowed, shoulders hunched, tight in a hard knot of pain which included the preening birds, the sunlight, the flowers. He said: 'Think you're old enough to go courting, hey?'

The girl tossed her head at the old-fashioned phrase and sulked, 'Oh, Grandad!'

'Think you want to leave home, hey? Think you can go running around the fields at night?'

Her smile made him see her, as he had every evening of this warm end-of-summer month, swinging hand in hand along the road to the village with that red-handed, redthroated, violent-bodied youth, the son of the postmaster. Misery went to his head and he shouted angrily: 'I'll tell your mother!'

'Tell away!' she said, laughing, and went back to the gate.

He heard her singing, for him to hear:

I've got you under my skin,

I've got you deep in the heart of . . .'

'Rubbish,' he shouted. 'Rubbish. <u>Impudent</u> little bit of rubbish!'

Growling under his breath he turned towards the dovecote, which was his refuge from the house he shared with his daughter and her husband and their children. But now the house would be empty. Gone all the young girls with their laughter and their squabbling and their teasing. He would be left, uncherished and alone, with that square-fronted, calm-eyed woman, his daughter.

He stopped, muttering, before the dovecote, resenting the absorbed cooing birds.

From the gate the girl shouted: 'Go and tell! Go on, what are you waiting for?'

Obstinately he made his way to the house, with quick, pathetic persistent glances of appeal back at her. But she never looked around. Her defiant but anxious young body stung him into love and repentance. He stopped, 'But I never meant . . .' he muttered, waiting for her to turn and run to him. 'I didn't mean . . .'

She did not turn. She had forgotten him. Along the road came the young man Steven, with something in his hand. A present for her? The old man stiffened as he watched the gate swing back, and the couple embrace. In the brittle shadows of the frangipani tree his granddaughter, his darling, lay in the arms of the postmaster's son, and her hair flowed back over his shoulder.

'I see you!' shouted the old man spitefully. They did not move. He stumped into the little whitewashed house, hearing the wooden veranda creak angrily under his feet. His daughter was sewing in the front room, threading a needle held to the light.

He stopped again, looking back into the garden. The couple were now <u>sauntering</u> among the bushes, laughing. As he watched he saw the girl escape from the youth with a sudden mischievous movement, and run off through the flowers with him in pursuit. He heard shouts, laughter, a scream, silence.

'But it's not like that at all,' he muttered miserably. 'It's not like that. Why can't you see? Running and giggling, and kissing and kissing. You'll come to something quite different.'

He looked at his daughter with <u>sardonic</u> hatred, hating himself. They were caught and finished, both of them, but the girl was still running free.

'Can't you *see*?' he demanded of his invisible granddaughter, who was at that moment lying in the thick green grass with the postmaster's son.

His daughter looked at him and her eyebrows went up in tired <u>forbearance</u>.

'Put your birds to bed?' she asked, humouring him.

'Lucy,' he said urgently, 'Lucy . . .'

'Well, what is it now?'

'She's in the garden with Steven.'

'Now you just sit down and have your tea.'

He stumped his feet alternately, thump, thump, on the hollow wooden floor and shouted: 'She'll marry him. I'm telling you, she'll be marrying him next!'

His daughter rose swiftly, brought him a cup, set him a plate.

'I don't want any tea. I don't want it, I tell you.'

'Now, now,' she crooned. 'What's wrong with it? Why not?'

'She's eighteen. Eighteen!'

'I was married at seventeen and I never regretted it.'

'Liar,' he said. 'Liar. Then you should regret it. Why do you make your girls marry? It's you who do it. What do you do it for? Why?'

'The other three have done fine. They've three fine husbands. Why not Alice?'

'She's the last,' he mourned. 'Can't we keep her a bit longer?'

'Come, now, Dad. She'll be down the road, that's all. She'll be here every day to see you.'

'But it's not the same.' He thought of the other three girls, transformed inside a few months from charming <u>petulant</u> spoiled children into serious young matrons.

'You never did like it when we married,' she said. 'Why not? Every time, it's the same. When I got married you made me feel like it was something wrong. And my girls the same. You get them all crying and miserable the way you go on. Leave Alice alone. She's happy.' She sighed, letting her eyes linger on the sunlit garden. 'She'll marry next month. There's no reason to wait.'

'You've said they can marry?' he said <u>incredulously</u>.

'Yes, Dad, why not?' she said coldly, and took up her sewing.

His eyes stung, and he went out on to the veranda. Wet spread down over his chin and he took out a handkerchief and mopped his whole face. The garden was empty.

From around the corner came the young couple; but their faces were no longer set against him. On the wrist of the postmaster's son balanced a young pigeon, the light gleaming on its breast.

'For me?' said the old man, letting the drops shake off his chin. 'For me?'

'Do you like it?' The girl grabbed his hand and swung on it. 'It's for you, Grandad. Steven brought it for you.' They hung about him, affectionate, concerned, trying to charm away his wet eyes and his misery. They took his arms and directed him to the shelf of birds, one on each side, enclosing him, petting him, saying wordlessly that nothing would be changed, nothing could change, and that they would be with him always. The bird was proof of it, they said, from their lying happy eyes, as they thrust it on him. 'There, Grandad, it's yours. It's for you.'

They watched him as he held it on his wrist, stroking its soft, sun-warmed back, watching the wings lift and balance.

'You must shut it up for a bit', said the girl intimately. 'Until it knows this is its home.'

'Teach your grandmother to suck eggs,' growled the old man.

Released by his half-deliberate anger, they fell back, laughing at him. 'We're glad you like it.' They moved off, now serious and full of purpose, to the gate, where they hung, backs to him, talking quietly. More than anything could, their grown-up seriousness shut him out, making him alone; also, it quietened him, took the sting out of their tumbling like puppies on the grass. They had forgotten him again. Well, so they should, the old man reassured himself, feeling his throat clotted with tears, his lips trembling. He held the new bird to his face, for the caress of its silken feathers. Then he shut it in a box and took out his favourite.

'*Now* you can go, he said aloud. He held it poised, ready for flight, while he looked down the garden towards the boy and the girl. Then, clenched in the pain of loss, he lifted the bird on his wrist, and watched it soar. A whirr and a spatter of wings, and a cloud of birds rose into the evening from the dovecote.

At the gate Alice and Steven forgot their talk and watched the birds.

On the veranda, that woman, his daughter, stood gazing, her eyes shaded with a hand that still held her sewing.

It seemed to the old man that the whole afternoon had stilled to watch his gesture of self-command, that even the leaves of the trees had stopped shaking.

Dry-eyed and calm, he let his hands fall to his sides and stood erect, staring up into the sky.

The cloud of shining silver birds flew up and up, with a shrill cleaving of wings, over the dark ploughed land and the darker belts of trees and the bright folds of grass, until they floated high in the sunlight, like a cloud of <u>motes</u> of dust.

They wheeled in a wide circle, tilting their wings so there was flash after flash of light, and one after another they dropped from the sunshine of the upper sky to shadow, one after another, returning to the shadowed earth over trees and grass and field, returning to the valley and the shelter of night.

The garden was all a fluster and a flurry of returning birds. Then silence, and the sky was empty.

The old man turned, slowly, taking his time; he lifted his eyes to smile proudly down the garden at his granddaughter. She was staring at him. She did not smile. She was wide-eyed, and pale in the cold shadow, and he saw the tears run shivering off her face.

GLOSSARY
dovecote: a pigeon house
frangipani: a type of tree
courting: dating
veranda: porch
teaching grandmother to suck eggs: a common expression meaning 'tell me something I don't already know'
matrons: married women

Speaking and Listening

Hotseat
- As a class, elect one person in the class to play the part of the old man. This person should sit in the hotseat and answer questions as if he/she is this character.
- The actor in the hotseat should base his/her performance on what he/she has learnt about the old man from the story.
- You may wish to ask the old man about his attitude to young people, his views on marriage and about his relationships with his family.

Style Guide

Conflict: For a story to engage the reader, the character must conflict with either:
- another character
- the world
- him/herself (inner conflict)

It is this conflict that creates the story as it establishes the problems and obstacles that the character must try to deal with.

In Doris Lessing's *Flight*, we see conflict between the old man and his granddaughter, Alice. We also see him at odds with his own daughter. The tension between these characters makes for a fascinating situation.

Reading for Meaning

1. Why is the old man upset with his granddaughter and daughter?
2. (a) Kurt Vonnegut's third rule for creative writing is, 'Every character should want something, even if it is only a glass of water' (see page 105). In *Flight*, what do each of the following characters want?
   (i) Alice
   (ii) Steven
   (iii) The old man
   (b) Explain how conflict is created by the fact that different characters want different things.
3. Do you feel sorry for the grandfather in the story? Why / why not?
4. What do you understand by the story's final sentences?
   'She [Alice] was staring at him. She did not smile. She was wide-eyed, and pale in the cold shadow, and he saw the tears run shivering off her face.'
5. (a) Explain why Doris Lessing called this story *Flight*.
   (b) Suggest another title for this story. Explain why you have chosen this alternative title.

Language Lab

Symbolism: A symbol is an image that stands for or represents an idea. In *Flight*, the image of the homing pigeon is used to represent the granddaughter, Alice. It helps the reader to understand how the grandfather feels about Alice.

1. When the old man first sees Alice he is holding his favourite pigeon.
   The reader is told:
   'His mood shifted. He deliberately held out his wrist for the bird to take flight, and caught it again at the moment it spread its wings. He felt the plump shape strive and strain under his fingers, and, in a sudden access of troubled spite, shut the bird into a small box and fastened the bolt, "Now you stay there," he muttered.'
   Basing your answer on this extract, in what ways does the old man treat his granddaughter in a similar way to his favourite pigeon?

2. Later in the story the old man decides to release his favourite homing pigeon. Does this signal a change in his attitude to his granddaughter? Explain your answer.

3. Doris Lessing uses many interesting words to bring this story to life. The words (1–12) below are underlined in the extract. Write down the words and match them with the correct meaning (a–l). Use a dictionary if you need to.

1.	preening	(a)	patience
2.	lulled	(b)	disrespectful / rude
3.	shrewd	(c)	arranging and cleaning feathers
4.	strive	(d)	sneering / cynical
5.	pert	(e)	specks / small particles
6.	impudent	(f)	soothed / quieted
7.	sauntering	(g)	with disbelief
8.	sardonic	(h)	lively
9.	forbearance	(i)	piercingly intelligent
10.	petulant	(j)	sulky, bad-tempered
11.	incredulously	(k)	walking leisurely
12.	motes	(l)	try hard

Writer's Workshop

Debate Speech: In *Flight*, the grandfather is very protective of his granddaughter, Alice, and worries deeply about her. Write a debate speech for or against one of the following motions:

- Parents today are too protective of their children

or

- In today's world, parents need to be more vigilant than ever.

Turn to Chapter 6, pages 212–214 to learn how to organise a debate.

Links

This story looks at how romantic interests are a key part of growing up. This story can be linked to other texts in this book and elsewhere:

In this book: Simon Armitage's poem, *I Am Very Bothered When I Think* (page 172)

Elsewhere: John Duignan's film, *Flirting*; Wes Anderson's film, *Moonrise Kingdom*

The Tell-Tale Heart

Edgar Allan Poe

Edgar Allan Poe (1809–1849) was an American writer, most famous for his short stories and poetry. His stories often deal with dark subject matter and horrifying themes. He is often credited with writing the first detective story, *The Murders in the Rue Morgue*.

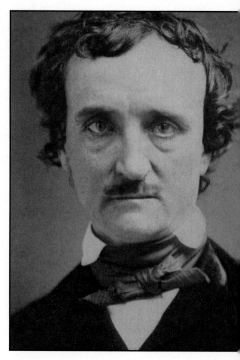

Poe's personal life was difficult. His biological father abandoned him; Poe's mother died from TB when he was three; he fought with and was later disowned by his foster father; his wife died also from TB and Poe suffered with alcoholism and had financial struggles throughout his life. Poe died in mysterious circumstances after being found distressed and injured on the streets of Baltimore.

The Tell-Tale Heart is a classic psychological story. Poe makes great use of an unreliable narrator (see Chapter 1, page 14) to relay the story. The story's tension mounts brilliantly as it powers to its crescendo.

TRUE! – nervous – very, very dreadfully nervous I had been and am; but why will you say that I am mad? The disease had sharpened my senses – not destroyed – not dulled them. Above all was the sense of hearing acute. I heard all things in the heaven and in the earth. I heard many things in hell. How, then, am I mad? Hearken! and observe how healthily – how calmly, I can tell you the whole story.

It is impossible to say how first the idea entered my brain; but, once conceived, it haunted me day and night. Object there was none. Passion there was none. I loved the old man. He had never wronged me. He had never given me insult. For his gold I had no desire. I think it was his eye! yes, it was this! One of his eyes resembled that of a vulture – a pale blue eye with a film over it. Whenever it fell upon me my blood ran cold; and so by degrees – very gradually – I made up my mind to take the life of the old man, and thus rid myself of the eye for ever.

Now this is the point. You fancy me mad. Madmen know nothing. But you should have seen me. You should have seen how wisely I proceeded – with what caution – with what foresight – with what dissimulation I went to work! I was never kinder to the old man than during the whole week before I killed him. And every night, about midnight, I turned the latch of his door and opened it – oh, so gently!

And then, when I had made an opening sufficient for my head, I put in a dark lantern all closed, closed so that no light shone out, and then I thrust in my head. Oh, you would have laughed to see how cunningly I thrust it in! I moved it slowly – very, very slowly, so that I might not disturb the old man's sleep. It took me an hour to place my whole head within the opening so far that I could see him as he lay upon his bed. Ha! – would a madman have been so wise as this? And then when my head was well in the room I undid the lantern cautiously – oh, so cautiously – cautiously (for the hinges creaked), I undid it just so much that a single thin ray fell upon the vulture eye. And this I did for seven long nights – every night just at midnight – but I found the eye always closed, and so it was impossible to do the work, for it was not the old man who vexed me but his Evil Eye. And every morning, when the day broke, I went boldly into the chamber and spoke courageously to him, calling him by name in a hearty tone, and inquiring how he had passed the night. So you see he would have been a very profound old man, indeed, to suspect that every night, just at twelve, I looked in upon him while he slept.

Upon the eighth night I was more than usually cautious in opening the door. A watch's minute hand moves more quickly than did mine. Never before that night had I felt the extent of my own powers – of my sagacity. I could scarcely contain my feelings of triumph. To think that there I was, opening the door little by little, and he not even to dream of my secret deeds or thoughts. I fairly chuckled at the idea; and perhaps he heard me – for he moved on the bed suddenly as if startled. Now you may think that I drew back – but no. His room was as black as pitch with the thick darkness (for the shutters were close fastened through fear of robbers), and so I knew that he could not see the opening of the door, and I kept pushing it on steadily, steadily.

I had my head in, and was about to open the lantern, when my thumb slipped upon the tin fastening, and the old man sprang up in the bed, crying out, 'Who's there?' I kept quite still and said nothing. For a whole hour I did not move a muscle, and in the meantime I did not hear him lie down. He was still sitting up in the bed, listening – just as I have done night after night hearkening to the death watches in the wall.

Presently, I heard a slight groan, and I knew it was the groan of mortal terror. It was not a groan of pain or of grief – oh, no! – it was the low stifled sound that arises from the bottom of the soul when overcharged with awe. I knew the sound well. Many a night, just at midnight, when all the world slept, it has welled up from my own bosom, deepening, with its dreadful echo, the terrors that distracted me.

I say I knew it well. I knew what the old man felt, and pitied him although I chuckled at heart. I knew that he had been lying awake ever since the first slight noise when he had turned in the bed. His fears had been ever since growing upon him. He had been trying to fancy them causeless, but could not. He had been saying to himself, 'It is nothing but the wind in the chimney – it is only a mouse crossing the floor,' or, 'It is merely a cricket which has made a single chirp.' Yes he had been trying to comfort himself with these suppositions; but he had found all in vain. All in vain; because Death, in approaching him, had stalked with his black shadow before him, and enveloped the victim. And it was the mournful influence of the unperceived shadow that caused him to feel – although he neither saw nor heard – to feel the presence of my head within the room.

When I had waited a long time, very patiently, without hearing him lie down, I resolved to open a little – a very, very little crevice in the lantern. So I opened it – you cannot imagine how stealthily, stealthily – until, at length a single dim ray, like the thread of the spider, shot out from the crevice and fell upon the vulture eye.

It was open – wide, wide open – and I grew furious as I gazed upon it. I saw it with perfect distinctness – all a dull blue, with a hideous veil over it that chilled the very marrow in my bones; but I could see nothing else of the old man's face or person, for I had directed the ray, as if by instinct, precisely upon the damned spot.

And now have I not told you that what you mistake for madness is but over-acuteness of the senses? – now, I say, there came to my ears a low, dull, quick sound, such as a watch makes when enveloped in cotton. I knew that sound well too. It was the beating of the old man's heart. It increased my fury, as the beating of a drum stimulates the soldier into courage.

But even yet I refrained and kept still. I scarcely breathed. I held the lantern motionless. I tried how steadily I could maintain the ray upon the eye. Meantime the hellish tattoo of the heart increased. It grew quicker and quicker, and louder and louder, every instant. The old man's terror must have been extreme! It grew louder, I say, louder every moment! – do you mark me well? I have told you that I am nervous: so I am. And now at the dead hour of the night, amid the dreadful silence of that old house, so strange a noise as this excited me to uncontrollable terror. Yet, for some minutes longer, I refrained and stood still. But the beating grew louder, louder! I thought the heart must burst. And now a new anxiety seized me – the sound would be heard by a neighbour! The old man's hour had come! With a loud yell I threw open the lantern and leaped into the room. He shrieked once – once only. In an instant I dragged him to the floor, and pulled the heavy bed over him. I then smiled gaily, to find the deed so far done. But, for many minutes, the heart beat on with a muffled sound. This, however, did not vex me; it would not be heard through the wall. At length it ceased. The old man was dead. I removed the bed and examined the corpse. Yes, he was stone, stone dead. I placed my hand upon the heart and held it there many minutes. There was no pulsation. He was stone dead. His eye would trouble me no more.

If still you think me mad, you will think so no longer when I describe the wise precautions I took for the concealment of the body. The night waned, and I worked hastily, but in silence. First of all I dismembered the corpse. I cut off the head and the arms and the legs.

I then took up three planks from the flooring of the chamber, and deposited all between the scantlings. I then replaced the boards so cleverly, so cunningly, that no human eye – not even his – could have detected anything wrong. There was nothing to wash out – no stain of any kind – no blood-spot whatever. I had been too wary for that. A tub had caught all – ha! ha!

When I had made an end of these labours, it was four o'clock – still dark as midnight. As the bell sounded the hour, there came a knocking at the street door. I went down to open it with a light heart, – for what had I now to fear? There entered three men, who introduced themselves, with perfect suavity, as officers of the police. A shriek had been heard by a neighbour during the night; suspicion of foul play had been aroused; information had been lodged at the police office, and they (the officers) had been deputed to search the premises.

I smiled – for what had I to fear? I bade the gentlemen welcome. The shriek, I said, was my own in a dream. The old man, I mentioned, was absent in the country. I took my visitors all over the house. I bade them search – search well. I led them, at length, to his chamber. I showed them his treasures, secure, undisturbed. In the enthusiasm of my confidence, I brought chairs into the room, and desired them here to rest from their fatigues, while I myself, in the wild audacity of my perfect triumph, placed my own seat upon the very spot beneath which reposed the corpse of the victim. The officers were satisfied. My manner had convinced them. I was singularly at ease. They sat, and while I answered cheerily, they chatted of familiar things. But, ere long, I felt myself getting pale and wished them gone. My head ached, and I fancied a ringing in my ears; but still they sat, and still chatted. The ringing became more distinct – it continued and became more distinct. I talked more freely to get rid of the feeling; but it continued and gained definitiveness – until, at length, I found that the noise was not within my ears.

No doubt I now grew very pale; but I talked more fluently, and with a heightened voice. Yet the sound increased – and what could I do? It was a low, dull, quick sound – much such a sound as a watch makes when enveloped in cotton. I gasped for breath – and yet the officers heard it not. I talked more quickly – more vehemently; but the noise steadily increased. I arose and argued about trifles, in a high key and with violent gesticulations; but the noise steadily increased. Why would they not be gone? I paced the floor to and fro with heavy strides, as if excited to fury by the observations of the men – but the noise steadily increased. O God! what could I do? I foamed – I raved – I swore! I swung the chair upon which I had been sitting, and grated it upon the boards, but the noise arose over all and continually increased.

It grew louder – louder – louder! And still the men chatted pleasantly, and smiled. Was it possible they heard not? Almighty God! – no, no? They heard! – they suspected! – they knew! – they were making a mockery of my horror! – this I thought, and this I think. But anything was better than this agony! Anything was more tolerable than this derision! I could bear those hypocritical smiles no longer! I felt that I must scream or die! – and now – again! hark! louder! louder! louder! louder! –– 'Villains!' I shrieked, 'dissemble no more! I admit the deed! – tear up the planks! – here, here! – it is the beating of his hideous heart!'

GLOSSARY

stealthily: cautiously
crevice: narrow opening
suavity: charm
deputed: appointed

audacity: nerve, defiance
derision: mockery
dissemble: pretend

Speaking and Listening

Audio Reading: *The Tell-Tale Heart* is a story that benefits from being read aloud. Listen to the actor Christopher Lee read this story (15 minutes) with his characteristic deep voice.

This reading is available with subtitles by going to www.mentorbooks.ie/resources and looking in the TY English section. Alternatively, you may find this film on YouTube.

As a class, discuss this reading of the story:

- Is Christopher Lee successful in bringing this story to life?
- Do the additions of a soundtrack and sound effects add to your enjoyment of the story?
- If you were to choose five images to accompany this reading, what would they be?

Reading for Meaning

1. Summarise the actions of the narrator in this story.
2. (a) Towards the end of the story the narrator complains of a loud noise. Where does he believe the noise is coming from?
   (b) What do you think is the source of the noise?

3. Go back to Chapter 1, page 14 and read the Style Guide about 'The Unreliable Narrator'. In what ways can we consider the narrator of *The Tell-Tale Heart* to be an unreliable narrator?
4. How does Edgar Allan Poe create tension in this story?
5. Why do you think Edgar Allan Poe called this story *The Tell-Tale Heart* ?
6. '*The Tell-Tale Heart* is a psychologically rich tale that offers us dark insight into murder and madness.' Discuss this statement offering examples from the story.

Language Lab

1. (a) Poe uses repetition throughout this story. Find three examples of repetition.
   (b) What effect does the use of repetition have on the reader?
2. This story was originally published in 1843, and therefore contains a number of interesting words. Using a dictionary, write the following words (1–10) and match them with their definitions (a–j).

1. Dissimulation	(a) Covered / wrapped in
2. Vexed	(b) Foresight / wisdom
3. Profound	(c) Animated gestures
4. Sagacity	(d) Having deep insight or intelligence
5. Suppositions	(e) Bothered / annoyed / irritated
6. Enveloped	(f) Concealment / disguise
7. Waned	(g) Passionately / acted with great insistence or enthusiasm
8. Reposed	(h) Decreased in power or intensity
9. Vehemently	(i) Something that is supposed or presumed
10. Gesticulations	(j) Lying in death / at rest

Writer's Workshop

Report: Imagine you are one of the police officers in the story. Write the police report you would submit about the case.

Short Story: *The Tell-Tale Heart* explores the darker side of humanity. Write your own dark tale using the following sentence in your story: 'Slowly but surely the man rose from the shadowed corner where he lay.'

Biographical Research: Using the internet, research Edgar Allan Poe's life. Write a short biography. You might find it interesting to learn about the strange circumstances surrounding his death.

Links

Poe's classic story has murder at its centre; in particular, it examines the mindset of a murderer. This story can be linked to other texts in this book and elsewhere:

In this book: Shakespeare's 'Tomorrow, and Tomorrow, and Tomorrow' (from *Macbeth*) (page 226)

Elsewhere: Alfred Hitchcock's film, *Shadow of a Doubt*; search online for Ray Bradbury's short story, *The Fruit at the Bottom of the Bowl*

Eveline

James Joyce

James Joyce (1882–1941) is one of Ireland's most celebrated writers. His novel *Ulysses* is often considered one of the most influential books of the twentieth century.

When first published, Joyce's work was seen as controversial. *Ulysses* was banned in the United States and the UK, and the Irish government used customs law to prevent it being brought into Ireland.

However, his reputation as a great author has outlived this controversy and James Joyce is regarded as a major literary figure.

The story below, *Eveline,* presents a torn character who wrestles with a life-changing decision.

She sat at the window watching the evening invade the avenue. Her head was leaned against the window curtains and in her nostrils was the odour of dusty cretonne. She was tired.

Few people passed. The man out of the last house passed on his way home; she heard his footsteps clacking along the concrete pavement and afterwards crunching on the cinder path before the new red houses. One time there used to be a field there in which they used to play every evening with other people's children. Then a man from Belfast bought the field and built houses in it – not like their little brown houses but bright brick houses with shining roofs. The children of the avenue used to play together in that field – the Devines, the Waters, the Dunns, little Keogh the cripple, she and her brothers and sisters. Ernest, however, never played: he was too grown up. Her father used often to hunt them in out of the field with his blackthorn stick; but usually little Keogh used to keep *nix* and call out when he saw her father coming. Still they seemed to have been rather happy then. Her father was not so bad then; and besides, her mother was alive. That was a long time ago; she and her brothers and sisters were all grown up; her mother was dead. Tizzie Dunn was dead, too, and the Waters had gone back to England. Everything changes. Now she was going to go away like the others, to leave her home.

Home! She looked round the room, reviewing all its familiar objects which she had dusted once a week for so many years, wondering where on earth all the dust came from. Perhaps she would never see again those familiar objects from which she had never dreamed of being divided. And yet during all those years she had never found out the name of the priest whose yellowing photograph hung on the wall above the broken harmonium beside the coloured print of the promises made to Blessed Margaret Mary Alacoque. He had been a school friend of her father. Whenever he showed the photograph to a visitor her father used to pass it with a casual word:

'He is in Melbourne now.'

She had consented to go away, to leave her home. Was that wise? She tried to weigh each side of the question. In her home anyway she had shelter and food; she had those whom she had known all her life about her. Of course she had to work hard, both in the house and at business. What would they say of her in the Stores when they found out that she had run away with a fellow? Say she was a fool, perhaps; and her place would be filled up by advertisement. Miss Gavan would be glad. She had always had an edge on her, especially whenever there were people listening.

'Miss Hill, don't you see these ladies are waiting?'

'Look lively, Miss Hill, please.'

She would not cry many tears at leaving the Stores.

But in her new home, in a distant unknown country, it would not be like that. Then she would be married – she, Eveline. People would treat her with respect then. She would not be treated as her mother had been. Even now, though she was over nineteen, she sometimes felt herself in danger of her father's violence. She knew it was that that had given her the palpitations. When they were growing up he had never gone for her like he used to go for Harry and Ernest, because she was a girl; but latterly he had begun to threaten her and say what he would do to her only for her dead mother's sake. And now she had nobody to protect her. Ernest was dead and Harry, who was in the church decorating business, was nearly always down somewhere in the country. Besides, the invariable squabble for money on Saturday nights had begun to weary her unspeakably. She always gave her entire wages – seven shillings – and Harry always sent up what he could but the trouble was to get any money from her father. He said she used to squander the money, that she had no head, that he wasn't going to give her his hard-earned money to throw about the streets, and much more, for he was usually fairly bad on Saturday night. In the end he would give her the money and ask her had she any intention of buying Sunday's dinner. Then she had to rush out as quickly as she could and do her marketing, holding her black leather purse tightly in her hand as she elbowed her way through the crowds and returning home late under her load of provisions. She had hard work to keep the house together and to see that the two young children who had been left to her charge went to school regularly and got their meals regularly. It was hard work – a hard life – but now that she was about to leave it she did not find it a wholly undesirable life.

She was about to explore another life with Frank. Frank was very kind, manly, open-hearted. She was to go away with him by the night-boat to be his wife and to live with him in Buenos Ayres where he had a home waiting for her. How well she remembered the first time she had seen him; he was lodging in a house on the main road where she used to visit. It seemed a few weeks ago. He was standing at the gate, his peaked cap pushed back on his head and his hair tumbled forward over a face of bronze. Then they had come to know each other. He used to meet her outside the Stores every evening and see her home. He took her to see *The Bohemian Girl* and she felt elated as she sat in an unaccustomed part of the theatre with him. He was awfully fond of music and sang a little. People knew that they were courting and, when he sang about the lass that loves a sailor, she always felt pleasantly confused. He used to call her Poppens out of fun. First of all it had been an excitement for her to have a fellow and then she had begun to like him. He had tales of distant countries. He had started as a deck boy at a pound a month on a ship of the Allan Line going out to Canada. He told her the names of the ships he had been on and the names of the different services. He had sailed through the Straits of Magellan and he told her stories of the terrible Patagonians. He had fallen on his feet in Buenos Ayres, he said, and had come over to the old country just for a holiday. Of course, her father had found out the affair and had forbidden her to have anything to say to him.

'I know these sailor chaps,' he said.

One day he had quarrelled with Frank and after that she had to meet her lover secretly.

The evening deepened in the avenue. The white of two letters in her lap grew indistinct. One was to Harry; the other was to her father. Ernest had been her favourite but she liked Harry too. Her father was becoming old lately, she noticed; he would miss her. Sometimes he could be very nice. Not long before, when she had been laid up for a day, he had read her out a ghost story and made toast for her at the fire. Another day, when their mother was alive, they had all gone for a picnic to the Hill of Howth. She remembered her father putting on her mother's bonnet to make the children laugh.

Her time was running out but she continued to sit by the window, leaning her head against the window curtain, inhaling the odour of dusty cretonne. Down far in the avenue she could hear a street organ playing. She knew the air. Strange that it should come that very night to remind her of the promise to her mother, her promise to keep the home together as long as she could. She remembered the last night of her mother's illness; she was again in the close dark room at the other side of the hall and outside she heard a melancholy air of Italy. The organ-player had been ordered to go away and given sixpence. She remembered her father strutting back into the sickroom saying:

'Damned Italians! Coming over here!'

As she mused, the pitiful vision of her mother's life laid its spell on the very quick of her being – that life of commonplace sacrifices closing in final craziness. She trembled as she heard again her mother's voice saying constantly with foolish insistence:

'Derevaun Seraun! Derevaun Seraun!'

She stood up in a sudden impulse of terror. Escape! She must escape! Frank would save her. He would give her life, perhaps love, too. But she wanted to live. Why should she be unhappy? She had a right to happiness. Frank would take her in his arms, fold her in his arms. He would save her.

She stood among the swaying crowd in the station at the North Wall. He held her hand and she knew that he was speaking to her, saying something about the passage over and over again. The station was full of soldiers with brown baggages. Through the wide doors of the sheds she caught a glimpse of the black mass of the boat, lying in beside the quay wall, with illumined portholes. She answered nothing. She felt her cheek pale and cold and, out of a maze of distress, she prayed to God to direct her, to show her what was her duty. The boat blew a long mournful whistle into the mist. If she went, tomorrow she would be on the sea with Frank, steaming towards Buenos Ayres. Their passage had been booked. Could she still draw back after all he had done for her? Her distress awoke a nausea in her body and she kept moving her lips in silent fervent prayer.

A bell clanged upon her heart. She felt him seize her hand:

'Come!'

All the seas of the world tumbled about her heart. He was drawing her into them: he would drown her. She gripped with both hands at the iron railing.

'Come!'

No! No! No! It was impossible. Her hands clutched the iron in frenzy. Amid the seas she sent a cry of anguish.

'Eveline! Evvy!'

He rushed beyond the barrier and called to her to follow. He was shouted at to go on but he still called to her. She set her white face to him, passive, like a helpless animal. Her eyes gave him no sign of love or farewell or recognition.

GLOSSARY

cretonne: heavy material

nix: keep watch

harmonium: type of organ

palpitations: feeling of your heart racing

Derevaun Seraun: Either: 1. a gibberish phrase Joyce invented for the story 2. a phonetic spelling of the Irish for 'The end of pleasure is pain'.

Reading for Meaning

1. 'She had consented to go away, to leave her home. Was that wise? She tried to weigh each side of the question.'
    (a) List all of the reasons Eveline considers for leaving home.
    (b) List all of the reasons Eveline considers for not leaving.
    (c) Why do you think Eveline decides to stay in the end?
2. In the story's closing, Eveline looks coldly at Frank as he boards the ship: 'She set her white face to him, passive…Her eyes gave him no sign of love or farewell or recognition.' Why do you think she behaves this way?
3. In the opening paragraph it says, 'Her head was leaned against the window curtains . . .' Later in the story it says, '. . . she continued to sit by the window, leaning her head against the window curtain . . .'
    In your view, what is the significance of this subtle change from 'was leaned' to 'leaning'?
4. This story is from James Joyce's book *Dubliners*. Many of the characters in the book are described as experiencing 'paralysis' (inability to act). What do you think is the cause of Eveline's paralysis?

Style Guide

Point of View: In this story, James Joyce presents Eveline's point of view. The reader comes to appreciate her thoughts and feelings, and looks at the world through her eyes. You will notice that Joyce does not use the first-person (I sat, I felt) to do this but instead adopts a third-person narrative (She sat, Eveline felt). Although Eveline is not telling the story herself, the narrative offers Eveline's point of view. Look at the following example:

> She had consented to go away, to leave her home. Was that wise? She tried to weigh each side of the question. In her home anyway she had shelter and food; she had those whom she had known all her life about her. Of course she had to work hard, both in the house and at business. What would they say of her in the Stores when they found out that she had run away with a fellow? Say she was a fool, perhaps; and her place would be filled up by advertisement. Miss Gavan would be glad. She had always had an edge on her, especially whenever there were people listening.

'Miss Hill, don't you see these ladies are waiting?'
'Look lively, Miss Hill, please.'
She would not cry many tears at leaving the Stores.

Here we can see how Eveline feels about her job and is conscious of what people may say about her. The third-person narrative is shaped by Eveline's character; you can see this particularly in the use of questions: 'What would they say of her in the Stores when they found out that she had run away with a fellow?'

When you are writing your own stories, whether in the first or third-person, consider whose viewpoint in being offered.

Language Lab

1. Eveline's point of view (see Style Guide) is presented throughout this story. For each of the following, write down a phrase from the story that shows Eveline's point of view. The first is done for you
   (a) Eveline dislikes her job. → 'She would not cry many tears at leaving the Stores.'
   (b) Eveline is unsure if it is a good idea to leave home.
   (c) Eveline feels that she lacks respect in her life.
   (d) Eveline sees Frank as a kind man.
   (e) Eveline feels trapped in her life and feels the need to break free.
2. Why do you think James Joyce does not offer Frank's or Eveline's father's point of view?

Writer's Workshop

Personal Letters:
- Imagine you are Frank. Ten years have passed since you left Eveline on the dock. Write a personal letter to Eveline.
- Now imagine you are Eveline. Write a personal letter responding to Frank. Go to page 83 to learn about personal letters.

Speaking and Listening

Interview: Many families living in Ireland have experienced emigration. This may be because they have left their own country to come to Ireland or through relatives who have gone abroad. Interview a person at home, a relative or family friend about this issue. This person may have emigrated themselves or may know somebody who has. Find out about his/her experience of emigration.
- Write down five questions you will ask.
- Record or note the answers given.
- Write down any follow-up questions you may ask and the interviewee's responses.
- Share any interesting stories with your class.

Links

In James Joyce's *Eveline*, the protagonist is wrestling with a difficult decision. This story can be linked to other texts in this book and elsewhere:
In this book: James Dillard's *A Doctor's Dilemma* (page 62)
Elsewhere: Roland Joffé's film, *The Mission*

The Story of an Hour

Kate Chopin

Kate Chopin (1850–1904) began writing novels, short stories and articles as an outlet for depression.

However, during her life Chopin achieved only moderate success as her work was ahead of its time. Many critics saw it as immoral and scandalous.

Chopin's work increased in popularity after her death. She helped pioneer feminist writing. *The Story of an Hour* shows the bravery of Chopin's writing as she reflects honestly on issues relating to the role of women in nineteenth-century society.

Knowing that Mrs. Mallard was afflicted with a heart trouble, great care was taken to break to her as gently as possible the news of her husband's death.

It was her sister Josephine who told her, in broken sentences; veiled hints that revealed in half concealing. Her husband's friend Richards was there, too, near her. It was he who had been in the newspaper office when intelligence of the railroad disaster was received, with Brently Mallard's name leading the list of 'killed.' He had only taken the time to assure himself of its truth by a second telegram, and had hastened to forestall any less careful, less tender friend in bearing the sad message.

She did not hear the story as many women have heard the same, with a paralyzed inability to accept its significance. She wept at once, with sudden, wild abandonment, in her sister's arms. When the storm of grief had spent itself she went away to her room alone. She would have no one follow her.

There stood, facing the open window, a comfortable, roomy armchair. Into this she sank, pressed down by a physical exhaustion that haunted her body and seemed to reach into her soul.

She could see in the open square before her house the tops of trees that were all aquiver with the new spring life. The delicious breath of rain was in the air. In the street below a peddler was crying his wares. The notes of a distant song which some one was singing reached her faintly, and countless sparrows were twittering in the eaves.

There were patches of blue sky showing here and there through the clouds that had met and piled one above the other in the west facing her window. She sat with her head thrown back upon the cushion of the chair, quite motionless, except when a sob came up into her throat and shook her, as a child who has cried itself to sleep continues to sob in its dreams.

She was young, with a fair, calm face, whose lines bespoke repression and even a certain strength. But now there was a dull stare in her eyes, whose gaze was fixed away off yonder on one of those patches of blue sky. It was not a glance of reflection, but rather indicated a suspension of intelligent thought. There was something coming to her and she was waiting for it, fearfully. What was it? She did not know; it was too subtle and elusive to name. But she felt it, creeping out of the sky, reaching toward her through the sounds, the scents, the color that filled the air.

Now her bosom rose and fell tumultuously. She was beginning to recognize this thing that was approaching to possess her, and she was striving to beat it back with her will – as powerless as her two white slender hands would have been. When she abandoned herself a little whispered word escaped her slightly parted lips. She said it over and over under her breath: 'free, free, free!' The vacant stare and the look of terror that had followed it went from her eyes. They stayed keen and bright. Her pulses beat fast, and the coursing blood warmed and relaxed every inch of her body.

She did not stop to ask if it were or were not a monstrous joy that held her. A clear and exalted perception enabled her to dismiss the suggestion as trivial. She knew that she would weep again when she saw the kind, tender hands folded in death; the face that had never looked save with love upon her, fixed and gray and dead. But she saw beyond that bitter moment a long procession of years to come that would belong to her absolutely. And she opened and spread her arms out to them in welcome.

There would be no one to live for during those coming years; she would live for herself. There would be no powerful will bending hers in that blind persistence with which men and women believe they have a right to impose a private will upon a fellow-creature. A kind intention or a cruel intention made the act seem no less a crime as she looked upon it in that brief moment of illumination. And yet she had loved him – sometimes. Often she had not. What did it matter! What could love, the unsolved mystery, count for in face of this possession of self-assertion which she suddenly recognized as the strongest impulse of her being!

'Free! Body and soul free!' she kept whispering. Josephine was kneeling before the closed door with her lips to the keyhole, imploring for admission. 'Louise, open the door! I beg, open the door – you will make yourself ill. What are you doing, Louise? For heaven's sake open the door.'

'Go away. I am not making myself ill.' No; she was drinking in a very elixir of life through that open window. Her fancy was running riot along those days ahead of her. Spring days, and summer days, and all sorts of days that would be her own. She breathed a quick prayer that life might be long. It was only yesterday she had thought with a shudder that life might be long.

She arose at length and opened the door to her sister's importunities. There was a feverish triumph in her eyes, and she carried herself unwittingly like a goddess of Victory. She clasped her sister's waist, and together they descended the stairs. Richards stood waiting for them at the bottom.

Some one was opening the front door with a latchkey. It was Brently Mallard who entered, a little travel-stained, composedly carrying his grip-sack and umbrella. He had been far from the scene of accident, and did not even know there had been one. He stood amazed at Josephine's piercing cry; at Richards' quick motion to screen him from the view of his wife.

But Richards was too late.

When the doctors came they said she had died of heart disease – of the joy that kills.

GLOSSARY	
afflicted: troubled	**tumultuously:** stormily
intelligence: news	**exalted:** raised, elevated
forestall: prevent, pre-empt	**fancy:** imagination
wares: goods for sale	**importunities:** pleas

1. (a) Describe Mrs. Mallard's initial reaction to the news that her husband has died.
    (b) How do her feelings about the situation change?
2. When Mrs. Mallard realises she is free to live on her own, her emotions are described as a 'monstrous joy'. What do you think is meant by this phrase?
3. (a) In your own words, describe Mrs. Mallard's view from the window.
    (b) Do you think the details of the view described by the narrator reflect Mrs. Mallard's thoughts?
4. What kind of relationship do you think Mrs. Mallard has with her husband?
5. Which one of the following statements do you feel is the best description of what *The Story of an Hour* is about? Explain your choice.
    - 'This story shows us that in life there can be a tension between how we should feel and what we do feel.'
    - '*The Story of an Hour* bravely gives voice to ideas and thoughts that can often be hidden or suppressed.'
    - 'This story shows that Kate Chopin is a feminist writer who expresses the unspoken reality of what it was to be a woman in her time.'

Writer's Workshop

Diary: Imagine Mrs. Mallard wrote in her diary when she locked herself in her room. Write the diary entry she would have composed. Consider her thoughts on her marriage, her future possibilities and how she balances her feelings of loss and her new possibilities.

Style Guide

Characterisation: An interesting character is a vital part of any good story. *The Story of an Hour* revolves around the thoughts and feelings of its central character, the intriguing Mrs. Mallard. A reader comes to know a character through his/her:

- **Physical Appearance:** an author may signpost a character's personality by how they look. For example, many villains are given a sinister appearance so that the reader distrusts them. In *The Story of an Hour*, Mrs. Mallard is shown to be young and pretty. This encourages sympathy from the reader.
- **Behaviour:** what a character says or does clearly establishes the kind of individual he/she is. How a character speaks can also be revealing. A character may show the capacity to change or develop; this gives a character greater depth. Mrs. Mallard's shock at the news of her husband's death shows that she is genuinely upset. When she locks herself in her room, the reader learns that she is a private person who wishes to face the situation independently.

- **Thoughts:** the author may give the reader insight into what a character is thinking. A character's motivation or ambition is an important part of who he/she is. What is most intriguing about Mrs. Mallard is how she grows to see her husband's death as an opportunity and guiltily welcomes the change in her life.
- **Treatment at the hands of other characters:** how other personalities in the story behave around a character reveals much to the reader. The concern afforded Mrs. Mallard by the other characters shows that she is much loved by her friends and relatives.

Links

Controversial for its time, *The Story of an Hour* is an important feminist text which looks at society's expectations of women. This story can be linked to other texts in this book and elsewhere:

In this book: Malala Yousafzai's speech, *One Pen Can Change the World* (page 201); James Joyce's story, *Eveline* (page 135)

Elsewhere: Niki Caro's film *Whale Rider*; Henrik Ibsen's, *A Doll's House*; Search online for Sojourner Truth's speech, *Ain't I a Woman?*

Korea

John McGahern

John McGahern (1934–2006) is one of Ireland's most celebrated writers. His early life was difficult. His mother died when the writer was only nine. He and his siblings were raised by their brutish father, a Garda Sergeant. However, McGahern's academic talent and love of literature allowed him to transcend his upbringing. He became a school teacher (like his mother) and started to write.

However, McGahern's writing was controversial and his second novel *The Dark* was banned for some time due to its sexual content. McGahern was subsequently forced out of his job.

Despite this, praise for McGahern's novels and his masterful short stories increased.

The following story, *Korea*, illustrates the power of McGahern's writing in its dark vision of family life.

'You saw an execution then too, didn't you?' I asked my father, and he started to tell as he rowed. He'd been captured in an ambush in late 1919, and they were shooting prisoners in Mountjoy as reprisals at that time. He thought it was he who'd be next, for after a few days they moved him to the cell next to the prison yard. He could see out through the bars. No rap to prepare himself came to the door that night, and at daybreak he saw the two prisoners they'd decided to shoot being marched out: a man in his early thirties, and what was little more than a boy, sixteen or seventeen, and he was weeping. They blindfolded the boy, but the man refused the blindfold. When the officer shouted, the boy clicked to attention, but the man stayed as he was, chewing very slowly. He had his hands in his pockets.

'Take your hands out of your pockets,' the officer shouted again, irritation in the voice.

The man slowly shook his head.

'It's a bit too late now in the day for that,' he said.

The officer then ordered them to fire, and as the volley rang, the boy tore at his tunic over the heart, as if to pluck out the bullets, and the buttons of the tunic began to fly into the air before he pitched forward on his face.

The other heeled quietly over on his back: it must have been because of the hands in the pockets. The officer dispatched the boy with one shot from the revolver as he lay face downward, but he pumped five bullets in rapid succession into the man, as if to pay him back for not coming to attention.

'When I was on my honeymoon years after, it was May, and we took the tram up the hill of Howth from Sutton Cross,' my father said as he rested on the oars. 'We sat on top in the open on the wooden seats with the rail around that made it like a small ship. The sea was below, and smell of the sea and furze-bloom all about, and then I looked down and saw the furze pods bursting, and the way they burst in all directions seemed shocking like the buttons when he started to tear at his tunic. I couldn't get it out of my mind all day. It destroyed the day.'

'It's a wonder their hands weren't tied?' I asked him as he rowed between the black navigation pan and the red where the river flowed into Oakport.

'I suppose it was because they were considered soldiers.'

'Do you think the boy stood to attention because he felt that he might still get off if he obeyed the rules?'

'Sounds a bit highfalutin' to me. Comes from going to school too long,' he said aggressively, and I was silent. It was new to me to hear him talk about his own life at all. Before, if I asked him about the war, he'd draw fingers across his eyes as if to tear a spider web away, but it was my last summer with him on the river, and it seemed to make him want to talk, to give of himself before it ended.

Hand over hand I drew in the line that throbbed with fish; there were two miles of line, a hook on a lead line every three yards. The licence allowed us a thousand hooks, but we used more. We were the last to fish this freshwater for a living.

As the eels came in over the side I cut them loose with a knife into a wire cage, where they slid over each other in their own oil, the twisted eel hook in their mouths. The other fish – pike choked on hooked perch they'd tried to swallow, bream, roach – I slid up the floorboards towards the bow of the boat. We'd sell them in the village or give them away. The hooks that hadn't been taken I cleaned and stuck in rows round the side of the wooden box. I let the line fall in its centre. After a mile he took my place in the stern and I rowed. People hadn't woken yet, and the early morning cold and mist were on the river. Outside of the slow ripple of the oars and the threshing of the fish on the line beaded with running drops of water as it came in, the river was dead silent, except for the occasional lowing of cattle on the banks.

'Have you any idea what you'll do after this summer?' he asked.

'No. I'll wait and see what comes up,' I answered.

'How do you mean what comes up?'

'Whatever result I get in the exam. If the result is good, I'll have choices. If it's not, there won't be choices. I'll have to take what I can get.'

'How good do you think they'll be?'

'I think they'll be all right, but there's no use counting chickens, is there?'

'No,' he said, but there was something calculating in the face; it made me watchful of him as I rowed the last stretch of the line. The day had come, the distant noises of the farms and the first flies on the river, by the time we'd lifted the large wire cage out of the bulrushes, emptied in the morning's catch of eels, and sunk it again.

'We'll have enough for a consignment tomorrow,' he said.

Each week we sent the live eels to Billingsgate in London.

'But say, say even if you do well, you wouldn't think of throwing this country up altogether and going to America?' he said, the words fumbled for as I pushed the boat out of the bulrushes after sinking the cage of eels, using the oar as a pole, the mud rising a dirty yellow between the stems.

'Why America?'

'Well, it's the land of opportunity, isn't it, a big, expanding country? There's no room for ambition in this poky place. All there's room for is to make holes in pints of porter.'

I was wary of the big words. They were not in his own voice.

'Who'd pay the fare?'

'We'd manage that. We'd scrape it together somehow.'

'Why should you scrape for me to go to America if I can get a job here?'

'I feel I'd be giving you a chance I never got. I fought for this country. And now they want to take away even the licence to fish. Will you think about it anyhow?'

'I'll think about it,' I answered.

Through the day he trimmed the brows of ridges in the potato field while I replaced hooks on the line and dug worms, pain of doing things for the last time as well as the boredom the knowledge brings that soon there'll be no need to do them, that they could be discarded almost now. The guilt of leaving came: I was discarding his life to assume my own, a man to row the boat would eat into the decreasing profits of the fishing, and it was even not certain he'd get renewal of his licence. The tourist board had opposed the last application. They said we impoverished the coarse fishing for tourists – the tourists who came every summer from Liverpool and Birmingham in increasing numbers to sit in aluminium deck-chairs on the riverbank and fish with rods. The fields we had would be a bare living without the fishing.

I saw him stretch across the wall in conversation with the cattle-dealer Farrell as I came round to put the worms where we stored them in clay in the darkness of the lavatory. Farrell leaned on the bar of his bicycle on the road. I passed into the lavatory thinking they were talking about the price of cattle, but as I emptied the worms into the box, the word Moran came, and I carefully opened the door to listen. It was my father's voice. He was excited.

'I know. I heard the exact sum. They got ten thousand dollars when Luke was killed. Every American soldier's life is insured to the tune of ten thousand dollars.'

'I heard they get two hundred and fifty dollars a month each for Michael and Sam while they're serving,' he went on.

'They're buying cattle left and right,' Farrell's voice came as I closed the door and stood in the darkness, in the smell of shit and piss and the warm fleshy smell of worms crawling in too little clay. The shock I felt was the shock I was to feel later when I made some social blunder, the splintering of a self-esteem and the need to crawl into a lavatory to think.

Luke Moran's body had come from Korea in a leaden casket, had crossed the stone bridge to the slow funeral bell with the big cars from the embassy behind, the coffin draped in the Stars and Stripes. Shots had been fired above the grave before they threw in the clay. There were photos of his decorations being presented to his family by a military attaché.

He'd scrape the fare, I'd be conscripted there, each month he'd get so many dollars while I served, and he'd get ten thousand if I was killed.

In the darkness of the lavatory between the boxes of crawling worms before we set the night line for the eels I knew my youth had ended.

I rowed as he let out the night line, his fingers baiting each twisted hook so beautifully that it seemed a single movement. The dark was closing from the shadow of Oakport to Nutley's boathouse, bats made ugly whirls overhead, the wings of duck shirred as they curved down into the bay.

'Have you thought about what I said about going to America?' he asked, without lifting his eyes from the hooks and the box of worms.

'I have.'

The oars dipped in the water without splash, the hole whirling wider in the calm as it slipped past him on the stern seat.

'Have you decided to take the chance, then?'

'No. I'm not going.'

'You won't be able to say I didn't give you the chance when you come to nothing in this fool of a country. It'll be your own funeral.'

'It'll be my own funeral,' I answered, and asked after a long silence, 'As you grow older, do you find your own days in the war and jails coming much back to you?'

'I do. And I don't want to talk about them. Talking about the execution disturbed me no end, those cursed buttons bursting into the air. And the most I think is that if I'd conducted my own wars, and let the fool of a country fend for itself, I'd be much better off today. I don't want to talk about it.'

I knew this silence was fixed for ever as I rowed in silence till he asked, 'Do you think, will it be much good tonight?'

'It's too calm,' I answered.

'Unless the night wind gets up,' he said anxiously.

'Unless a night wind,' I repeated.

As the boat moved through the calm water and the line slipped through his fingers over the side I'd never felt so close to him before, not even when he'd carried me on his shoulders above the laughing crowd to the Final. Each move he made I watched as closely as if I too had to prepare myself to murder.

Reading for Meaning

1. (a) What is your impression of the father in this story?
   (b) Describe the relationship he has with his son.
2. After overhearing his father's conversation with Farrell, the narrator says, 'I knew my youth had ended.' What do you think he means by this?
3. (a) Comment on the story's final paragraph. Do you find it strange, believable, saddening?
   (b) What point do you think the author is making in this paragraph?
4. 'Korea is a shocking portrayal of the greed and self-interest that can be found in the human heart.' Discuss this statement making reference to the story.

Writer's Workshop

Story/Drama: Imagine the narrator of the story decides to confront his father. Write the scene that takes place. You may write your scene as a drama or as a piece of prose.

Links

In this story, John McGahern looks at how sometimes parents fail to live up to their responsibilities to love and care for their children. You can link *Korea* in terms of its subject matter to other texts in this book and elsewhere.

In this book: Louis MacNeice's poem, *Prayer Before Birth* (page 154)
Elsewhere: Jeanette Winterson's memoir, *Why Be Happy When You Can Be Normal?*

Chapter 5:
Poetry: A Packsack of Invisible Keepsakes

Poetry

Poems are intense concentrations of language. The unique pattern of words, sounds and images on the page dares the reader to take another look, as if the poem itself is saying, 'I am unique. I am different. Do not ignore me.' In this chapter, you will discover a wide range of poetic voices with each poem offering a unique perspective on the world.

The poems collected in this chapter are divided into six topics: Growing Up; Parents and Children; Love; Death and Time; A Modern World; and Nature and Animals. However, it would be impossible to reduce these poems to just these categories. These poems should offer us a sense of how varied our human experiences can be.

It may be impossible to adequately define everything that poetry is. However, in his 38 Definitions of Poetry, the poet Carl Sandburg, describes poetry as 'a packsack of invisible keepsakes' – something to take with you, something elusive, something to be treasured. Hopefully some of the poems in this chapter will find their way into your packsack as you make your way through life.

Oranges

Gary Soto

The first time I walked
With a girl, I was twelve,
Cold, and weighted down
With two oranges in my jacket.
December. Frost cracking
Beneath my steps, my breath
Before me, then gone,
As I walked toward
Her house, the one whose
Porch light burned yellow
Night and day, in any weather.
A dog barked at me, until
She came out pulling
At her gloves, face bright
With rouge. I smiled,
Touched her shoulder, and led
Her down the street, across
A used car lot and a line
Of newly planted trees,
Until we were breathing
Before a drug store. We
Entered, the tiny bell
Bringing a saleslady
Down a narrow aisle of goods.
I turned to the candies
Tiered like bleachers,
And asked what she wanted –
Light in her eyes, a smile
Starting at the corners

Of her mouth. I fingered
A nickel in my pocket,
And when she lifted a chocolate
That cost a dime,
I didn't say anything.
I took the nickel from
My pocket, then an orange,
And set them quietly on
The counter. When I looked up,
The lady's eyes met mine,
And held them, knowing
Very well what it was all
About.

Outside,
A few cars hissing past,
Fog hanging like old
Coats between the trees.
I took my girl's hand
In mine for two blocks,
Then released it to let
Her unwrap the chocolate.
I peeled my orange
That was so bright against
The gray of December
That, from some distance,
Someone might have thought
I was making a fire in my hands.

GLOSSARY

drug store: an American pharmacy that also sells items you
    might find in a shop such as sweets and newspapers
candies: sweets
bleachers: tiered seating often found in a stadium
nickel: a five-cent coin
dime: a ten-cent coin
gray: American spelling of 'grey'

Speaking and Listening

Mime: This poem contains lots of meaningful physical actions.

1. As a class, recreate *Oranges* through mime (acting without speaking). Choose three students to act out the drama.
2. When miming the boy's part make it clear to your audience that the boy does not have enough money to pay for the chocolate bar. Using body language and facial expressions, communicate the boy's nervousness and inexperience.
3. You may wish to use props or words written on large sheets of paper.

Reading for Meaning

1. Explain what occurred between the speaker and the sales assistant.
2. (a) Describe the weather and season in which this poem is set.
   (b) Why do you think the poet chose this type of weather and season as the backdrop to the poem?
3. What do you understand by the final image in which the speaker talks about 'making a fire' in his hands?
4. The speaker never directly mentions any emotions that he is feeling. How do you think he felt during the events described?
5. How would you describe the behaviour of the boy in the poem: brave, foolish, romantic, cheeky, risky?
6. 'Gary Soto's *Oranges* sums up the newness, bravery and creativity of being young.' Discuss this statement making reference to the poem.

Language Lab

1. (a) The poet, Gary Soto, makes interesting comparisons using similes (see Chapter 4, page 95) in this poem. Write down two examples.
   (b) Do you think these are effective similes? Why / why not?
2. (a) The poet adds to the scene by appealing to the senses (see Chapter 4, page 95). Write down examples of this from the poem.
   (b) How do the poet's appeals to the senses add to the scene?
3. (a) This poem presents interesting contrasts between light and dark. List all of the examples of this that you can find.
   (b) Why do you think the poet makes these contrasts? Think about the atmosphere and the poem's themes.

Writer's Workshop

Personal Composition: In *Oranges*, Gary Soto tells a personal story to say something about being young. Write a personal composition about a memory that you have from your childhood. Try to choose something that is meaningful. Use descriptive language (see Chapter 4, page 95) to create atmosphere. You may wish to look back at Chapter 1 for tips about personal writing.

Links

Oranges beautifully brings to life a childhood moment when the possibilities of the future burn brightly. This poem can be linked to other texts in this book and elsewhere:

In this book: Michael Morpurgo's story, *No Trumpets Needed* (page 112)

Elsewhere: John Carney's coming-of-age film, *Sing Street*

Legend

Gillian Clarke

The rooms were mirrors
for that luminous face,
the morning windows ferned
with cold. Outside
a level world of snow.

Voiceless birds in the trees
like notes in the books
in the piano stool.
She let us suck top-of-the-milk
burst from the bottles like corks.

Then wrapped shapeless
we stumped to the park
between the parapets of snow
in the wake of the shovellers,
cardboard rammed in the tines of garden forks.

The lake was an empty rink
and I stepped out,
pushing my sister first
onto its creaking floor.
When I brought her home,

shivering, wailing, soaked,
they thought me a hero.
But I still wake at night,
to hear the Snow Queen's knuckles crack,
black water running fingers through the ice.

GLOSSARY

luminous: shining / bright

ferned: Clarke has created this verb to describe the look of the ice frozen on the window.
   A fern is a type of green plant.

top-of-the-milk: years ago, milk was delivered to houses in glass bottles. In cold weather the milk
   at the top of the bottle froze, forming an ice cube

parapets: a defensive wall as in a castle

tines: prongs of a garden fork

Reading for Meaning

1. Explain what occurs in this poem.
2. (a) Why was the speaker called a 'hero' when she got home?
   (b) How do you think she feels about this?
3. (a) Why do you think the poem is called *Legend*?
   (b) Suggest an alternative title for the poem and explain why you think this new title would be fitting.
3. One critic wrote about this poem, '*Legend* is about guilt: how it hides itself from view and then surfaces, most often when we are all alone.' Discuss this comment by making reference to the poem.

Language Lab

1. Describe the mood (see page 163) of the first two stanzas. In your answer, pay attention to the details offered in the stanzas.
2. (a) The poet uses a number of interesting comparisons in this poem. Write down three.
   (b) For each, state if the comparison is a simile or metaphor.
   (c) Which of your three chosen comparisons do you think is best?

Speaking and Listening

Listen to the Poet: Listen to Gillian Clarke read this poem at www.poetryarchive.org. As a class discuss this reading. Does the poet do a good job of giving voice to the emotions in the poem?

Writer's Workshop

Composition: Imagine you are the speaker in this poem and you find a photo of yourself as a child taken twenty years ago. Write a personal composition in which you remember the events described in *Legend*. Explore how you felt then and how you feel now.

Links

Gillian Clarke's *Legend* explores ideas around guilt and regret. This poem can be linked to other texts in this book and elsewhere:
In this book: Ruth Stone's poem, *Another Feeling* (page 192)
Elsewhere: Joe Wright's film, *Atonement*

Prayer Before Birth

Louis MacNeice

I am not yet born; O hear me.
Let not the bloodsucking bat or the rat or the stoat or the
  club-footed ghoul come near me.

I am not yet born; console me.
I fear that the human race may with tall walls wall me,
  with strong drugs dope me, with wise lies lure me,
    on black racks rack me, in blood-baths roll me.

I am not yet born; provide me
With water to dandle me, grass to grow for me, trees to talk
  to me, sky to sing to me, birds and a white light
    in the back of my mind to guide me.

I am not yet born; forgive me
For the sins that in me the world shall commit, my words
  when they speak me, my thoughts when they think me,
    my treason engendered by traitors beyond me,
      my life when they murder by means of my
        hands, my death when they live me.

I am not yet born; rehearse me
In the parts I must play and the cues I must take when
  old men lecture me, bureaucrats hector me, mountains
    frown at me, lovers laugh at me, the white
      waves call me to folly and the desert calls
        me to doom and the beggar refuses
        my gift and my children curse me.

I am not yet born; O hear me,
Let not the man who is beast or who thinks he is God
  come near me.

I am not yet born; O fill me
With strength against those who would freeze my
  humanity, would dragoon me into a lethal automaton,
    would make me a cog in a machine, a thing with
      one face, a thing, and against all those
        who would dissipate my entirety, would
          blow me like thistledown hither and
            thither or hither and thither
              like water held in the
                hands would spill me.

Let them not make me a stone and let them not spill me.
  Otherwise kill me.

GLOSSARY

console: give comfort

dandle: pet / pamper

engendered: to be produced or brought into existence

bureaucrats: officials who work to rigid guidelines without exercising personal judgement

hector: bully / torment

dragoon: persecute by armed forces

automaton: robot / a non-thinking person

dissipate: disperse / scatter / break up / squander

Speaking and Listening

Listen to the Poet: Go to www.poetryarchive.org and listen to Louis MacNeice read this poem. As a class, discuss the tone used in this reading. What emotions does MacNeice convey with his voice?

Reading for Meaning

1. Explain how the poet's attitude towards the world is largely negative.
2. Rewrite each of the following phrases in your own words:
   (a) 'provide me / With water to dandle me, grass to grow for me, trees to talk / to me, sky to sing to me, birds and a white light / in the back of my mind to guide me'
   (b) 'O fill me / With strength against those who would freeze my / humanity, would dragoon me into a lethal automaton, / would make me a cog in a machine, a thing with / one face'
3. In the fourth stanza, MacNeice writes, 'forgive me / For the sins that in me the world shall commit.' What do you think he means by this line?
4. Choose a phrase that you find striking or memorable (other than the ones in Q2 and Q3). Explain why you find this phrase striking.
5. This poem was written in the 1940s. Do you think that the poet's view of the world is relevant today? In your answer, discuss the challenges facing the world today.
6. MacNeice once said, 'The writer today should be not so much the mouthpiece of a community . . . as its conscience.' How does this quotation apply to *Prayer Before Birth*?

Writer's Workshop

Letter: Write a letter to Louis MacNeice in response to this poem. Include one of the following sentences:

- I feel that there is much more room for hope for the world than your poem *Prayer Before Birth* suggests.
- I found your poem *Prayer Before Birth* to be a worrying but accurate depiction of the world.

Style Guide

Refrain: A refrain is a line or phrase that is repeated throughout a poem. In *Prayer Before Birth*, the refrain, 'I am not yet born' emphasises the speaker's vulnerability and frames the child's plea for a better world.

Tone: One of the ways that we can understand the emotion of a poem is through the tone. For example, a poet may be feeling joy, anger, sadness and/or nostalgia when writing and this may be reflected in the tone of the poem.

When somebody speaks, we may notice the person's tone of voice. This can be understood by the manner in which they talk: somebody who is shouting is likely to be speaking in an angry tone. In written language, we have to rely solely on the words to understand the tone. Look at how the basic meaning of the following two sentences is the same but the tones differ:

> I would like you to leave please. → assertive, polite tone
>
> Get the hell out of here, right now! → angry, threatening tone

In *Prayer Before Birth*, the tone is one of pleading and outrage. The speaker, an unborn child, prays to humanity for a better world to be born into: 'O hear me,' 'console me', 'provide me.' This is coupled with a tone of disgust at the bleak reality of the world: 'on black racks rack me, in blood-baths roll me,' 'those who would freeze my humanity...would dragoon me...would make me a cog in a machine.'

Links 🔗

Prayer Before Birth is a plea to make the world a safer and fairer place. It asks what society would you like to be born into. This poem can be linked to other texts in this book and elsewhere:

In this book: Kurt Vonnegut's short story, *Harrison Bergeron* (page 99); India Knight's *Who's Deprived Now?* (page 53)

Elsewhere: Search online for a video version of John Rawls's thought experiment, *The Veil of Ignorance*

Cinders

Roger McGough

After the pantomime, carrying you back to the car
On the coldest night of the year
My coat, black leather, cracking in the wind.

Through the darkness we are guided by a star
It is the one the Good Fairy gave you
You clutch it tightly, your magic wand.

And I clutch you tightly for fear you blow away
For fear you grow up too soon and – suddenly,
I almost slip, so take it steady down the hill.

Hunched against the wind and hobbling
I could be mistaken for your grandfather
And sensing this, I hold you tighter still.

Knowing that I will never see you dressed for the Ball
Be on hand to warn you against Prince Charmings
And the happy ever afters of pantomime.

On reaching the car I put you into the baby seat
And fumble with straps I have yet to master
Thinking, if only there were more time. More time.

You are crying now. Where is your wand?
Oh no. I can't face going back for it
Let some kid find it in tomorrow's snow.

Waiting in the wings, the witching hour.
Already the car is changing. Smells sweet
Of ripening seed. We must go. Must go.

Style Guide

Imagery: In literature, imagery refers to the pictures the author paints using words. These images help to focus the reader on particular ideas or may help the author to express emotion.

In *Cinders*, Roger McGough uses powerful images to convey his feelings and to highlight the poem's central theme. The image of a man struggling, against the weather and the hill, suggests the idea that the speaker is dealing with large forces, namely time itself. This is made clear by the images of a change: 'ripening seed,' 'the car is changing'. The idea of resisting time is stressed through the images of holding on: 'I clutch you tightly for fear you blow away,' 'I hold you tighter still,' 'You clutch it tightly, your magic wand.'

The central image of Cinderella ('Cinders') refers to the idea of change, as midnight ('the witching hour') looms. Through these images, Roger McGough explores his feelings that time moves quickly, stealing the magic of youth and pulling us into adulthood.

Language Lab

1. Explain what effect the following imagery (see Style Guide above) from the poem has on you. You may wish to discuss what the images make you feel or think about. Focus your answer on key words.
   (a) 'After the pantomime, carrying you back to the car
       On the coldest night of the year
       My coat, black leather, cracking in the wind'
   (b) 'Through the darkness we are guided by a star
       It is the one the Good Fairy gave you
       You clutch it tightly, your magic wand.'
   (c) 'Waiting in the wings, the witching hour.
       Already the car is changing. Smells sweet
       Of ripening seed.'
2. Choose another image from the poem that you feel is powerful or memorable. Explain why you find it so.

Reading for Meaning

1. Do you think the poet captures the scene and atmosphere well in this poem?
2. Describe the tone (see page 156) used by the speaker in this poem.
3. What do you learn about the relationship between the speaker and his child in this poem?
4. The speaker says, 'if only there were more time.' What worry is he expressing here?
5. Does this poem speak to you personally? Why / why not?

Speaking and Listening

Comparative Discussion

1. Read John McGahern's short story, *Korea* in Chapter 4, pages 144–147.
2. As a class discuss how the parent-child relationships in *Cinders* and *Korea* are very different. What does this suggest about the authors of these texts?
3. Which text do the class prefer, *Korea* or *Cinders*? Why?

Writer's Workshop

Write your Own: Taking inspiration from *Cinders*, write a poem from the perspective of your parent or guardian. Try to capture your parent's/guardian's thoughts and feelings. It may help if you base your poem on one event from your childhood. Try to include interesting imagery in your poem.

Links

Cinders explores how precious, yet short, childhood innocence is. This poem can be linked to other texts in this book and elsewhere:

In this book: Francis P. Church's, *Yes, Virginia, there is a Santa Claus* (page 87); Paweł Kuczyński's cartoon B (page 241)

Elsewhere: Search online for Eavan Boland's poem, *This Moment*

Parents and Children

Those Winter Sundays

Robert Hayden

Sundays too my father got up early
and put his clothes on in the blueblack cold,
then with cracked hands that ached
from labor in the weekday weather made
banked fires blaze. No one ever thanked him.

I'd wake and hear the cold splintering, breaking.
When the rooms were warm, he'd call,
and slowly I would rise and dress,
fearing the chronic angers of that house,

Speaking indifferently to him,
who had driven out the cold
and polished my good shoes as well.
What did I know, what did I know
of love's austere and lonely offices?

GLOSSARY
austere: strict / forbidding / self-denying
offices: duties / services carried out for another / position of responsibility

Reading for Meaning

1. The poem begins with the words, 'Sundays too my father got up early'. What does the word 'too' suggest?
2. (a) What chores did the father perform for his son?
   (b) How does Robert Hayden show that these chores were unpleasant?
3. What kind of relationship do you think the father and son had?
4. (a) Describe the tone of the poem's final two lines.
   (b) What does this suggest about how the son feels?

Writer's Workshop

Write your Own: Write your own poem from the point of view of the father. Try to consider how he felt about his son and the work that was done around the house.

Comparative Analysis: Read Alden Nowlan's poem *Weakness* on page 168. In both *Weakness* and *Those Winter Sundays*, the speakers re-evaluate their fathers. Compare these poems in terms of how the fathers are presented and how the speakers reconsider their fathers.

Speaking and Listening

Learn and Recite: Memorise the poem *Those Winter Sundays*. Your teacher will call on some students to recite it for the class. Be prepared to say the poem with emotion, emphasising and pausing at appropriate moments.

Links

Those Winter Sundays urges the reader to re-evaluate the often thankless support parents give their children. This poem can be linked to other texts in this book and elsewhere:

In this book: Martina King's tale, *Waiting* (page 32)

Elsewhere: Search online for W.B. Yeats's poem, *Song of the Old Mother*

The Back Seat of My Mother's Car

Julia Copus

We left before I had time
to comfort you, to tell you that we nearly touched
hands in that vacuous half-dark. I wanted
to stem the burning waters running over me like tiny
rivers down my face and legs, but at the same time I was reaching out
for the slit in the window where the sky streamed in,
cold as ether, and I could see your fat mole-fingers grasping
the dusty August air. I pressed my face to the glass;
I was calling to you – Daddy! – as we screeched away into
the distance, my own hand tingling like an amputation.
You were mouthing something I still remember, the noiseless words
piercing me like that catgut shriek that flew up, furious as a sunset
pouring itself out against the sky. The ensuing silence
was the one clear thing I could decipher –
the roar of the engine drowning your voice,
with the cool slick glass between us.

With the cool slick glass between us,
the roar of the engine drowning, your voice
was the one clear thing I could decipher –
pouring itself out against the sky, the ensuing silence
piercing me like that catgut shriek that flew up, furious as a sunset.
You were mouthing something: I still remember the noiseless words,
the distance, my own hand tingling like an amputation.
I was calling to you, Daddy, as we screeched away into
the dusty August air. I pressed my face to the glass,
cold as ether, and I could see your fat mole-fingers grasping
for the slit in the window where the sky streamed in
rivers down my face and legs, but at the same time I was reaching out
to stem the burning waters running over me like tiny
hands in that vacuous half-dark. I wanted
to comfort you, to tell you that we nearly touched.
We left before I had time.

Speaking and Listening

Group Reading

- Read this poem as a class group.
- Taking turns, members of your class should read a line or phrase from the poem.
- You should read until you come to a punctuation mark (comma, full stop or dash) and then allow someone else to read.
- Some class members may need to read more than once.
- It is important to listen so that you know when it is your turn to read.

Reading for Meaning

1. This poem takes place over a few seconds. What do you think is happening in the life of the little girl speaking in the poem?
2. (a) The form of this poem is called 'specular' after the Latin for 'mirror'. Explain how the poem has a mirror-like structure.
   (b) What effect does this structure have on the reader? What does it make you feel or think about?
3. Explain what you understand by each of the following phrases from the poem:
   (a) 'my own hand tingling like an amputation'
   (b) 'I wanted / to stem the burning waters running over me like tiny / rivers down my face and legs'
   (c) 'the ensuing silence / piercing me like that catgut shriek that flew up, furious as a sunset'
4. Aside from the examples in Question 3, choose two phrases from the poem that you feel are striking. Write down these phrases and explain why you find them so.
5. 'This poem uses rich poetic language to describe a moment that is brief but utterly devastating.' Discuss this statement making reference to the poem.

Style Guide

Mood: We can understand the emotions of a poem from the tone (see page 156) and the mood. The mood refers to the emotions of the poem as a whole; it is the overall feeling of a poem. This is linked to tone but is not the same thing. For example, a poet may write in a mock angry tone and this could create a humorous mood.

In short, think of tone as the emotions in the speaker's language. The mood is the emotion experienced by the reader.

In *The Back Seat of My Mother's Car*, the mood is one of panic and great loss. The car 'screeched away' before the speaker had time to say goodbye; this creates a highly charged mood where the separation of child and father is made more powerful. The mood of loss is intensified by phrases such as 'my own hand tingling like an amputation' and the image of the child who says, 'I pressed my face to the glass'. Overall the mood experienced by the reader is one of intense loss.

Writer's Workshop

Visual Collage: Create a visual representation of this poem using images (printed or drawn by you). Include lines from the poem in your collage. Try to capture the main ideas and emotions in the poem.

Links

This poem deals with a very painful moment in the speaker's life: the break-up of her parents' marriage. This poem can be linked to other texts such as Robert Benton's very moving film, *Kramer vs Kramer*; Henrik Ibsen's play, *A Doll's House*

My Papa's Waltz

Theodore Roethke

The whiskey on your breath
Could make a small boy dizzy;
But I hung on like death:
Such waltzing was not easy.

We romped until the pans
Slid from the kitchen shelf;
My mother's countenance
Could not unfrown itself.

The hand that held my wrist
Was battered on one knuckle;
At every step you missed
My right ear scraped a buckle.

You beat time on my head
With a palm caked hard by dirt,
Then waltzed me off to bed
Still clinging to your shirt.

GLOSSARY
countenance: face

Speaking and Listening

Listen to the Poet: When Theodore Roethke reads *My Papa's Waltz*, he uses a 'waltzing' rhythm. To listen to Roethke recite his poem, go to www.mentorbooks.ie/resources and look in the TY English section. Alternatively, you may find this reading on YouTube.

Reading for Meaning

1. This poem lends itself to different interpretations. Describe the subject matter of this poem as you see it.

2. Write down two phrases or images from the poem that you find interesting and explain why you find them so.

3. One commentator wrote of *My Papa's Waltz*: 'The father-son relationship is intimate and loving yet by the end of the poem we find ourselves uneasy and a little worried.' Do you agree with this statement? Explain your answer.

Writer's Workshop

Class Comment Thread: When a piece of writing is published on a website, the site often allows readers to contribute their thoughts by means of a comment thread. Usually you can approve or disapprove of a comment by clicking the thumbs-up or thumbs-down buttons. Contributors to comment threads often give themselves nicknames and write in an informal manner. Some poetry websites also include a comment thread facility. Look at the comment thread below for *My Papa's Waltz*.

JohnJoe

I think this poem is about physical abuse. The father is clearly drunk and the boy is frightened as he 'hung on like death'. For me the language suggests that the boy might be beaten: 'my right ear scraped a buckle' and 'You beat time on my head'. I think the boy is confused because he loves his dad but his father might have a tendency for drunken violence.

| Like | Reply | edit | Recommend | Hide |

WhasssUp!!!

@**JohnJoe** you've got it all wrong! This is a tender poem about a boy who fondly remembers helping his dad who'd had a few drinks. Roethke never says the boy was hit, his 'ear scrapes a buckle' because he is much shorter than his father. The father isn't beating his son; he's keeping 'time' to the music.

| Like | Reply | edit | Recommend | Hide |

GhostInTheMachine

@**JohnJoe**, it's like you're reading a different poem. How can't you see the beauty of this tender moment?

| Like | Reply | edit | Recommend | Hide |

JohnJoe

Why is the mother upset then? 'My mother's countenance / Could not unfrown itself'. Clearly she does not approve of this drunken, abusive father and she has to rely on her young son to help.

| Like | Reply | edit | Recommend | Hide |

GhostInTheMachine

She's just upset because the dad is messing and is a bit tipsy.

| Like | Reply | edit | Recommend | Hide |

SarahSarah

I'm with **@JohnJoe**, the 'battered hand' to me is a bit threatening and suggests that the father may have used his fists.

| Like | Reply | edit | Recommend | Hide |

WhasssUp!!!

@SarahSarah, he's a working man. Roethke's father owned greenhouses and produced flowers.

| Like | Reply | edit | Recommend | Hide |

SarahSarah

Well you wouldn't say 'battered' if that's the case.

| Like | Reply | edit | Recommend | Hide |

GhostInTheMachine

Just look at the tone; it's gentle, sweet and loving. There's no violence here.

| Like | Reply | edit | Recommend | Hide |

JohnJoe

Sounds to me like the boy is scared and confused.

| Like | Reply | edit | Recommend | Hide |

Class Comment Thread

1. As a class continue this comment thread.
2. Use the white board as the comment thread space.
3. Take it in turns to leave your seats and write on the board offering your comments on *My Papa's Waltz*.
4. The rest of the class may hold their thumbs up or down to indicate if they approve or disapprove of a comment.
5. Nobody may talk until the class comment thread is finished.
6. As a class, discuss the comment thread when it is completed.

Links

The complexity of the father-son relationship is central to *My Papa's Waltz*. This poem can be linked to other texts in this book and elsewhere:

In this book: Alden Nowlan's poem, *Weakness* (page 168)

Elsewhere: Search online for Raymond Carver's short story, *Bicycles, Muscles, Cigarettes*

Weakness

Alden Nowlan

Old mare whose eyes
are like cracked marbles,
drools blood in her mash,
shivers in her jute blanket.

My father hates weakness worse than hail;
in the morning
   without haste
he will shoot her in the ear, once,
shovel her under in the north pasture.

Tonight
   leaving the stables
he stands his lantern on an overturned water pail,
turns,
   cursing her for a bad bargain,
and spreads his coat
carefully over her sick shoulders

GLOSSARY
jute: a coarse material often used for making sacks

Reading for Meaning

1. Do you think Alden Nowlan successfully describes the horse's physical state in the first stanza?
2. When the speaker says that his father hates 'weakness worse than hail,' what kind of weakness do you think he is referring to?
3. What is your impression of the father in this poem?
4. Why do you think Alden Nowlan chose to entitle this poem *Weakness*?
5. Write a paragraph beginning with the following statement: 'This poem shows that kindness can be found in the most surprising of places.'

Biographical Note

Poets' lives and experiences help to shape the content and emotions of their poems. In *Weakness*, Alden Nowlan draws on memories of his father for inspiration.

Alden Nowlan was born into extreme poverty in Canada. His mother left the family home when he was very young and Nowlan was raised by his father and grandmother. Nowlan's family were tough individuals who saw no value in education, let alone poetry. He completed only four years of school.

As a teenager, Nowlan discovered the library located eighteen miles from his home. He hitchhiked there every weekend and read in secret, hiding the fact from his father. As the poet remembers, 'My father would as soon have seen me wear lipstick.'

Links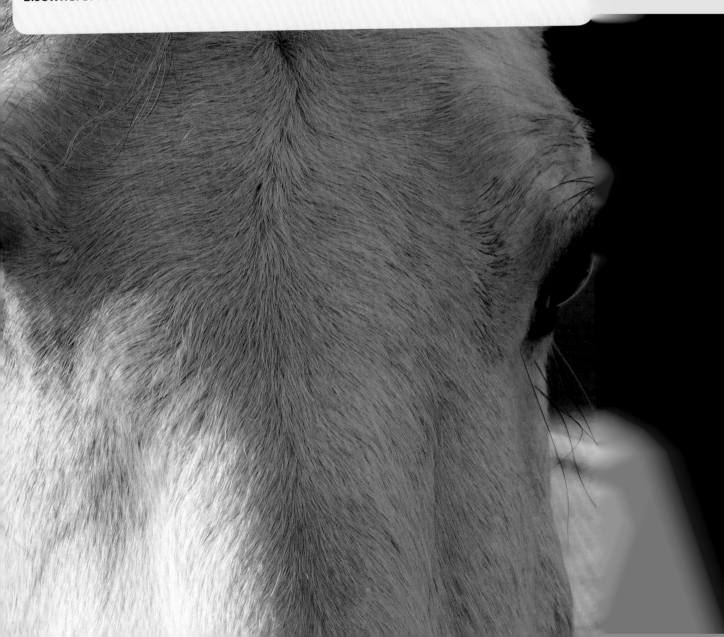

In *Weakness*, the speaker's view of his father is changed by a single, simple gesture. This poem can be linked to other texts in this book and elsewhere:

In this book: Robert Hayden's poem, *Those Winter Sundays* (page 160)
Elsewhere: Phil Alden Robinson's film, *Field of Dreams*

My Mistress' Eyes are Nothing Like the Sun

William Shakespeare

My mistress' eyes are nothing like the sun;
Coral is far more red than her lips' red;
If snow be white, why then her breasts are dun;
If hairs be wires, black wires grow on her head.
I have seen roses damasked, red and white,
But no such roses see I in her cheeks;
And in some perfumes is there more delight
Than in the breath that from my mistress reeks.
I love to hear her speak, yet well I know
That music hath a far more pleasing sound;
I grant I never saw a goddess go;
My mistress, when she walks, treads on the ground.
　　And yet, by heaven, I think my love as rare
　　As any she belied with false compare.

GLOSSARY
dun: dull greyish brown
damasked: containing layers of colour
belie: to show to be false / contradict

Reading for Meaning

1. In your own words, describe the woman depicted in *My Mistress' Eyes are Nothing Like the Sun*.
2. (a) In this poem, Shakespeare gives an image of his mistress through a series of contrasts. Find three examples of such contrasts.
    (b) Do you feel that these contrasts are an effective way of describing the woman in the poem?

3. The poem ends with a rhyming couplet: 'And yet, by heaven, I think my love as rare / As any she belied with false compare'. What do you think Shakespeare means by these lines?
4. Do you feel the woman in the poem would be complimented or insulted by this sonnet?

Style Guide

Sonnet: A sonnet is a fourteen-line poem. Sonnets date back to the thirteenth century and often deal with large themes such as love. The sonnet form requires poets to write with great skill and control. There are two main types of sonnet: Petrarchan and Shakespearean.

Petrarchan sonnets are named after the Italian poet Petrarch. They are divided into an eight-line section called an octet, followed by a six-line stanza called a sestet.

A *Shakespearean sonnet* is written using iambic pentameter (see below). It has three four-line sections called quatrains, followed by a rhyming couplet. The rhyming scheme for a Shakespearean sonnet is ababcdcdefefgg.

Iambic Pentameter: Iambic pentameter is a type of rhythm often found in Shakespeare's works. A line of iambic pentameter contains ten syllables, five of which are stressed. If you read the line below and clap your hands to every DUM, you will hear where the stresses lie.

da	DUM	da	DUM	da	DUM	da	DUM	da	DUM

When this is applied to a line from the poem it sounds like this:

da	DUM	da	DUM	da	DUM	da	DUM	da	DUM
My	mis-	tress'	eyes	are	noth-	ing	like	the	sun

Traditionally, iambic pentameter has been a very popular rhythm in poetry because it reflects the rhythms of human speech while retaining the musicality of poetry.

Writer's Workshop

Letter: You are the 'mistress' in the poem. Write a personal letter (see Chapter 3, page 83) to the poet in response to the sonnet written about you.

Sonnet: Following the Style Guide above, write your own sonnet. You may explore any theme that is of interest to you.

Links

This sonnet queries the value of physical perfection and asks questions about the true nature of love. This poem can be linked to other texts in this book and elsewhere:

In this book: Eavan Boland's poem, *Quarantine* (page 174)

Elsewhere: Search online for the classic song, *My Funny Valentine*

I Am Very Bothered When I Think

Simon Armitage

I am very bothered when I think
of the bad things I have done in my life.
Not least that time in the chemistry lab
when I held a pair of scissors by the blades
and played the handles
in the naked lilac flame of the Bunsen burner;
then called your name, and handed them over.

O the unrivalled stench of branded skin
as you slipped your thumb and middle finger in,
then couldn't shake off the two burning rings. Marked,
the doctor said, for eternity.

Don't believe me, please, if I say
that was just my butterfingered way, at thirteen,
of asking you if you would marry me.

Reading for Meaning

1. Why is the speaker in the poem 'very bothered'?
2. What does the poet mean when he says, 'that was just my butterfingered way, at thirteen, / of asking you if you would marry me'?
3. Considering what the poet says in the final stanza, what is the significance of the phrases 'finger' and 'burning rings' in the second stanza?
4. Describe the tone (see page 156) used in this poem.
5. Do you feel the poem realistically describes the way young people try to attract the attention of someone they are romantically interested in?
6. In the tradition of Shakespeare's sonnets, the title of this poem is the first line. Suggest an alternative title for this poem. Explain why you chose this title.

Style Guide

Sonnet: Simon Armitage classifies this poem as a sonnet. Like all sonnets it is fourteen lines long. Some of the lines are in iambic pentameter (see page 171). As with many sonnets, the theme is love. However, it also explores the ideas of guilt and regret. Like most sonnets, the first line is intriguing and encourages the reader to wonder and ask questions. Here we are intrigued to know why the poet is bothered.

The rhyme pattern and the rhythm are less consistent than traditional sonnets. This shows how a traditional form can be brilliantly adapted to express a very modern idea.

Writer's Workshop

A Poetic Reply: Write a poem from the perspective of the girl in *I Am Very Bothered When I Think*, beginning with the phrase, 'I too am bothered when I think'.

Links

Simon Armitage's poem draws on the sonnet form. In terms of its structure, it can be linked to other texts in this book and elsewhere:

In this book: Shakespeare's *My Mistress' Eyes Are Nothing Like the Sun* (page 170)

Elsewhere: Search online for other sonnets such as: Elizabeth Barrett Browning's *Grief*, John Donne's *Death Be Not Proud*, John Keats's *Bright Star*, Gerard Manley Hopkins's *The Windhover*, A. Mary F. Robinson's *Neurasthenia*, Christina Rossetti's *Remember*, Edna St Vincent Millay's *Time Does Not Bring Relief; You Have All Lied*

Quarantine

Eavan Boland

In the worst hour of the worst season
    of the worst year of a whole people
a man set out from the workhouse with his wife.
He was walking — they were both walking — north.

She was sick with famine fever and could not keep up.
    He lifted her and put her on his back.
He walked like that west and west and north.
Until at nightfall under freezing stars they arrived.

In the morning they were both found dead.
    Of cold. Of hunger. Of the toxins of a whole history.
But her feet were held against his breastbone.
The last heat of his flesh was his last gift to her.

Let no love poem ever come to this threshold.
    There is no place here for the inexact
praise of the easy graces and sensuality of the body.
There is only time for this merciless inventory:

Their death together in the winter of 1847.
    Also what they suffered. How they lived.
And what there is between a man and woman.
And in which darkness it can best be proved.

GLOSSARY
workhouse: during the Famine, a place where poor people
    could work in exchange for food. Conditions were harsh and
    the poor were treated cruelly
inventory: catalogue / list
1847: the worst year of the Great Famine in Ireland

Reading for Meaning

1. Explain what happened to the husband and wife in this poem.
2. 1847 was the worst year of the Great Famine in Ireland. In your view, is Eavan Boland successful in capturing how grim this moment in Irish history was?
3. If this is a poem that explores the meaning of love, why do you think Boland writes, 'Let no love poem ever come to this threshold. / There is no place here for the inexact / praise of the easy graces and sensuality of the body'?
4. One commentator said of this poem, 'Love is only truly on show, when everything else is gone.' Explain how this comment applies to *Quarantine*.

Writer's Workshop

History Poem: The far past can be a great source of poetic inspiration. Choose a historical moment that you find interesting; this may be something you have studied in school or learnt about elsewhere. Taking inspiration from Boland's *Quarantine*, write a poem based on your chosen historical event.

Style Guide

Theme: The theme of a piece of literature is its message or the central idea that is explored. This is woven into the fabric of the text through images, subject matter and language. A good starting point for thinking about a text's theme is to ask, 'What is the author trying to say or explore?'

The themes of a piece of literature provide a link between the imagined world of the text and real life. They allow the writer to make a comment on life or his/her world.

In *Quarantine*, Eavan Boland asks the question, 'what does love mean?' For her love is more than just romance or empty physical attraction ('inexact / praise of the easy graces and sensuality of the body') – love is about true connection, it is what offers comfort in the most trying of situations: 'what there is between a man and woman. / And in which darkness it can best be proved.'

Links

In *Quarantine*, we see how love and human decency can survive even in the most barren and bleak environments. This poem can be linked to other texts in this book and elsewhere:
In this book: Michael Morpurgo's short story, *No Trumpets Needed* (page 112)
Elsewhere: Cormac McCarthy's novel, *The Road*

The Vacuum

Howard Nemerov

The house is so quiet now
The vacuum cleaner sulks in the corner closet,
Its bag limp as a stopped lung, its mouth
Grinning into the floor, maybe at my
Slovenly life, my dog-dead youth.

I've lived this way long enough,
But when my old woman died her soul
Went into that vacuum cleaner, and I can't bear
To see the bag swell like a belly, eating the dust
And the woollen mice, and begin to howl

Because there is old filth everywhere
She used to crawl, in the corner and under the stair.
I know now how life is cheap as dirt,
And still the hungry, angry heart
Hangs on and howls, biting at air.

Reading for Meaning

1. Consider all of the meanings of the word 'vacuum'. Why do you think the poet called this poem *The Vacuum*?
2. Describe the emotions and thoughts expressed in this poem. Use quotations to support your ideas.
3. What do you understand by the final phrase of the poem: 'I know now how life is cheap as dirt, / And still the hungry, angry heart / Hangs on and howls, biting at air'?

Style Guide

Alliteration: Alliteration is the repetition of consonant sounds at the start of words or in stressed syllables. It occurs in words that are placed close together. Alliteration depends on the repetition of consonant sounds, not letters. This is why '**kn**ow **n**othing' is alliterative but 'climate change' is not.

Alliteration is used in poetry, branding, tongue twisters, newspaper headlines, advertising and song lyrics. Look at the following examples:

- **Brands:** <u>K</u>odak <u>C</u>ameras, <u>R</u>ange <u>R</u>over, <u>W</u>eight <u>W</u>atchers
- **Newspaper Headlines:** <u>S</u>now<u>s</u>torm <u>S</u>ends <u>C</u>ity into <u>S</u>hutdown
- **Slogans:** <u>F</u>ila: <u>F</u>unctional. <u>F</u>ashionable. <u>F</u>ormidable
- **Poetry:** *And the <u>s</u>ilken, <u>s</u>ad, un<u>c</u>ertain rustling of each purple curtain Thrilled me – <u>f</u>illed me with <u>f</u>antastic terrors never <u>f</u>elt be<u>f</u>ore* – from *The Raven*, Edgar Allan Poe

In *The Vacuum*, Howard Nemerov uses alliteration to give a musical quality to the poem: 'The va<u>c</u>uum <u>c</u>leaner sul<u>k</u>s in the <u>c</u>orner <u>c</u>loset'; 'And still the <u>h</u>ungry, angry <u>h</u>eart / <u>H</u>angs on and <u>h</u>owls, biting at air.'

Language Lab

1. Howard Nemerov makes use of a number of language devices in *The Vacuum*. Find examples in the poem of each of the following:
   (a) appeals to the senses (see Chapter 4, page 95)
   (b) personification (see Chapter 4, page 95)
   (c) simile (see Chapter 4, page 95)
2. Explain the effect each of these language devices have in the poem.
3. Describe the tone (see page 156) used in *The Vacuum*.

Writer's Workshop

Poetry Analysis: The last four poems in this section of the chapter all explore the idea of love. Read all four poems again. Choose the one that you feel is the most meaningful. Write an analysis of the poem using the following ideas:

- Subject matter
- Theme
- Language
- Emotions
- Imagery

Links

The feeling of loss when somebody you love dies is an incredibly powerful human emotion. This poem can be linked to other texts in this book and elsewhere:

In this book: Fleur Adcock's poem, *For Meg* (page 178)

Elsewhere: Search online for Tony Harrison's poem, *Long Distance II*

Death and Time

For Meg
(In Memory of Meg Sheffield 1940 – 1997)
Fleur Adcock

Half the things you did were too scary for me.
Skiing? No thanks. Riding? I've never learnt.
Canoeing? I'd be sure to tip myself out
and stagger home, ignominiously wet.
It was my son, that time in Kathmandu,
who galloped off with you to the temple at Bodnath
in a monsoon downpour, both of you on horses
from the King of Nepal's stables. Not me.

And as for the elephants – my God, the elephants!
How did you get me up on to one of those?
First they lay down; the way to climb aboard
was to walk up a gross leg, then straddle a sack
(that's all there was to sit on), while the creature
wobbled and swayed through the jungle for slow hours.
It felt like riding on the dome of St Paul's
in an earthquake. This was supposed to be a treat.

You and Alex and Maya, in her best sari,
sat beaming at the wildlife, you with your camera
proficiently clicking. You were pregnant at the time.
I clung with both hot hands to the bit of rope
that was all there was to cling to. The jungle steamed.
As soon as we were back in sight of the camp
I got off and walked through a river to reach it.
You laughed, but kindly. We couldn't all be like you.

Now you've done the scariest thing there is;
and all the king's horses, dear Meg, won't bring you back.

GLOSSARY

ignominiously: humiliatingly

monsoon: a seasonal wind of the Indian Ocean or the season in which it occurs

sari: a long flowing garment traditionally worn by women in India, Pakistan and other parts of Asia

proficiently: competently

Reading for Meaning

1. What is your impression of Meg and how does she differ from the poet?
2. What do we learn about Meg in the poem's final stanza?
3. (a) The tone and mood (see pages 156 and 163) of this poem change in the final stanza. Compare the tone and mood of the first three stanzas with the tone and mood of the last stanza.

   (b) How did this shift in tone and mood affect you as a reader?
4. The last line of the poem refers to a children's nursery rhyme. Why do you think Adcock made this reference?
5. 'This poem celebrates a life well lived, but also cries out for the loss of that life.' Explain how this statement describes *For Meg*.

Writer's Workshop

Essay: Although literature often deals with upsetting and dark subjects, it can help us to understand and work through difficult moments in life. Write an essay in which you discuss the importance of literature (writing or reading it) in people's lives.

Speaking and Listening

Listen to the Poet

- Go to www.poetryarchive.org and listen to Fleur Adcock introduce and then read *For Meg*.
- As a class, discuss Adcock's introduction. Do the details she offered change or add to the experience of reading the poem?

Links

Meg was clearly a vital, fun-loving individual; this makes her death even harder to bear. This poem can be linked to other texts in this book and elsewhere:

In this book: Bernard Farrell's *The Boy Soprano* (page 23)

Elsewhere: Roberto Benigni's much-loved film, *Life is Beautiful (La Vita è Bella)*

The Immortals

Rita Ann Higgins

The boy racers
quicken on the Spiddal road
in Barbie Pink souped-ups
or roulette red Honda Civics.
With few fault lines or face lifts to rev up about
only an unwritten come hither of thrills
with screeching propositions and no full stops –
if you are willing to ride the ride.

Hop you in filly in my passion wagon.
Loud music and cigarette butts are shafted into space.
We'll speed hump it all the way baby
look at me, look at me
I'm young, I'm immortal, I'm free.

Gemmas and Emmas
stick insects or supermodels
regulars at 'Be a Diva'
for the perfect nails
eyebrows to slice bread with
and landing strips to match.

They wear short lives
they dream of never slowing down-pours
while half syllable after half syllable
jerk from their peak capped idols lips.
Their skinny lovers melt into seats
made for bigger men
Look at me, look at me
I'm young, I'm immortal, I'm free.
The boy racers never grow older or fatter.

On headstones made from Italian marble
they become 'our loving son Keith'
'our beloved son Jonathan,' etcetera etcetera.
On the Spiddal road
itching to pass out the light
they become Zeus, Eros, Vulcan, Somnus

GLOSSARY

quicken: 1. become faster 2. become alive 3. stir up

souped-ups: made more powerful (particularly applies to modified cars)

roulette: a game of chance played using a spinning wheel with numbers in red and black

filly: girl (slang); formally it is a name for a young female horse

Zeus, Eros, Vulcan, Somnus: Greek and Roman gods: Zeus (supreme Greek god), Eros (Greek god of love), Vulcan (Roman god of fire), Somnus (Roman god of sleep)

Reading for Meaning

1. Describe the scene on the Spiddal Road that the poet portrays.
2. Do you think the poet is successful in capturing the energy and attitude of the 'immortals'?
3. The line, 'I'm young, I'm immortal, I'm free,' is repeated twice. Does the poet agree with this sentiment?
4. Do you think the poet is sympathetic or judgemental in her attitude to the young people described in the poem?

Language Lab

1. Look at the multiple meanings of the word 'quicken' in the glossary. Why do you think Rita Ann Higgins chose this word?
2. Why are the Honda Civics described as 'roulette red'?
3. (a) Why are the young men compared to gods in the final line?
   (b) What is significant about the particular gods (see glossary) that the poet has chosen to reference?

Style Guide

Irony: There are three main types of irony:

- **Dramatic irony:** when the audience knows something that the characters do not. For example, in Shakespeare's *Othello*, the audience knows that Othello's trusted 'friend' Iago is in fact a villain poisoning Othello's thoughts.
- **Situational irony:** when the outcome of a situation is very different from what was expected. For example, in *The Wizard of Oz*, the powerful wizard turns out to be an old man with no special powers hiding behind a curtain.
- **Verbal irony:** a statement which indicates the opposite is true. For example, in Rita Ann Higgins's *The Immortals*, the title is verbally ironic. The reader understands that the boy racers are anything but immortal. Their lives are likely to be cut short: 'They wear short lives' and 'never grow older.' The image of their headstones cements this idea and underlines the irony of the title. The use of irony allows Higgins to comment on the recklessness and arrogance of the boy racers.

Writer's Workshop

Describing the Crowd: In *The Immortals*, Rita Ann Higgins brilliantly depicts a crowd of people through well-chosen details and powerful language. Write a poem or descriptive composition that depicts a crowd of strangers. Try to look at the whole group rather than focussing intently on individuals.

Links

The Immortals looks at how some young people break rules and often take quite dangerous risks. This poem can be linked to other texts in this book and elsewhere:

In this book: 'They're Speakin' of Witchcraft' (extract from Arthur Miller's *The Crucible*, page 218)

Elsewhere: Rob Reiner's film, *Stand by Me*; Richard Kelly's film, *Donnie Darko*; search online for Graham Greene's short story, *The Destructors*

Ozymandias

Percy Bysshe Shelley

I met a traveller from an antique land

Who said: Two vast and trunkless legs of stone

Stand in the desert… Near them, on the sand,

Half sunk, a shattered visage lies, whose frown,

And wrinkled lip, and sneer of cold command,

Tell that its sculptor well those passions read

Which yet survive, stamped on these lifeless things,

The hand that mocked them, and the heart that fed:

And on the pedestal these words appear:

'My name is Ozymandias, king of kings:

Look on my works, ye Mighty, and despair!'

Nothing beside remains. Round the decay

Of that colossal wreck, boundless and bare

The lone and level sands stretch far away.

GLOSSARY
Ozymandias: another name for the Egyptian pharaoh, Ramses II
trunkless: without a body
antique: ancient
visage: face / appearance
colossal: huge / resembling Colossus (a huge bronze statute)

Reading for Meaning

1. What does the inscription on the pedestal suggest about the personality of Ozymandias?
2. Considering the setting of the poem, explain how there is great irony (see page 181) in the pedestal's inscription.
3. Explain what this poem has in common with a Shakespearian sonnet in terms of its structure and rhythm. Look back to pages 170–171 to help you.
4. What do you think is the theme of the poem?

Writer's Workshop

Diary: Imagine Ozymandias kept a diary. Basing your answer on the information in the poem, write a diary entry for the day the monument was completed.

Speaking and Listening

Learn and Recite: Memorise the poem *Ozymandias*. Your teacher will call on some students to recite it for the class. Be prepared to say the poem with emotion, emphasising and pausing at appropriate moments.

Links

No matter how great and powerful an individual may be, time and mortality eventually catch up with everyone. This poem can be linked to other texts in this book and elsewhere:
In this book: Sara Teasdales's poem, *There Will Come Soft Rains* (page 190)
Elsewhere: David Fincher's film, *The Curious Case of Benjamin Button*; search online for Shakespeare's sonnet, *Like as the waves make towards the pebbled shore*

A Modern World

The One Twenty Pub

Wisława Szymborska

(Translated by Dennis O'Driscoll)

The bomb is primed to go off at one twenty.
A time-check: one sixteen.
There's still a chance for some to join
the pub's ranks, for others to drop out.

The terrorist watches from across the street.
Distance will shield him
from the impact of what he sees:

A woman, turquoise jacket on her shoulder,
enters; a man with sunglasses departs.
Youths in tee-shirts loiter without intent.

One seventeen and four seconds.
The scrawny motorcyclist, revving up
to leave, won't believe his luck;
but the tall man steps straight in.

One seventeen and forty seconds.
That girl, over there with the walkman
– now the bus has cut her off.
One eighteen exactly.
Was she stupid enough to head inside?
Or wasn't she? We'll know before long,
when the dead are carried out.

It's one nineteen.
Nothing much to report
until a muddled barfly hesitates,
fumbles with his pockets, and, like
a blasted fool, stumbles back
at one nineteen and fifty seconds
to retrieve his goddamn cap.

One twenty
How time drags when…
Any moment now.

Not yet.
Yes.
    Yes,
        there
            it
                goes.

GLOSSARY
barfly: a person who spends a lot of time in bars

Reading for Meaning

1. (a) Describe the patrons who enter and exit the pub.
   (b) How does Wisława Szymborska show that these are very ordinary people?
   (c) Why do you think she chooses to emphasise their ordinariness?
2. The terrorist describes the motorcyclist as 'scrawny', the girl as 'stupid' and a man as a 'muddled barfly'. Why do you think the terrorist uses such negative words to describe the people?
3. Describe the attitude of the terrorist.
4. How does the poet build the tension in the poem?
5. This could be any pub, anywhere, at any time period. Why do you think the poet chooses not to identify a particular place, group of people or terrorist organisation?
6. The final four lines of the poem are placed in a slanting pattern on the page. What effect does this create?

Writer's Workshop

Speech: Write a speech with the following title: 'Violent terrorism solves nothing'.

Speaking and Listening

Research: Wisława Szymborska won the Nobel Prize for Literature in 1996.
Individually: Go to www.nobelprize.org. Read about her life and some of her other poems.
As a class: Discuss what you read. Which of her poems stands out for you? What did you learn about the poet as a person?

Links

This poem looks at the troubling fact that violence can often be found in the modern world. This poem can be linked to other texts in this book and elsewhere:
In this book: Lansing Lamont's *Testing the Bomb* (page 65)
Elsewhere: Peter Weir's film, *Witness*

The Fisherman

William Butler Yeats

Although I can see him still,
The freckled man who goes
To a grey place on a hill
In grey Connemara clothes
At dawn to cast his flies,
It's long since I began
To call up to the eyes
This wise and simple man.
All day I'd looked in the face
What I had hoped 'twould be
To write for my own race
And the reality;
The living men that I hate,
The dead man that I loved,
The craven man in his seat,
The insolent unreproved,
And no knave brought to book
Who has won a drunken cheer,
The witty man and his joke
Aimed at the commonest ear,
The clever man who cries
The catch-cries of the clown,
The beating down of the wise
And great Art beaten down.

Maybe a twelvemonth since
Suddenly I began,
In scorn of this audience,
Imagining a man,
And his sun-freckled face
And grey Connemara cloth,
Climbing up to a place
Where stone is dark under froth,
And the down-turn of his wrist
When the flies drop in the stream;
A man who does not exist,
A man who is but a dream;
And cried, 'Before I am old
I shall have written him one
Poem maybe as cold
And passionate as the dawn.'

GLOSSARY

'twould: it would

insolent: disrespectful

unreproved: not corrected

no knave brought to book: none of the dishonest rogues have been punished

catch-cries: expressions used to attract attention or gain support

in scorn of this audience: despite the audience of modern people (described in stanza 1)

Reading for Meaning

1. (a) Some readers comment that the fisherman in this poem is Yeats's image of an ideal Irishman. What qualities does the fisherman have that make him ideal?

   (b) Considering this, why do you think Yeats describes the fisherman as, 'A man who does not exist, / A man who is but a dream'?

2. In the second half of the first stanza, Yeats turns his attention away from the simple fisherman to 'the reality'. Describe his attitude to the reality of people in his society in 1919.

3. In *The Fisherman*, Yeats is reflecting about Ireland and Irishness. Do you think he is optimistic or pessimistic about Ireland? Explain your answer.

4. What do you understand by the poem's final four lines?

5. This poem was written in 1919. Do you think it is still relevant today? Why / why not?

Writer's Workshop

Video: Your class has decided to make a video to accompany the text of this poem. Describe what this video would look like. You may wish to refer to the images, music, colour, voiceover or any other feature of video. Refer to the poem throughout your answer.

Links ⟨⟩⟨⟩

In *The Fisherman*, Yeats asks questions about what it means to be Irish. This poem can be linked to other texts in this book and elsewhere:

In this book: Peter Cunningham's article, *Paddy's Day* (page 56)

Elsewhere: Search online for the short film, *Yu Ming is Ainm Dom*

Hotel Room, 12ᵗʰ Floor

Norman MacCaig

This morning I watched from here
a helicopter skirting like a damaged insect
the Empire State Building, that
jumbo size dentist's drill, and landing
on the roof of the PanAm skyscraper.
But now midnight has come in
from foreign places. Its uncivilised darkness
is shot at by a million lit windows, all
ups and acrosses.

But midnight is not
so easily defeated. I lie in bed, between
a radio and a television set, and hear
the wildest of warwhoops continually ululating through
the glittering canyons and gulches –
police cars and ambulances racing
to broken bones, the harsh screaming
from coldwater flats, the blood
glazed on the sidewalks.

The frontier is never
somewhere else. And no stockades
can keep the midnight out.

GLOSSARY
Empire State Building: a famous building in New York City
PanAm: an American airline
ululating: howling or wailing
canyon: deep valley
gulches: ravines; steep valleys
stockades: wooden fortresses

Language Lab

1. Norman MacCaig uses similes and metaphors (see Chapter 4, page 95) to great effect in this poem. Write down one simile and one metaphor from the first stanza and comment on their effectiveness.

2. (a) The poet brings the city to life by appealing to the senses. Find three examples where the poet makes use of sound in his description of the city.

   (b) Do you think the sounds the speaker hears are real or are they his imagined fears?

Reading for Meaning

1. (a) *Hotel Room, 12th Floor* contains a number of violent images and references to the wild west. Identify three examples of this.

   (b) What do these references say about the poet's impression of New York?

2. Midnight is referred to in all three stanzas. What do you think midnight represents in the poem?

3. The words 'no' and 'never' in the final stanza indicate that a strong conclusion has been reached. What conclusion do you think the speaker comes to in this poem?

Writer's Workshop

Visual Collage: Create a visual representation of this poem using images (printed or drawn by you). Include lines from the poem in your collage. Try to capture the main ideas and emotions in the poem.

Links

The city setting is a major feature of *Hotel Room, 12th Floor*. In terms of its urban setting, this poem can be linked to other texts in this book and elsewhere:

In this book: Steven Roe's photograph, *Seoul, North Korea* (page 246)

Elsewhere: Jim Sheridan's film, *In America*

Nature and Animals

There Will Come Soft Rains

Sara Teasdale

There will come soft rains and the smell of the ground,
And swallows circling with their shimmering sound;

And frogs in the pools singing at night,
And wild plum trees in tremulous white,

Robins will wear their feathery fire
Whistling their whims on a low fence-wire;

And not one will know of the war, not one
Will care at last when it is done.

Not one would mind, neither bird nor tree
If mankind perished utterly;

And Spring herself, when she woke at dawn,
Would scarcely know that we were gone.

GLOSSARY
tremulous: quivering
whims: a sudden impulse or thought
perished: died

Reading for Meaning

1. What type of atmosphere is created in the first three stanzas?
2. Why do you think the poet doesn't mention 'the war' until the fourth stanza?
3. According to the poem, what would the world be like if 'mankind perished utterly'?
4. Although it is not stated directly, what do you think the poet's view of humanity is?
5. Why do you think the poet chose the title, *There Will Come Soft Rains*?
6. Do you think this is a pessimistic or optimistic poem?

Language Lab

1. This poem contains attractive and pleasing imagery. Choose two images that you find appealing and explain why you find them so.
2. (a) Write down two examples of alliteration (page 176) from the poem.
   (b) What effect does the use of alliteration have?
3. (a) Where does Sara Teasdale use personification (see Chapter 4, page 95) in *There Will Come Soft Rains*?
   (b) What effect does this have?

Speaking and Listening

Short Story: Ray Bradbury wrote a short story based on this poem also called *There Will Come Soft Rains*.

To listen to a reading of this story, go to www.mentorbooks.ie/resources and then look in the TY English section. Alternatively, you may find this reading on YouTube.

Short Film: Directed by Paul Cotter, this short film (5 mins) is based on Ray Bradbury's short story.

To watch this film, go to www.mentorbooks.ie/resources and then look in the TY English section. Alternatively, you may find this film on YouTube.

1. Listen to the short story or watch the short film inspired by this poem.
2. Discuss these adaptations as a class.
3. Do you think these adaptations effectively capture the theme of Teasdale's poem?

Writer's Workshop

Short Story: As you can see in the Speaking and Listening task above, the poem *There Will Come Soft Rains* has inspired other artists to create their own work. Choose another poem from this book and write your own short story inspired by the poem.

Links

Humanity's capacity for self-destruction is a key concern of Teasdale's poem. This poem can be linked to other texts in this book and elsewhere:

In this book: Lansing Lamont's *Testing the Bomb* (page 65)
Elsewhere: David Mitchell's novel, *Cloud Atlas*

Another Feeling

Ruth Stone

Once you saw a drove of young pigs

crossing the highway. One of them

pulling his body by the front feet,

the hind legs dragging flat.

Without thinking,

you called the Humane Society.

They came with a net and went for him.

They were matter of fact, uniformed;

there were two of them,

their truck ominous, with a cage.

He was hiding in the weeds. It was then

you saw his eyes. He understood.

He was trembling.

After they took him, you began to suffer regret.

Years later, you remember his misfit body

scrambling to reach the others.

Even at this moment, your heart

is going too fast; your hands sweat.

Speaking and Listening

Group Reading

- Read this poem as a class group.
- Taking turns, members of your class should read a line or phrase from the poem.
- You should read until you come to a punctuation mark (comma, full stop or dash) and then allow someone else to read.
- Some class members may need to read more than once.
- It is important to listen so that you know when it is your turn to read.

Reading for Meaning

1. Why do you think the person in the poem 'began to suffer regret'?
2. Do you agree that the 'Humane Society' is presented negatively?
3. How does the reader know that the memory of what happened to the pig is a disturbing one?
4. Why do you think this poem is written in the second person ('you') rather than the first person ('I')?
5. In life it is often difficult to work out what is the right thing to do. How does this poem show that our moral choices are not always clear and obvious?

Writer's Workshop

Composition / Poem: In *Another Feeling*, the speaker describes a feeling of regret and guilt about a decision that was made. Write a poem or a composition that deals with the idea of regret.

Links

Concern for animals is a central theme of *Another Feeling*. This poem can be linked to other texts in this book and elsewhere:

In this book: Romesh Ranganathan's article, *Zoos are Prisons for Animals* (page 47)

Elsewhere: Richard Adams's novel, *Watership Down;* John Montague's poem, *Killing the Pig*

Mushrooms

Sylvia Plath

Overnight, very
Whitely, discreetly,
Very quietly

Our toes, our noses
Take hold on the loam,
Acquire the air.

Nobody sees us,
Stops us, betrays us;
The small grains make room.

Soft fists insist on
Heaving the needles,
The leafy bedding,

Even the paving.
Our hammers, our rams,
Earless and eyeless,

Perfectly voiceless,
Widen the crannies,
Shoulder through holes. We

Diet on water,
On crumbs of shadow,
Bland-mannered, asking

Little or nothing.
So many of us!
So many of us!

We are shelves, we are
Tables, we are meek,
We are edible,

Nudgers and shovers
In spite of ourselves.
Our kind multiplies:

We shall by morning
Inherit the earth.
Our foot's in the door.

GLOSSARY
loam: rich soil
meek: submissive / weak and compliant
Inherit the earth: an allusion to Psalm 37 from the King
    James Bible: 'the meek shall inherit the earth'

Reading for Meaning

1. (a) How are the mushrooms portrayed as powerful in this poem?
   (b) How are the mushrooms depicted as vulnerable?
   (c) Which of the mushrooms' qualities do you feel is stressed more, their power or their vulnerability?
2. Who do you think the mushrooms are supposed to represent?
3. 'The mushrooms in this poem are portrayed as persistent and vaguely menacing.' Do you agree with this statement?
4. In your view, what is the theme of this poem?

Style Guide

Assonance: Assonance is the repetition of vowel sounds in neighbouring words. It is often found in poetry, advertising slogans, song lyrics – particularly rap music. As with alliteration (see page 176) it is the sounds, not the letters that are important. Look at the following examples:

- **Slogan:** It beats…as it sweeps…as it cleans – 1950s advertising slogan for Hoover Vacuum Cleaners
- **Proverb:** The early bird catches the worm
- **Poetry:** So twice five miles of fertile ground / With walls and towers were girdled round – from *Kubla Khan* by Samuel Taylor Coleridge

Mushrooms (see Language Lab below) contains many examples of assonance which give the poem a musical quality.

Language Lab

1. (a) In *Mushrooms*, Sylvia Plath makes much use of assonance (see Style Guide above), e.g. 'fists insist' and 'our toes, our noses / Take hold on the loam'. Find two more examples of this in the poem.
   (b) Do you agree that the use of assonance adds a pleasing quality to the poem?
2. The poet uses personification to give the mushrooms human qualities. Find three examples of this in the poem.
3. (a) Write down two phrases from the poem that you feel accurately capture the idea of mushrooms.
   (b) Explain how these phrases effectively portray mushrooms.

Writer's Workshop

Personification in Poetry: Sylvia Plath makes great use of personification (see Chapter 4, page 95) in *Mushrooms*. Write your own poem from the perspective of an object or something from nature. Make use of personification in your poem.

At the Bomb Testing Site
William Stafford

At noon in the desert a panting lizard
waited for history, its elbows tense,
watching the curve of a particular road
as if something might happen.

It was looking at something farther off
than people could see, an important scene
acted in stone for little selves
at the flute end of consequences.

There was just a continent without much on it
under a sky that never cared less.
Ready for a change, the elbows waited.
The hands gripped hard on the desert.

Reading for Meaning

1. How important is the title of this poem?
2. How does William Stafford create an air of tension and expectancy in the poem?
3. (a) The poet gives the lizard some human qualities. Find an example of this.
    (b) What effect does this have on the reader?
4. What do you think the poet means when he says, 'little selves / at the flute end of consequences'?
5. What point is William Stafford making about humanity?

Writer's Workshop

What Happened Next? Echoing William Stafford's style, write a fourth stanza for this poem.

Speaking and Listening

Debate: As a class debate the following motion: 'Humanity has little respect for the environment and the creatures that live in it'. Go to Chapter 6, pages 212–214 for tips about how to organise a debate.

Links

Humanity's capacity for destruction is a central focus of this poem. This poem can be linked to other texts in this book and elsewhere:
In this book: Lansing Lamont's, *Testing the Bomb* (page 65)
Elsewhere: Davis Guggenheim's documentary, *An Inconvenient Truth*

POETRY PROJECTS

Project 1: An Anthology of the Class's Work

Task
- As a class, your task is to create an anthology of the class's poems.
- Each student in the class must compose a poem to be included in the anthology.
- Each student must write a short introduction to another person's poem.

Guidelines
- Set a date for the submission of the poems.
- Consider having a theme for your anthology (maybe: transition, identity, the future etc.)
- Decide who should write the introductions for which poems.
- You may want to appoint an editor, design team, production team, chairperson (for meetings), secretary (for meetings).

Project 2: Study of a Poet

This project allows you to independently explore a poet's work. The poems you include in your project will say something about you. To complete this project, you will need access to the internet.

Task

Choose a poet (from this book or elsewhere) that you find interesting and write a report on that poet.

Project Guidelines
Your study should contain all of the following:
- A short **biography** of the poet. Where is the poet from? Has his/her life been interesting, unusual or controversial? Has the poet won any major awards?
- An **anthology** of four or five poems by the poet that you found interesting. These will be printed from the internet, photocopied from books or copied from other sources.
- An **overview** of the poet's work. Look at the themes the poet explores, interesting stylistic features and the poet's subject matter.
- A **personal response** to one poem. Write an in-depth response to one poem. You may wish to discuss the poem's theme, subject matter, imagery, language, emotions, mood, tone or any other features you find interesting.
- A **bibliography**. This is a list of all the books and websites that you used while writing this project.

Research Guidelines
- To get you started, some website addresses have been suggested below. These contain helpful information about many poets and samples of their work.
- Do not rely solely on the websites listed here. You will need to visit other websites, use the library or find books at home to complete your study.
- Keep a list of every website you visit for your bibliography (see above).
- **Plagiarism:** This is when you claim somebody else's work is your own. It is important that you do not plagiarise. Use the internet to find information and ideas, but these must be expressed in your own words.

Helpful Websites
The following websites contain useful information and anthologise thousands of poems.
> www.poetryireland.ie
> www.poetryarchive.org
> www.poets.org
> www.poetryfoundation.org
> www.poetsgraves.co.uk

Chapter 6:
Say It Out Loud – Speeches, Debating and Drama

Most of the texts that you have explored in this book live only on the page. However, some texts are written to be said out loud, to be performed.

This chapter is divided into three sections: Speeches, Debating and Drama. These are some of the oldest forms of literature. The Ancient Greeks valued the power of oratory (the art of public speaking) as well as the importance of staged drama. Speeches, debates and drama take the focus of language but combine it with performance, so that meaning is offered not just through the words, but also by the performer who breathes life into them.

In this chapter you will hopefully come to appreciate these art forms and even be encouraged to perform yourself.

Gerald sensed that more than just his reputation was riding on the success of the presentation.

Speeches

Whether it is in the political world, at a wedding, at an award ceremony, at a press conference, during a debate or at school, public speaking is a vital part of life today. In this section, you will explore the language and style of speech writing. To start we should look at speech openings.

Speech Openings

There are many ways to begin a speech. However, a strong lively opening will grab the audience's interest. Unfortunately, some speech-makers start in a manner that is dull and fails to excite or interest the audience. For example, the opening line, 'Thank you so much for that kind introduction. I have been really looking forward to the opportunity to talk to you all…' lacks flair, energy or bite. A good speech opening should hook the audience. Many speakers begin with something that is amusing, shocking, imaginative or personal.

A strong speech opening may:

- include a quotation
- ask a question of the audience
- tell an anecdote (see Chapter 1, page 9)
- be deeply personal
- shock the audience

Reading for Meaning

Take a look at the following speech openings and explain why they could be considered effective ways of beginning a speech:

(a) I want to ask you a question: how many of you have ever dreamed of a world without poverty, a world where everybody has enough? I am here today to tell you that this dream can become a reality.

(b) Sadly, in the next ten minutes, one species on planet Earth will become extinct. In the twenty minutes I spend talking to you, two species will cease to exist. By this time tomorrow one hundred and fifty more will have disappeared. By this day next year, it will be about 55,000.

(c) James Dean once said, 'I can't change the direction of the wind, but I can adjust my sails to always reach my destination.'

(d) Unlike most of you here today, I was not born in a hospital. There were no doctors when I came into this wold; there were no nurses, no anaesthetic, no sterile sheets. There were no teddy bears nor balloons, no congratulation cards nor visiting relatives. When I was born, the sky was lit up by scud missiles and my mother's labour screams couldn't compete with the roar of gunfire. For I was born in a warzone.

(e) The factory owner Henry Ford hired an expert to go through his plant. He said, 'Find the non-productive people. Tell me who they are, and I will fire them!'

After surveying the whole factory, the expert returned to Ford's office. 'I've found a problem with one of your administrators,' he said. 'Every time I walked by, he was sitting with his feet propped up on the desk. The man never does a thing. I definitely think you should consider getting rid of him!'

When Henry Ford learned the name of the man the expert was referring to, Ford shook his head and said, 'I can't fire him. I pay that man to do nothing but think – and that's what he's doing.'

I am here today to talk to you about the importance of deep thinkers.

Writer's Workshop

Openings: You have been asked to write a speech about the experience of being a teenager in Ireland today. Using what you have learned about speech openings, write three different openings to your speech. Make use of the five opening techniques described on the previous page.

The Language of Speeches

Successful speeches are carefully crafted to win over the audience. Speech-writers use language that strengthens their arguments, persuades or entertains. The following language devices are commonly found in speeches. You should refer back to this list when analysing speeches and when writing your own.

- **Rhetorical questions:** These are questions in which the answer is already implied. They are used to make a statement. For example, instead of the statement, 'I don't believe that,' a rhetorical question can be used: 'Do you expect me to believe that?' Asking questions of an audience is an effective and persuasive tool when making speeches and debating.
- **Repetition:** This can help to emphasise a point.
- **Hyperbole (exaggeration):** Used appropriately, exaggeration can stir an audience.
- **Humour:** When it is suitable, a joke can help to entertain and win over a crowd.
- **Identification with the audience:** Sometimes speakers may want to identify with the crowd. Speakers, therefore, often say 'we' to include the audience in the speech. The speaker may also use references or place names known to the audience.
- **Metaphor:** Metaphorical language can add colour to a speech. Look at Martin Luther King's Freedom's Ring (I Have a Dream) speech on pages 207–209 for an excellent example of this.
- **Anecdote/Illustration:** Sometimes an idea may need an example to bring it to life or to make a point more relevant. Speech-writers often use an anecdote to illustrate a point.
- **Facts:** It is difficult to argue with hard facts; they help to strengthen a point.
- **Emotive language:** Language that stirs the emotions may help to rouse an audience. For example, a speech about animal rights may use emotive language to evoke sympathy in the audience: 'These helpless animals are subjected to torture on a daily basis.'
- **Anticipatory statements:** By predicting the counter-argument and dismissing it, a speaker can deal with any potential opposition to their ideas.

One Pen Can Change the World

Malala Yousafzai

Malala Yousafzai is the youngest ever Nobel Prize recipient. She became a political activist at the age of eleven when she began writing a blog about life under the Taliban in Pakistan. A documentary was later made about her and she became famous following a number of interviews with her in the media. When she was 15, a Taliban gunman boarded her school bus, asked for her by name and shot her in the head. Yousafzai survived and became a world-famous advocate for education and women's rights.

The text below is from the speech that Malala Yousafzai gave to the United Nations on 12 July 2013, the date of her 16th birthday and 'Malala Day' at the UN.

Dear friends, on 9 October 2012, the Taliban shot me on the left side of my forehead. They shot my friends, too. They thought that the bullets would silence us, but they failed. And out of that silence came thousands of voices. The terrorists thought they would change my aims and stop my ambitions. But nothing changed in my life except this: weakness, fear and hopelessness died. Strength, power and courage were born.

I am the same Malala. My ambitions are the same. My hopes are the same. And my dreams are the same. Dear sisters and brothers, I am not against anyone. Neither am I here to speak in terms of personal revenge against the Taliban or any other terrorist group. I am here to speak for the right of education for every child. I want education for the sons and daughters of the Taliban and all the terrorists and extremists. I do not even hate the Talib who shot me. Even if there was a gun in my hand and he was standing in front of me, I would not shoot him.

Dear sisters and brothers, we realise the importance of light when we see darkness. We realise the importance of our voice when we are silenced. In the same way, when we were in Swat, the north of Pakistan, we realised the importance of pens and books when we saw the guns. The wise saying, 'The pen is mightier than the sword;' it is true. The extremists are afraid of books and pens. The power of education frightens them. They are afraid of women. The power of the voice of women frightens them. This is why they killed fourteen innocent students in the recent attack in Quetta. And that is why they kill female teachers. That is why they are blasting schools every day because they were, and they are, afraid of change and equality that we will bring to our society. And I remember that there was a boy in our school who was asked by a journalist why are

201

the Taliban against education? He answered very simply by pointing to his book, he said, 'A Talib doesn't know what is written inside this book.'

Today I am focusing on women's rights and girls' education because they are suffering the most. We call upon all governments to ensure free, compulsory education all over the world for every child. We call upon all the governments to fight against terrorism and violence. To protect children from brutality and harm. We call upon the developed nations to support the expansion of education opportunities for girls in the developing world. We call upon all communities to be tolerant, to reject prejudice based on caste, creed, sect, colour, religion or agenda to ensure freedom and equality for women so they can flourish. We cannot all succeed when half of us are held back. We call upon our sisters around the world to be brave, to embrace the strength within themselves and realise their full potential.

Dear brothers and sisters, we want schools and education for every child's bright future. We will continue our journey to our destination of peace and education. No one can stop us. We will speak up for our rights and we will bring change to our voice. We believe in the power and the strength of our words. Our words can change the whole world because we are all together, united for the cause of education. And if we want to achieve our goal, then let us empower ourselves with the weapon of knowledge and let us shield ourselves with unity and togetherness.

Dear brothers and sisters, we must not forget that millions of people are suffering from poverty and injustice and ignorance. We must not forget that millions of children are out of their schools. We must not forget that our sisters and brothers are waiting for a bright, peaceful future.

So let us wage a global struggle against illiteracy, poverty and terrorism; let us pick up our books and our pens; they are the most powerful weapons. One child, one teacher, one book and one pen can change the world. Education is the only solution. Education first.

Reading for Meaning

1. What is your impression of Malala Yousafzai from this speech?
2. What do you think is the main message of this speech?
3. This speech refers to a boy who was questioned about the Taliban by a journalist.
   (a) What did the boy say?
   (b) What do you think the boy meant by this comment?
4. Do you agree with Yousafzai that 'the pen is mightier than the sword'? Why / why not?

Language Lab

1. How does Malala Yousafzai try to connect with the audience in her speech?
2. (a) Write down two examples of repetition in this speech.
   (b) What effect does this have on the listeners?
3. Yousafzai uses a number of contrasts in the opening paragraph, for example: 'out of that silence came thousands of voices.' Why do you think she uses these contrasts in her speech?

Style Guide

Rousing / Stirring Language: Often the function of a speech is to appeal to people's hearts. Speech-writers therefore commonly use language that stirs the audience emotionally. This is true of this speech by Malala Yousafzai. She uses stirring phrases such as, 'But nothing changed in my life except this: weakness, fear and hopelessness died. Strength, power and courage were born' and 'One child, one teacher, one book and one pen can change the world.' Powerful, emotive phrases like this will resonate with the audience and encourage them to agree with the speech's message.

Speaking and Listening

Watch the Speaker: Watch Malala Yousafzai deliver this powerful speech to the UN (17 mins) by going to www.mentorbooks.ie/resources and then look in the TY English section. Alternatively, you can watch Malala Yousafzai deliver this speech on YouTube.

Writer's Workshop

Research Report: Malala Yousafzai is a celebrated advocate for human rights. Using the internet, find out more about her. Present a report on her life and her achievements.

Links

It is upsetting to confront the reality that sometimes children are the victims of war and political violence. This speech can be linked to other texts in this book and elsewhere:
In this book: Michael Morpurgo's short story, *No Trumpets Needed* (page 112)
Elsewhere: Search online for Rosita Boland's poem, *Butterflies*

A Call for Revolution (from *Animal Farm*)

George Orwell

George Orwell's novel *Animal Farm* is an allegory (symbolic story) for the communist revolution that happened in Russia early in the twentieth century. In this stirring speech from the book, an old pig called Major calls on the other animals to rise up against the farmer and take control of the farm.

'I do not think, comrades, that I shall be with you for many months longer, and before I die, I feel it my duty to pass on to you such wisdom as I have acquired. I have had a long life, I have had much time for thought as I lay alone in my stall, and I think I may say that I understand the nature of life on this earth as well as any animal now living. It is about this that I wish to speak to you.

'Now, comrades, what is the nature of this life of ours? Let us face it: our lives are miserable, laborious, and short. We are born, we are given just so much food as will keep the breath in our bodies, and those of us who are capable of it are forced to work to the last atom of our strength; and the very instant that our usefulness has come to an end we are slaughtered with hideous cruelty. No animal in England knows the meaning of happiness or leisure after he is a year old. No animal in England is free. The life of an animal is misery and slavery: that is the plain truth.

'But is this simply part of the order of nature? Is it because this land of ours is so poor that it cannot afford a decent life to those who dwell upon it? No, comrades, a thousand times no! The soil of England is fertile, its climate is good, it is capable of affording food in abundance to an enormously greater number of animals than now inhabit it. This single farm of ours would support a dozen horses, twenty cows, hundreds of sheep – and all of them living in a comfort and a dignity that are now almost beyond our imagining. Why then do we continue in this miserable condition? Because nearly the whole of the produce of our labour is stolen from us by human beings. There, comrades, is the answer to all our problems. It is summed up in a single word – Man. Man is the only real enemy we have. Remove Man from the scene, and the root cause of hunger and overwork is abolished for ever.

'Man is the only creature that consumes without producing. He does not give milk, he does not lay eggs, he is too weak to pull the plough, he cannot run fast enough to catch rabbits. Yet he is lord of all the animals. He sets them to work, he gives back to them the bare minimum that will prevent them from starving, and the rest he keeps for himself. Our labour tills the soil, our dung fertilises it, and yet there is not one of us that owns more than his bare skin. You cows that I see before me, how many thousands of gallons of milk have you given during this last year? And what has happened to that milk which should have been breeding up sturdy calves? Every drop of it has gone down the throats of our enemies. And you hens, how many eggs have you laid in this last year, and how many of those eggs ever hatched into chickens? The rest have all gone to market to bring in money for Jones and his men.

'And even the miserable lives we lead are not allowed to reach their natural span ... no animal escapes the cruel knife in the end. You young porkers who are sitting in front of me, every one of you will scream your lives out at the block within a year. To that horror we all must come – cows, pigs, hens, sheep, everyone. Even the horses and the dogs have no better fate. You, Boxer, the very day that those great muscles of yours lose their power, Jones will sell you to the knacker, who will cut your throat and boil you down for the foxhounds. As for the dogs, when they grow old and toothless, Jones ties a brick round their necks and drowns them in the nearest pond.

'Is it not crystal clear, then, comrades, that all the evils of this life of ours spring from the tyranny of human beings? Only get rid of Man, and the produce of our labour would be our own. Almost overnight we could become rich and free. What then must we do? Why, work night and day, body and soul, for the overthrow of the human race! That is my message to you, comrades: Rebellion! I do not know when that Rebellion will come, it might be in a week or in a hundred years, but I know, as surely as I see this straw beneath my feet, that sooner or later justice will be done. Fix your eyes on that, comrades, throughout the short remainder of your lives! And above all, pass on this message of mine to those who come after you, so that future generations shall carry on the struggle until it is victorious.

'Among us animals let there be perfect unity, perfect comradeship in the struggle. All men are enemies. All animals are comrades. I have little more to say. I merely repeat, remember always your duty of enmity towards Man and all his ways. Whatever goes upon two legs is an enemy. Whatever goes upon four legs, or has wings, is a friend.'

GLOSSARY
laborious: involving much work or effort
tills: prepares land for ploughing
Boxer: a horse in the story
produce: agricultural products
enmity: hostility, feud

Reading for Meaning

1. According to Major, what is life like for the animals?
2. What evidence does Major offer to suggest that human beings are useless?
3. What does Major propose that the animals should do to improve their own lives?
4. If you were one of the animals, how do you think you would feel listening to this speech?

Language Lab

1. (a) Find examples of emotive language in this speech that stirs the listener emotionally.
   (b) Do you think this type of language is effective?

2. (a) How does Major try to shock or scare the other animals?

    (b) Why do you think he does this?

3. (a) Major uses questions in his speech. Write down three examples.

    (b) What effect does his use of questions have?

4. There are a number of interesting words used in this speech.

    (a) Using a dictionary, find the meanings of the following words from the text:

comrades	fertile	sturdy
laborious	abundance	knacker
dwell	abolished	tyranny

    (b) For each, write a sentence that includes the word.

Writer's Workshop

What Happens Next? Imagine that the other animals meet after hearing Major's speech to discuss what they have heard. Write the scene that takes place. Make use of dialogue in your writing.

I Have a Dream

Martin Luther King

Dr Martin Luther King made this impassioned speech at an American civil rights rally in Washington D.C. in 1963. Five years later he was assassinated. Martin Luther King was a Baptist preacher who called for a peaceful, equal and respectful coexistence between all races. He won the Nobel Peace Prize the year after he made this speech. Today he stands as a symbol for civil rights and Americans celebrate his contribution to society on Martin Luther King Day which falls on the third Monday of each January.

Five score years ago, a great American, in whose symbolic shadow we stand today signed the Emancipation Proclamation. This momentous decree came as a great beacon of light of hope to millions of Negro slaves, who had been seared in the flames of withering injustice. It came as a joyous daybreak to end the long night of captivity.

But one hundred years later, we must face the tragic fact that the Negro still is not free. One hundred years later, the life of the Negro is still sadly crippled by the manacles of segregation and the chains of discrimination. One hundred years later, the Negro lives on a lonely island of poverty in the midst of a vast ocean of material prosperity. One hundred years later, the Negro is still languishing in the corners of American society and finds himself an exile in his own land. And so we've come here today to dramatise a shameful condition. In a sense we have come to our nation's capital to cash a cheque. When the architects of our republic wrote the magnificent words of the Constitution and the Declaration of Independence, they were signing a promissory note to which every American was to fall heir. This note was a promise that all men, yes, black men as well as white men, would be guaranteed the unalienable rights of life, liberty, and the pursuit of happiness. It is obvious today that America has defaulted on this promissory note, insofar as her citizens of colour are concerned. Instead of honouring this sacred obligation, America has given the Negro people a bad cheque, a cheque which has come back marked 'insufficient funds'.

But we refuse to believe that the bank of justice is bankrupt. We refuse to believe that there are insufficient funds in the great vaults of opportunity of this nation. And so we have come to cash this cheque, a cheque that will give us upon demand the riches of freedom and the security of justice.

We have also come to this hallowed spot to remind America of the fierce urgency of Now. This is no time to engage in the luxury of cooling off or to take the tranquillising drug of gradualism. Now is the time to make real the promises of democracy. Now is the time to rise from the dark and desolate valley of segregation to the sunlit path of racial justice. Now is the time to lift our nation from the quicksands of racial injustice to the solid rock of brotherhood. Now is the time to make justice a reality for all of God's children.

. . . Now is the time to make real the promises of democracy.

It would be fatal for the nation to overlook the urgency of the moment. This sweltering summer of the Negro's legitimate discontent will not pass until there is an invigorating autumn of freedom and equality. 1963 is not an end but a beginning. Those who hope that the Negro needed to blow off steam and will now be content will have a rude awakening if the nation returns to business as usual. There will be neither rest nor tranquillity in America until the Negro is granted his citizenship rights. The whirlwinds of revolt will continue to shake the foundations of our nation until the bright days of justice emerges.

And that is something that I must say to my people who stand on the warm threshold which leads into the palace of justice. In the process of gaining our rightful place we must not be guilty of wrongful deeds. Let us not seek to satisfy our thirst for freedom by drinking from the cup of bitterness and hatred. We must ever conduct our struggle on the high plane of dignity and discipline. We must not allow our creative protest to degenerate into physical violence. Again and again we must rise to the majestic heights of meeting physical force with soul force.

The marvellous new militancy which has engulfed the Negro community must not lead us to distrust all white people, for many of our white brothers, as evidenced by their presence here today, have come to realize that their destiny is tied up with our destiny. And they have come to realize that their freedom is inextricably bound to our freedom. We cannot walk alone.

And as we walk, we must make the pledge that we shall always march ahead. We cannot turn back. There are those who are asking the devotees of civil rights, 'When will you be satisfied?' We can never be satisfied as long as the Negro is the victim of the unspeakable horrors of police brutality. We can never be satisfied as long as our bodies, heavy with the fatigue of travel, cannot gain lodging in the motels of the highways and the hotels of the cities . . . We cannot be satisfied as long as a Negro in Mississippi cannot vote and a Negro in New York believes he has nothing for which to vote. No, no, we are not satisfied and we will not be satisfied until justice rolls down like waters and righteousness like a mighty stream.

I am not unmindful that some of you have come here out of great trials and tribulations. Some of you have come fresh from narrow jail cells. Some of you have come from areas where your quest for freedom left you battered by the storms of persecutions and staggered by the winds of police brutality.

You have been the veterans of creative suffering. Continue to work with the faith that unearned suffering is redemptive. Go back to Mississippi, go back to Alabama, go back to South Carolina, go back to Georgia, go back to Louisiana, go back to the slums and ghettos of our northern cities, knowing that somehow this situation can and will be changed. Let us not wallow in the valley of despair. I say to you today, my friends, even though we face the difficulties of today and tomorrow, I still have a dream. It is a dream deeply rooted in the American dream.

I have a dream that one day this nation will rise up and live out the true meaning of its creed: We hold these truths to be self-evident that all men are created equal.

I have a dream that one day on the red hills of Georgia the sons of former slaves and the sons of former slave owners will be able to sit down together at the table of brotherhood. I have a dream that one day even the state of Mississippi, a state sweltering with the heat of injustice, sweltering with the heat of oppression, will be transformed into an oasis of freedom and justice.

I have a dream that my four little children will one day live in a nation where they will not be judged by the colour of their skin but by the content of their character. I have a dream today!

I have a dream that one day, down in Alabama, with its vicious racists, with its governor having his lips dripping with the words of interposition and nullification; one day right down in Alabama little black boys and black girls will be able to join hands with little white boys and white girls as sisters and brothers. I have a dream today!

I have a dream that one day every valley shall be exalted, and every hill and mountain shall be made low, the rough places will be made plain, and the crooked places will be made straight, and the glory of the Lord shall be revealed and all flesh shall see it together.

This is our hope. This is the faith that I will go back to the South with. With this faith we will be able to hew out of the mountain of despair a stone of hope. With this faith we will be able to transform the jangling discords of our nation into a beautiful symphony of brotherhood. With this faith we will be able to work together, to pray together, to struggle together, to go to jail together, to stand up for freedom together, knowing that we will be free one day. And this will be the day, this will be the day when all of God's children will be able to sing with new meaning, 'My country 'tis of thee, sweet land of liberty, of thee I sing. Land where my fathers died, land of the Pilgrim's pride, from every mountainside, let freedom ring!' And if America is to be a great nation, this must become true.

And so let freedom ring from the prodigious hilltops of New Hampshire.

Let freedom ring from the mighty mountains of New York.

Let freedom ring from the heightening Alleghenies of Pennsylvania.

Let freedom ring from the snow-capped Rockies of Colorado.

Let freedom ring from the curvaceous slopes of California.

But not only that. Let freedom ring from Stone Mountain of Georgia.

Let freedom ring from Lookout Mountain of Tennessee.

Let freedom ring from every hill and molehill of Mississippi, from every mountainside, let freedom ring!

And when this happens, when we allow freedom to ring, when we let it ring from every village and every hamlet, from every state and every city, we will be able to speed up that day when all of God's children, black men and white men, Jews and Gentiles, Protestants and Catholics, will be able to join hands and sing in the words of the old Negro spiritual, 'Free at last, free at last. Thank God Almighty, we are free at last.'

– Washington D.C., 28 August 1963

Speaking and Listening

Watch the Speaker: Watch Martin Luther King deliver this rousing speech (6 mins) by going to www.mentorbooks.ie/resources and then looking in the TY English section. Alternatively, you can watch Dr King deliver this speech on YouTube.

Discuss: In groups, discuss Martin Luther King's delivery of this speech.
● Does the manner in which Dr King speaks add to the power of the speech?
● Comment on his use of pauses as he delivers this speech.
● Which moments of this speech stand out for you? What makes them stand out?

Reading for Meaning

1. What is Martin Luther King's message in this speech?
2. What kind of relationship does King want to see between black and white people?
3. How does Martin Luther King identify with the audience?
4. What effect does this speech have on you? Do you find it thought provoking / moving / powerful?

Language Lab

1. (a) Repetition is used to great effect in this speech. Identify two examples of this.
   (b) What effect does King's use of repetition have on the listener?
2. (a) This speech employs a number of striking metaphors. Identify two examples of metaphorical language in this speech.
   (b) Do you feel that these metaphors are effective?
3. Choose a phrase that you felt was particularly stirring or striking from this speech. Explain why you found this phrase interesting.

Style Guide

Extended Metaphor: We have already seen how metaphor is a type of comparison often found in literature. When a metaphor is developed or sustained in a piece of writing, we call it an **extended metaphor**.

Martin Luther King uses extended metaphor masterfully in this speech. For example, he tells the audience that 'we have come to our nation's capital to cash a cheque', a 'promissory note' for equal rights. King then extends this metaphor: 'America has given the Negro people a bad cheque, a cheque which has come back marked "insufficient funds."' This metaphor is a sustained one, drawing attention to the fact that black Americans have been denied a promise of equality and liberty. King concludes this extended metaphor with the stirring image: 'But we refuse to believe that the bank of justice is bankrupt. We refuse to believe that there are insufficient funds in the great vaults of opportunity of this nation. And so we have come to cash this cheque, a cheque that will give us upon demand the riches of freedom and the security of justice.'

Writer's Workshop

Report: Research Martin Luther King online and present a report on what you have learned. Use a number of websites to find information. The website www.nobelprize.org is a helpful starting point.

Links

In this moving speech, Martin Luther King calls for a change to the structure of society so that all people are treated equally. This speech can be linked to other texts in this book and elsewhere:

In this book: George Orwell's *A Call for Revolution* (from *Animal Farm*, page 204)
Elsewhere: Ava DuVernay's film, *Selma*

Delivering a Speech

This chapter has explored the different techniques speech-writers employ to convey a message. However, we shouldn't forget that a speech is a live experience and more than just the words written on a page. *How* something is said can be as important as *what* is said. When delivering a speech try to:

1. **Connect with the audience:** Making eye contact, listening to the audience's reactions and speaking with enthusiasm will help you to win over your listeners.
2. **Use your body: Body language**, facial expressions and gestures are a visual way of emphasising your points and maintaining the audience's interest.
3. **Cadence:** By controlling the rise and fall of your voice (cadence), you can express emotion and set the tone of your speech.
4. **Pausing:** Adding a pause can have a dramatic effect on a speech.
5. **Pace:** The speed at which someone speaks can have a particular dramatic effect. When delivering a speech, you should consider the speed at which you speak.
6. **Movement:** 'Owning' the stage, podium or space though body movement can add power to a speech.
7. **Speak, don't read:** Try to make your speech sound natural. By using cue cards rather than a fully prepared script, your speech will avoid sounding artificial.

Writer's Workshop/ Speaking and Listening

Write and Deliver your Own Speech: Now that you have learned about some of the techniques used in delivering a speech, it is time to write and deliver your own. Write a three-minute speech based on one of the topics below and then deliver it to your class.

- Taking risks
- When I grow up…
- What music means to me
- If I had a time machine I would…
- Heroes
- Our parents made the world – our job is to change it
- Some traditions are worth keeping

Debating

One enjoyable way of speaking to a crowd is to take part in debating. Debating is a great way of practising all the skills you have developed in this chapter.

Although it can be nerve-wracking at first, you soon learn to get over the anxiety, particularly if you are well prepared and know the topic well.

There are lots of different ways of running a debating competition. Teams sizes can vary as can the length of time given to each speaker to talk. However, the rules outlined below are very typical of student competitions in Ireland.

Debate Motions

Debating teams are given a **motion** in advance of the competition. A motion is a topic that the teams will debate. It usually comes in the form of a statement such as, 'It is time for society to ban beauty contests.'

One team, called the **Proposition** will argue in favour of the motion. The other team, called the **Opposition**, argue against the motion. A good motion will allow for a strong debate, with both teams raising multiple points to support their arguments.

When preparing for a debate it is important that debaters think about the points they will raise, but debaters should also think about the points the other team may make.

The Rules

Two teams of four debate a motion that has been given to them in advance. A time limit is given on how long each speaker may talk for. Typically, this is 4 ½ minutes to talk. Speeches that are too long or too short are penalised.

Each team has a **captain** who introduces the team's argument and sums up at the end of the debate.

A **chairperson** is in charge of running the debate. The **timekeeper** ensures that the speakers are aware of the time by giving the speaker a warning when they have 30 seconds left. The timekeeper also makes a note if any speaker goes over time.

Procedure

● Chairperson welcomes the audience, teams and adjudicators, and introduces the motion.
● Captain of the Proposition (Speaker 1) opens by giving an overview of his/her team's argument
● Captain of the Opposition (Speaker 1) opens by giving an overview of his/her team's argument.
● Speaker 2 from the Proposition speaks.
● Speaker 2 from the Opposition speaks.
● Speaker 3 from the Proposition speaks.
● Speaker 3 from the Opposition speaks.
● Speaker 4 from the Proposition speaks.
● Speaker 4 from the Opposition speaks.

- Captain of the Opposition closes by summing up the team's argument and makes some final points.
- Captain of the Proposition closes by summing up the team's argument and makes some final points.
- Adjudicators add up scores and decide upon a winner.
- The Chairperson opens out the discussion to the audience.
- The Chief Adjudicator announces the winning team.

Refutation and Rebuttal

What separates debating from speechmaking is the art of **refutation** and **rebuttal**.

Refutation is when the speaker produces evidence to show that one of the other team's arguments is untrue. In the following example the debater uses factual evidence to refute a point: *Our opponents claim that obesity only affects a small minority of young people. However, the Irish Heart Foundation have shown, that shockingly, 1 in 5 Irish teenagers is overweight or obese.*

Rebuttal is when an argument is discredited by offering a stronger, more convincing argument. For example: *Speaker 3, you said that it is up to individual parents to decide what type of education their children need. I disagree, society as a whole has a responsibility to each of its citizens, and this does not stop short at the school gate.*

Refutation and Rebuttal are not needed during the captains' opening speeches.

Room Layout

During debates, the room should be laid out as indicated in the image to the right.

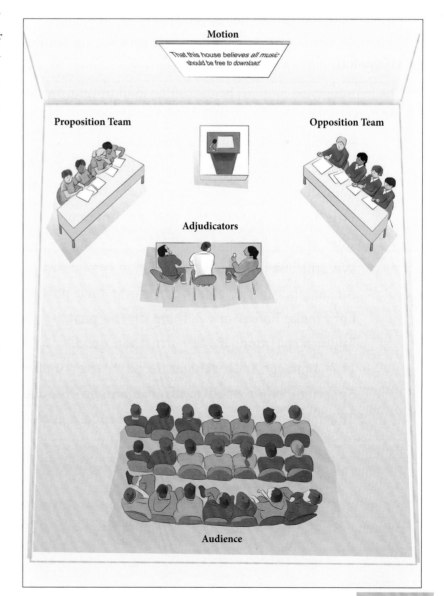

Scorecards

Adjudicators' debating scorecards can be downloaded from www.mentorbooks.ie/resources. Look in the TY English section.

Debating Scorecard

Motion: _____

		The Proposition								The Opposition			
Captain Opening	2nd Speaker	3rd Speaker	4th Speaker	Captain Closing	Totals		Captain Opening	2nd Speaker	3rd Speaker	4th Speaker	Captain Closing	Totals
10	10	10	10	10	50	**Quality of Speech Content**	10	10	10	10	10	50
	10	10	10	10	40	**Refutation & Rebuttal**		10	10	10	10	40
10	10	10	10	10	50	**Ability to Communicate**	10	10	10	10	10	50
		10			10	**Display of Teamwork** Marks are awarded for the whole team			10			10
					150	**Subtotal**						150
						Time Penalties Deduct 2 marks if a speaker goes beyond the set time. Deduct 2 marks for every 30 seconds after that.						
						Grand Total (Subtotal minus Time Penalties)						

Suggested Motions

Debate motions are written as statements or propositions. They can vary considerably: some are serious, others less so. A good topic will provoke vigorous debate and invite a number of different viewpoints.

The ten suggested motions below can be used in your own debates or can serve as models to write your own.

All music should be free to download.

Irish should be made an optional Leaving Certificate subject.

Social networking does more harm than good.

It is time to change the national anthem.

Zoos should be banned.

We still live in a sexist world.

All new parents should be made to take parenting lessons.

Let's make homework a thing of the past.

The internet does more harm than good.

It is time for Irish schools to ditch their uniforms.

Sporting bodies need to lift the ban on the use of performance enhancing drugs.

The Irish government should introduce a junk food tax as a matter of urgency.

Your English teacher may be able to give you advice for getting involved in school debating. The following websites should also prove useful:

www.idebate.org – Website for the International Debate Education Association (IDEA)

www.concern.net – Concern have a long tradition of running schools-based debating competition.

www.tcdphil.com – Trinity College's debating society 'The Phil' is the oldest debating society in the world and runs a competition pairing third and second-level students.

Drama

Four Yorkshiremen

Tim Brook-Taylor, John Cleese, Graham Chapman, Marty Feldman

Four Yorkshiremen was famously performed by the British comedy group, Monty Python. In this comedy sketch, four elderly men discuss their childhoods with hilarious results.

[It is sundown time at the tropical paradise. Four elderly men in tuxedos sit contemplating the sunset. A waiter pours some wine for one of them to taste.]

JOSHUA: Very passable. Not bad at all.

> *[The waiter pours the wine for the rest of them and then departs.]*

OBADIAH: Can't beat a good glass of Château de Chasselas, ey Josiah?

JOSHUA: Aye, you're right there Obadiah.

EZEKIEL: Who'd have thought… forty years ago… that we'd all be sittin' here, drinking Château de Chasselas?

JOSHUA: Aye. In those days, we were glad to have the price of a cup of tea.

OBADIAH: A cup o' *cold* tea.

EZEKIEL: Without milk or sugar.

JOSIAH: Or tea!

JOSHUA: Aye, and cracked cup at that.

EZEKIEL: We never had a cup. We used to have to drink out of a rolled-up newspaper.

OBADIAH: The best *we* could manage was to suck on a piece of damp cloth.

JOSIAH: But you know…we were happy in those days, although we were poor.

JOSHUA: Aye, *because* we were poor. My old Dad used to say, 'Money doesn't buy you happiness, son.'

EZEKIEL: He was right. I was happier then and I had *nothing*. We used to live in this tiny old tumbledown house, with great big holes in the roof.

OBADIAH: House? You were lucky to have a house! We used to live in one room, all twenty-six of us, no furniture. Half the floor was missing; we were all huddled together in one corner for fear of falling!

JOSIAH: You were lucky to have a room! We used to have to live in a corridor!

JOSHUA: Ooooh we used to *dream* of living in a corridor! That would have been a palace to us. We used to live in an old water tank on a rubbish tip. We got woken up every morning by having a load of rotting fish dumped all over us! House!? Hmph.

EZEKIEL: Well when I say 'house' … it was only a hole in the ground covered by a couple of foot of torn canvas, but it was a house to *us*.

OBADIAH: We were evicted from *our* hole in the ground. We had to go and live in a lake!

JOSIAH: You were lucky to have a lake. There were a hundred and sixty of us living in a small shoebox in the middle of the road.

JOSHUA: Cardboard box?

JOSIAH: Aye.

JOSHUA: You were lucky. We lived for three months in a brown paper bag in a septic tank. We used to have to get up at six o' clock in the morning, clean the bag, eat a crust of stale bread, work fourteen hours at the mill, day in, day out, for sixpence a week, come home, and Dad would thrash us to sleep with his belt!

OBADIAH: *Luxury!* We used to get out of the lake at three o' clock in the morning, clean it, eat a handful of hot gravel, go to work at the mill every day for tuppence a month, come home, and Dad would beat us around the head and neck with a broken bottle, *if we were lucky.*

[Pause]

JOSIAH: Well we had it tough. We used to have to get up out of the shoebox at twelve o' clock at night, and lick the road clean with our tongues. We had half a handful of freezing cold gravel, worked twenty-four hours a day at the mill for fourpence every six years, and when we got home, our Dad would slice us in two with a bread knife.

[Pause]

EZEKIEL: Right. I had to get up in the morning at ten o' clock at night, half an hour before I went to bed, eat a lump of cold poison, work twenty-nine hours a day at the mill, and pay the mill owner for permission to come to work, and when we got home, our Dad would kill us, and dance about on our graves singing 'Hallelujah.'

[Pause]

JOSHUA: But you try and tell the young people today that … and they won't believe ya'.

Reading for Meaning

1. (a) Find three examples of exaggeration in this piece.
   (b) Why do you think the men exaggerate the details of their childhood?
2. (a) What are the four men doing at the start of this comedy sketch?
   (b) In what way is this ironic?
3. (a) How are the older generation portrayed in this sketch?
   (b) Do you think there is any truth to this portrayal?
4. Do you find this piece funny?
5. Imagine you were asked to direct this comedy sketch for a school production. Write down the instructions you would give your actors.

Style Guide

Satire is a form of humorous writing that pokes fun at or ridicules an individual or group of people by exposing their flaws or foolishness.

In *Four Yorkshiremen*, the writers satirise the nostalgic conversations that older people have about their humble beginnings. The sketch reveals these memories to be exaggerated as each of the four speakers tries to outdo the others by describing the poverty of their childhood. This becomes increasingly ridiculous until Ezekiel declares that every night, 'our Dad would kill us, and dance about on our graves.'

The comedy sketch also exposes the hypocrisy of the men who begin their conversation discussing fine wines, 'Can't beat a good glass of Château de Chasselas', but then criticise young people for their privileged upbringings: 'But you try and tell the young people today that … and they won't believe ya.'

Speaking and Listening

Watch: Watch Monty Python perform this sketch (3½ mins) by going to www.mentorbooks. ie/resources and then looking in the TY English section. Alternatively, you can watch this sketch on Youtube.

'They're Speakin' of Witchcraft' (from *The Crucible*)

Arthur Miller

The Crucible is set in 1692 in Salem, Massachusetts in America. It is inspired by a real event, the Salem Witch Trials, in which more than two hundred people were accused of witchcraft some of whom were tried and executed. Seventeenth-century Salam was a deeply religious, puritanical society which disapproved of dancing and the arts.

This scene is set in the attic of the town preacher, Reverend Parris. His daughter Betty is lying ill and motionless on the bed. The previous evening, Parris discovered Betty, his niece Abigail and other girls in the town performing some type of ritual in the forest. There are also rumours of witchcraft in the town.

This extract begins with Parris' slave, Tituba, entering the room.

TITUBA: [*already taking a step backward*]: My Betty be hearty soon?

PARRIS: Out of here!

TITUBA: [*backing to the door*]: My Betty not goin' die...

PARRIS: [*scrambling to his feet in a fury*]: Out of my sight! [*She is gone*]. Out of my – [*He is overcome with sobs. He clamps his teeth against them and closes the door and leans against it, exhausted*]. Oh, my God! God help me! [*Quaking with fear, mumbling to himself through his sobs, he goes to the bed and gently takes BETTY's hand*]. Betty. Child. Dear child. Will you wake, will you open up your eyes! Betty, little one...
[*He is bending to kneel again when his niece, ABIGAIL WILLIAMS, seventeen, enters – a strikingly beautiful girl, an orphan, with an endless capacity for dissembling. Now she is all worry and apprehension and propriety.*]

ABIGAIL: Uncle? [*He looks to her.*] Susanna Walcott's here from Doctor Griggs.

PARRIS: Oh? Let her come, let her come.

ABIGAIL: [*leaning out the door to call to SUSANNA, who is down the hall a few steps*]: Come in, Susanna.
[*SUSANNA WALCOTT a little younger than ABIGAIL, a nervous, hurried girl, enters*].

PARRIS: [*eagerly*]: What does the doctor say, child?

SUSANNA: [*craning around PARRIS to get a look at BETTY*]: He bid me come and tell you, reverend sir, that he cannot discover no medicine for it in his books.

PARRIS: Then he must search on.

SUSANNA: Aye, sir, he have been searchin' his books since he left you, sir. But he bid me tell you, that you might look to unnatural things for the cause of it.

PARRIS: [*his eyes going wide*]: No – no. There be no unnatural cause here. Tell him I have sent for Reverend Hale of Beverly, and Mr. Hale will surely confirm that. Let him look to medicine and put out all thought of unnatural causes here. There be none.

SUSANNA: Aye, sir. He bid me tell you. [*She turns to go.*]

ABIGAIL: Speak nothin' of it in the village, Susanna.

PARRIS:	Go directly home and speak nothing of unnatural causes.
SUSANNA:	Aye, sir. I pray for her. [*She goes out.*]
ABIGAIL:	Uncle, the rumour of witchcraft is all about; I think you'd best go down and deny it yourself. The parlour's packed with people, sir. I'll sit with her.
PARRIS:	[*pressed, turns on her*]: And what shall I say to them? That my daughter and my niece I discovered dancing like heathen in the forest?
ABIGAIL:	Uncle, we did dance; let you tell them I confessed it – and I'll be whipped if I must be. But they're speakin' of witchcraft. Betty's not witched.
PARRIS:	Abigail, I cannot go before the congregation when I know you have not opened with me. What did you do with her in the forest?
ABIGAIL:	We did dance, uncle, and when you leaped out of the bush so suddenly, Betty was frightened and then she fainted. And there's the whole of it.
PARRIS:	Child. Sit you down.
ABIGAIL:	[*quavering, as she sits*]: I would never hurt Betty. I love her dearly.
PARRIS:	Now look you, child, your punishment will come in its time. But if you trafficked with spirits in the forest I must know it now, for surely my enemies will, and they will ruin me with it.
ABIGAIL:	But we never conjured spirits.
PARRIS:	Then why can she not move herself since midnight? This child is desperate! [*ABIGAIL lowers her eyes.*] It must come out – my enemies will bring it out. Let me know what you done there. Abigail, do you understand that I have many enemies?
ABIGAIL:	I have heard of it, uncle.
PARRIS:	There is a faction that is sworn to drive me from my pulpit. Do you understand that?
ABIGAIL:	I think so, sir.
PARRIS:	Now then, in the midst of such disruption, my own household is discovered to be the very centre of some obscene practice. Abominations are done in the forest –
ABIGAIL:	It were sport, uncle!
PARRIS:	[*pointing at BETTY*]: You call this sport? [*She lowers her eyes. He pleads*]: Abigail, if you know something that may help the doctor, for God's sake tell it to me. [*She is silent.*] I saw Tituba waving her arms over the fire when I came on you. Why was she doing that? And I heard a screeching and gibberish coming from her mouth. She were swaying like a dumb beast over that fire!
ABIGAIL:	She always sings her Barbados songs, and we dance.
PARRIS:	I cannot blink what I saw, Abigail, for my enemies will not blink it. I saw a dress lying on the grass.
ABIGAIL:	[*innocently*]: A dress?
PARRIS:	[*it is very hard to say*]: Aye, a dress. And I thought I saw – someone naked running through the trees!
ABIGAIL:	[*in terror*]: No one was naked! You mistake yourself, uncle!
PARRIS:	[*with anger*]: I saw it! [*He moves from her. Then, resolved*]: Now tell me true, Abigail. And I pray you feel the weight of truth upon you, for now my ministry's at stake, my ministry and perhaps your cousin's life. Whatever abomination you have done, give

me all of it now, for I dare not be taken unaware when I go before them down there.

ABIGAIL: There is nothin' more. I swear it, uncle.

PARRIS: [*studies her, then nods, half convinced*]: Abigail, I have sought here three long years to bend these stiff-necked people to me, and now, just now when some good respect is rising for me in the parish, you compromise my very character. I have given you a home, child, I have put clothes upon your back – now give me upright answer. Your name in the town – it is entirely white, is it not?

ABIGAIL: [*with an edge of resentment*]: Why, I am sure it is, sir. There be no blush about my name.

PARRIS: [*to the point*]: Abigail, is there any other cause than you have told me, for your being discharged from Goody Proctor's service? I have heard it said, and I tell you as I heard it, that she comes so rarely to the church this year for she will not sit so close to something soiled. What signified that remark?

ABIGAIL: She hates me, uncle, she must, for I would not be her slave. It's a bitter woman, a lying, cold, snivelling woman, and I will not work for such a woman!

PARRIS: She may be. And yet it has troubled me that you are now seven month out of their house, and in all this time no other family has ever called for your service.

ABIGAIL: They want slaves, not such as I. Let them send to Barbados for that. I will not black my face for any of them! [*With ill-concealed resentment at him*] Do you begrudge my bed, uncle?

PARRIS: No – no.

ABIGAIL: [*in a temper*]: My name is good in the village! I will not have it said my name is soiled! Goody Proctor is a gossiping liar!

Reading for Meaning

1. What is your impression of Reverend Parris from this scene?
2. Does this scene encourage you to be suspicious of Abigail?
3. This is the opening scene of the play. How does the playwright grab the audience's interest and encourage viewers to ask questions?
4. Although this scene takes place in the attic of a house, the audience are given an impression of the whole community. Basing your answer on what you learn of the society of the play, is seventeenth-century Salem a place you would like to live? Why / why not?

Style Guide

Dramatic tension is what keeps the audience of a play interested. It can also be found in other literary forms such as novels. Dramatic tension can occur in three different ways:

1. **Conflict:** Tension between characters, characters' challenges and conflict with the wider world are at the heart of drama. The play is the process whereby this conflict is resolved. This is one of the elements that keeps an audience fascinated: we want to know how a character will deal with these moments of conflict. In the extract above

we can see tension between the characters: Abigail and Parris in particular seem to be at odds with one another. Conflict is also created as the characters have to contend with their difficult social setting.

2. **Suspense:** Suspense occurs when the audience expects something to happen. Suspenseful moments draw this out; this amplifies the suspense as the audience wait for the expected moment. In this scene we anticipate how the rest of the community are going to view what happened in the forest and how the rumours of witchcraft will play out.

3. **Mystery:** Effective drama will plant questions in the minds of the audience. If information has been rationed out by the playwright, the audience will begin to wonder and want to find answers to their questions. In this scene we wonder: what really occurred in the forest? Why is Betty ill? Why did Abigail lose her job at the Proctors' farm?

Speaking and Listening

Freeze Frame Performance: Having read through the extract, perform the scene above making use of a freeze frame technique.

- Five actors in the class should play the roles of Parris, Abigail, Tituba, Susanna and Betty.
- You will also need two students to act as the 'minds' of Parris and Abigail.
- Perform the scene as scripted on pages 218–220. The actors should freeze when the teacher calls, 'Freeze'.
- During these frozen moments, the rest of the class may ask questions of the students acting as the 'minds' of Parris and Abigail. The 'minds' should stand beside their frozen counterparts and answer questions as if they are the character. Questions should focus on how a character is feeling, his/her motivation, worries and thoughts.

Writer's Workshop

What Happens Next? Imagine that in the next scene Parris leaves the room and Abigail speaks to Betty. In your scene, Betty may wake and respond or remain unresponsive. Try to deal with the suspicions the audience have of Abigail by this point of the play. As you have only read a small portion of the play, you will need to use your imagination to develop the action. Don't worry if you don't stay true to what really happens next in the play – let your imagination take you to new places.

Links

In this extract from *The Crucible*, we see how social expectations can bring pressure to bear on a character. This extract can be linked to other texts in this book and elsewhere:

In this book: Kate Chopin's *The Story of an Hour* (page 140)

Elsewhere: The full play of *The Crucible* by Arthur Miller; Elia Kazan's film, *On the Waterfront*

'And That Was That Night'
(from *Philadelphia, Here I Come!*)

Brian Friel

Set in Ireland in the 1960s, *Philadelphia, Here I Come!* tells the story of Gar O'Donnell as he prepares to emigrate to Philadelphia, leaving his father and friends behind in the small town of Ballybeg.

On stage, Gar is represented by two onstage roles: Public (the Gar the other characters can see and talk to) and Private (Gar's inner thoughts and feelings, invisible to the others on stage).

In the scene below Gar is meeting with his friends on the eve of his planned departure.

PUBLIC:	[*raising glass*] Well, boys, when you're lining out on the pitch, you can think of me, because I'll be thinking of you.
JOE:	[*earnestly*] Lucky bloody man, Gar. God, I wish I was in your –
NED:	[*quickly*] By the way, lads, who's the blondie thing I seen at the last Mass on Sunday?
TOM:	A big red-head?
NED:	Are you bloody well deaf! A blondie! She wouldn't be Maggie Hanna's niece, would she?
TOM:	There was two of them, sitting over near the box?
NED:	I seen one.
TOM:	'Cos they're English. Staying at the hotel. But the big red thing – she's one of Neil McFadden's girls.
NED:	Annie? Is Annie home?
JOE:	Aye, she is. So I heard the mammy saying.
NED:	Bloody great! That's me fixed up for the next two weeks! Were any of youse ever on that job?
JOE:	No, I wasn't, Ned.
TOM:	For god's sake, she wouldn't spit on you!
NED:	Game as they're going, big Annie. But you need the constitution of a horse. I had her for the fortnight she was home last year and she damned near killed me.
PUBLIC:	Big Annie from up beyond the quarry?
JOE:	You know, Gar – the one with the squint.
NED:	[*with dignity*] Annie McFadden has no squint.
PUBLIC:	Away and take a running race to yourself, Ned.
NED:	[*with quiet threat*] What do you mean?
PUBLIC:	You were never out with big Annie McFadden in your puff, man.
NED:	Are you calling me a liar?
PRIVATE:	[*wearily*] What's the point.
TOM:	[*quickly*] Oh, by god, Ned was there, Gar, manys and manys the time. Weren't you, Ned?
PUBLIC:	Have it your own way.
JOE:	[*nervously*] And maybe she got the squint straightened out since I saw her last. All the women get the squints straightened out nowadays. Dammit, you could walk from here to Cork nowadays and you wouldn't see a woman with a –

NED: I just don't like fellas getting snottery with me, that's all.

There follows an uneasy silence during which PRIVATE surveys the group.

PRIVATE: The boys…they weren't always like this, were they? There was a hell of a lot of crack, wasn't there? There was a hell of a lot of laughing, wasn't there?

TOM: [*briskly*] Bit of life about the place next week, lads – the Carnival. Too bad you'll miss it, Gar. By God it was a holy fright last year, night after night. [*to NED*] Remember?

GLOSSARY
crack: craic

NED: [*sulkily*] Bloody cows, the whole bloody lot of them!

TOM: Mind the night with the two wee Greenock pieces?

NED: [*thawing*] Aw, stop, stop!

TOM: Talk about hot things!

NED: Liveliest wee tramps I ever laid!

TOM: And the fat one from Dublin you picked up at the dance that night – the one that hauled you down into the ditch!

NED: I was never the same since.

TOM: [*to PUBLIC*] Whatever it is about him [*NED*], if there's a fast woman in the country, she'll go for Ned first thing. Lucky bugger! [*Pause.*] Aye, lucky bugger!

Another brief silence. These silences occur like regular cadences.
To defeat them someone always introduces a fresh theme.

PUBLIC: I'm for off tomorrow, boys.

NED: [*indifferently*] Aye, so, so…

TOM: Brooklyn, isn't it?

PUBLIC: Philadelphia.

TOM: Philadelphia. That's where Jimmy Crerand went to, isn't it? Philadelphia…

NED: [*quickly*] Mind the night Jimmy and us went down to the caves with them Dublin skivvies that was working up at the lodge? [*to PUBLIC*] Were you? – No, you weren't with us that night.

JOE: Was I there, Ned?

NED: You mind the size of Jimmy? – five foot nothing and scared of his shadow.

PUBLIC: Best goalie we ever had.

NED: One of the women was Gladys and the other was Emmy or something –

TOM: Dammit, I mind now! Gladys and Emmy – that was it, Ned!

NED: Anyhow the rest of us went in for a swim –

TOM: In the bloody pelt!

NED: – and your man Jimmy was left in the cave with the women; and what the hell do they do but whip the trousers off him!

JOE: No, I wasn't there that night.

NED: And the next thing we see is wee Jimmy coming shouting across the white strand and the two Dublin cows haring after him.

TOM: Not a stab on him!

NED: – and him squealing at the top of his voice, 'Save me, boys, save me!'

TOM:	Never drew breath till he reached home!
NED:	You [*Gar*] missed that night.
TOM:	'Save me, boys, save me!'
NED:	I don't think we went to bed that night at all.
TOM:	You may be sure we didn't.
NED:	Powerful.

Another silence descends. After a few seconds PRIVATE speaks.

PRIVATE: We were all there that night, Ned. And the girls' names were Gladys and Susan. And they sat on the rocks dangling their feet in the water. And we sat in the cave, peeping out at them. And then Jimmy Crerand suggested that we go in for a swim; and we all ran to the far end of the shore; and we splashed about like schoolboys. Then we came back to the cave, and wrestled with one another. And then out of sheer boredom, Tom, you suggested that we take the trousers off Crerand – just to prove how manly we all were. But when Ned started towards Jimmy – five foot nothing, remember? – wee Jimmy squared up and defied not only the brave Ned but the whole lot of us. So we straggled back home, one behind the other, and left the girls dangling their feet in the water. And that was that night.

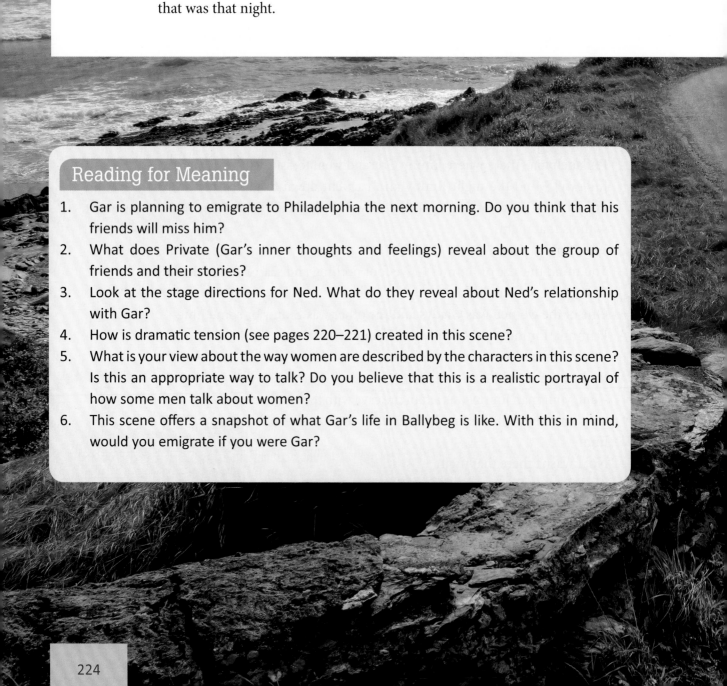

Reading for Meaning

1. Gar is planning to emigrate to Philadelphia the next morning. Do you think that his friends will miss him?
2. What does Private (Gar's inner thoughts and feelings) reveal about the group of friends and their stories?
3. Look at the stage directions for Ned. What do they reveal about Ned's relationship with Gar?
4. How is dramatic tension (see pages 220–221) created in this scene?
5. What is your view about the way women are described by the characters in this scene? Is this an appropriate way to talk? Do you believe that this is a realistic portrayal of how some men talk about women?
6. This scene offers a snapshot of what Gar's life in Ballybeg is like. With this in mind, would you emigrate if you were Gar?

Style Guide

Stage Directions: Stage directions are instructions given to actors, directors and producers by the playwright; they are usually enclosed in square brackets or typed in italics. Stage directions explain how a stage should look and how a character should behave or speak. For example, Brian Friel explains how the actors should behave and speak: [*raising glass*], [*quickly*], *There follows an uneasy silence during which PRIVATE surveys the group.*

Some playwrights give detailed stage directions, while some like to leave decisions to the director and actors by including few stage directions.

Speaking and Listening

Performance: As a class, put on a performance of this scene.

- Select five actors to play the parts in this scene (Public Gar, Private Gar, Ned, Tom, Joe).
- Discuss how to stage the scene: who will sit where? Should Private Gar sit or walk behind the other characters?
- Consider the tension between the characters. Who is the most powerful character on stage?
- Discuss the type of body language and tone of voice the actors should use. Consider the stage directions in your discussion.
- Perform this piece for the class.

Links

The experience of emigration is deeply intertwined with Irish society. In terms of its subject matter, this extract can be linked to other texts in this book and elsewhere:
In this book: James Joyce's story, *Eveline* (page 135)
Elsewhere: John Crowley's film, *Brooklyn*

'Tomorrow, and Tomorrow, and Tomorrow (from Macbeth)

William Shakespeare

This hugely intense soliloquy comes during the final act of *Macbeth*. Macbeth has comm[itted] murders and terrible acts of betrayal to secure his rule of Scotland. He has reigned over t[he] with a brutal and bloody hand. In this soliloquy, Macbeth has just learned of the death [of] Lady Macbeth. The soliloquy explores Macbeth's despair and sense of meaninglessness as [he is] increasingly weary of life.

Tomorrow, and tomorrow, and tomorrow,
Creeps in this petty pace from day to day[1]
To the last syllable of recorded time,
And all our yesterdays have lighted fools
The way to dusty death.[2] Out, out, brief candle!
Life's but a walking shadow, a poor player[3]
That struts and frets[4] his hour upon the stage
And then is heard no more. It is a tale
Told by an idiot, full of sound and fury,
Signifying nothing.

GLOSSARY
[1] **Creeps in…day to day:** Time crawls [on] day after the next.
[2] **And all our…dusty death:** All of ou[r ... has] just been a candle lighting the path t[o the] grave.
[3] **poor player:** bad/unfortunate actor
[4] **struts and frets:** parades and causes c[oncern]

Language Lab

1. (a) List all of the words that come at the end of each line: 'tomorrow', 'day'…
    (b) Looking at this list of ten words, what do they suggest about the themes explored in this soliloquy?
2. (a) List all of the words in this soliloquy associated with time.
    (b) What point is being made about the relationship between time and life?
3. Describe Macbeth's tone in this soliloquy.
4. This soliloquy makes use of a number of metaphors. Describe one metaphor and explain what point is being made by Macbeth.

Style Guide

Soliloquy: A soliloquy is a dramatic speech in which a character reveals his/her innermost thoughts to the audience. It is when a character thinks aloud on stage.

Sometimes what a character says in soliloquy can be at odds with their behaviour around other characters. This is because a soliloquy is an intimate, personal moment that is only shared with the audience. Soliloquies allow the audience insight into a character's motivations and feelings. The soliloquy allows the audience to understand a character's plans, ambition, motivation, confusion or despair. It reveals the heart of the character.

It is only when a character's most private thoughts are said on stage that we can truly appreciate the depth of his/her soul.

Speaking and Listening

Performance: Memorise either this Macbeth soliloquy or the Hamlet soliloquy on pages 228–229. Perform it for the class. Try to communicate the emotions and ideas included in the soliloquy.

Speaking and Listening

Watch and Discuss: Watch an excellent performance of this soliloquy (2 mins) by going to www.mentorbooks.ie/resources and then looking in the TY English section.
As a class, discuss the actor's performance.
● Was he successful in conveying the thoughts and feelings of Macbeth?
● Comment on the actor's: tone of voice, body language and facial expressions.

Writer's Workshop

Visual Text: Create a visual representation of this soliloquy either on paper or by using a digital format. Use pictures to reflect the imagery of the soliloquy. Include key words and phrases from the soliloquy. Try to capture the mood and themes of the soliloquy.

Links

The profound sense of hopelessness and world-weariness is the defining feature of this soliloquy. In terms of its tone and ideas, *'Tomorrow, and Tomorrow, and Tomorrow'* can be linked to other texts in this book and elsewhere:
In this book: William Stafford's poem, *At the Bomb Testing Site* (page 196)
Elsewhere: The full play of William Shakespeare's *Macbeth*; Robert Frost's poem, *Out, Out -*

'To Be, Or Not To Be' (from *Hamlet*)

William Shakespeare

This play tells the story of Hamlet, the Prince of Denmark. Hamlet has been visited by his father's ghost who tells his son that he was murdered by Claudius, Hamlet's uncle. Throughout this play, Hamlet agonises about what to do, how to bring about justice and avenge his father.

The soliloquy below is one of the most celebrated in all of Shakespeare. Here Hamlet reflects on the nature of life and death.

To be, or not to be[1] – that is the question:[2]

Whether 'tis nobler in the mind to suffer

The slings and arrows of outrageous fortune,[3]

Or to take arms against a sea of troubles

And by opposing end them?[4] To die: to sleep –

No more;[5] and by a sleep to say we end

The heartache and the thousand natural shocks

That flesh is heir to;[6] 'tis a consummation[7]

Devoutly to be wished. – To die: to sleep –

To sleep, perchance to dream – ay, there's the rub,[8]

For in that sleep of death what dreams may come

When we have shuffled off this mortal coil[9]

Must give us pause:[10] there's the respect

That makes calamity of so long life.[11]

For who would bear the whips and scorns of time,[12]

Th' oppressor's wrong, the proud man's contumely,[13]

The pangs of disprized[14] love, the law's delay,

The insolence of office[15] and the spurns

That patient merit of th' unworthy takes,

When he himself might his quietus make

With a bare bodkin?[16] Who would fardels bear,[17]

To grunt and sweat under a weary life,

But that the dread of something after death,

(The undiscovered country[18] from whose bourn[19]

GLOSSARY

[1] **To be, or not to be:** It is worth noting that Hamlet talks in general philosophical terms and avoids saying 'I' or 'me'

[2] **the question:** 1. whether life is worth living 2. whether he should commit suicide 3. whether he should take revenge against his uncle and in doing so lose his own life

[3] **slings and arrows…fortune:** the hardship and pain of misfortune / fate

[4] **to take arms…end them:** futilely fight against fate and in doing so, die in the process

[5] **To die…No more:** To die is just to sleep, nothing more

[6] **flesh is heir to:** that is part of being alive

[7] **consummation:** ending / conclusion

[8] **rub:** problem / obstacle. A 'rub' is an obstacle used in the game of bowls which impedes the bowl

[9] **shuffled off this mortal coil:** 1. discarded the turmoil of this life 2. discarded this mortal flesh

[10] **Must give us pause:** must make us stop and think

[11] **there's the respect…life:** there's the thought that makes calamities last so long (because we endure them rather than committing suicide)

[12] **whips and scorns of time:** 1. pain and insults of the times we live in 2. pain and insults of time / life

[13] **contumely:** insults

[14] **disprized:** despised

[15] **office:** positions of authority

[16] **When he himself…bodkin?:** when he could pay his account (i.e. take his own life) with a mere dagger

[17] **fardels bear:** put up with burdens

[18] **The undiscovered country:** i.e. the afterlife

[19] **bourn:** boundary

No traveller returns) puzzles[20] the will

And makes us rather bear those ills we have

Than fly to others that we know not of?

Thus conscience[21] does make cowards of us all,

And thus the native hue of resolution

Is sicklied o'er with the pale cast of thought,[22]

And enterprises of great pitch and moment

With this regard their currents turn awry,

And lose the name of action.[23]

[20] **puzzles:** bewilders and prevents actio

[21] **conscience:** conscious thought / refle

[22] **the native…thought:** the natural hea
of resolution is made sickly looking
pallid tinge of thought, i.e. thought
our ability to act decisively

[23] **enterprises of great pitch…action:** i
undertakings of great scope and sig
are diverted from their course and a
acted upon

Speaking and Listening

Watch and Discuss: Watch an excellent performance of this soliloquy (3 mins) by going to
www.mentorbooks.ie/resources and then looking in the TY English section.

As a class, discuss the actor's performance.

● Was he successful in conveying the thoughts and feelings of Hamlet?
● Comment on the actor's tone of voice, body language and facial expressions.

Language Lab

1. What do you think Hamlet means in each of the following phrases:
   (a) 'ay, there's the rub; / For in that sleep of death what dreams may come / When we
       have shuffled off this mortal coil'
   (b) 'the dread of something after death, / The undiscovered country from whose
       bourn / No traveller returns, puzzles the will / And makes us rather bear those ills
       we have / Than fly to others that we know not of'
   (c) 'the native hue of resolution / Is sicklied o'er with the pale cast of thought'
2. (a) Hamlet asks a number of questions in this soliloquy. Write down three examples.
   (b) What does his use of questions suggest about his state of mind?

Reading for Meaning

1. Outline the ideas and arguments explored in this soliloquy.
2. Describe Hamlet's emotions as he speaks in this soliloquy.
3. If you were directing *Hamlet*, how would you direct this scene? What advice would you give to the actor? How would you stage the scene? You may wish to refer to lighting, music, sound effects, props etc.
4. Basing your answer on this soliloquy, choose a modern actor to play the role of Hamlet. Explain what qualities, characteristics or previous roles make this actor suitable for playing this part. Refer to the soliloquy in your answer.

Writer's Workshop

21st-Century Soliloquy: Translate this soliloquy into modern English. Use sayings and expressions from your local area to give your translation a modern feel.

Links

Hamlet's meditation on death is a fascinating though dark exploration. In terms of its subject matter, this soliloquy can be linked to other texts in this book and elsewhere:

In this book: Percy Bysshe Shelly's poem, *Ozymandias* (page 182)

Elsewhere: David Wroblewski's retelling of *Hamlet* in his novel, *The Story of Edgar Sawtelle*

DRAMA PROJECTS

A Trip to the Theatre

Task

- As a class, organise and attend a dramatic performance in a local theatre.

- Individually, write a report on the trip.

Theatre Etiquette

- A trip to the theatre is not the same as going to the cinema. Theatres expect the audience to behave in a certain way; this is known as 'theatre etiquette'.

- Ensure mobile phones are turned off.

- Do not talk during the performance; it can be very distracting for the actors otherwise.

- Most theatres don't allow eating or drinking during the performance, so check beforehand.

- Ensure you are on time. Once the performance has started, audience members will not be admitted.

Report Guidelines

- Review the play. Go to page 73 to learn about writing a review. You may wish to comment on the play itself, the interpretation the director made, the actors, the stage, the use of music and sound, the lighting.

- It may be helpful to buy a programme while at the theatre. This will provide the actors' names and information about the production and the play itself.

Chapter 7:

Worth a Thousand Words
— Visual Texts: Film, Cartoons, Photography

In our daily lives we are exposed to a vast array of images. Television, film, the internet, advertising and artworks present us with thousands of images, each of which tries to communicate something to the viewer. It is essential that we understand how visual texts work in a world that requires high levels of visual literacy.

Although a visual text may not contain many or any words, it is still a text that we *read*. Appreciating image-based texts requires us to understand the visual language of images rather than words.

In this chapter you will practise your visual literacy as you appreciate a wide selection of visual texts. The chapter is divided into three sections: Film, Cartoons and Photography.

Film

Film is a hugely important part of modern culture. Whether it is short film, feature length film or documentary, there are few people who don't enjoy some form of cinema. Although most films include words as well as images, the emphasis on images in film make it a visual text – that is why we sometimes refer to cinema as 'the pictures'.

Genre

Sometimes it can be helpful to categorise different types of artistic works. We use the word 'genre' to describe the category or type of an artistic work. For example, in music, there are genres such as Rock, Electronic, Blues, Jazz; literature has genres such as Horror, Historical Fiction, Science Fiction and so on.

Tastes in film genre vary widely. Some enjoy the comedy genre; others may prefer action films. Film genre is a way of categorising films according to their plot, setting, characters, themes and style. Some of the most common film genre categories are: Drama, Comedy, Romance, Western, Science Fiction, Horror, Action, Historical, Satire, Disaster, Teen, Thriller. These classifications are often too simplistic. Many films can be seen as a blend of genres. For example, Romcom (Romantic-Comedy) is a very popular genre but Romcoms can also be classified as comedy, romance or drama.

Speaking and Listening

Talking about Genre

1. In groups, list three films in each of the following genres:

(a) Romcom	(b) Teen	(c) Action	(d) Disaster
(e) Sci-fi	(f) Super-hero	(g) Thriller	(h) Comedy

2. In your groups, discuss the following statement: 'My favourite film genre is…,' then discuss it as a class.

Film Posters

Film posters are marketing tools that encourage the public to go and see a film. Film companies use posters and other types of advertisements to create a 'buzz' around a film. Film posters make use of the follow design features to help market a film:

● **Tagline:** Film studios often include a line that sums up the theme or plot of the film. For example, the poster for the film *Jaws* uses the tagline, *You'll never get in the water again*. This suggests the terrifying nature of the film and offers something about the film's subject matter. The tagline for *Chicken Run* uses wordplay and also suggests something about the subject matter: *Escape, or die frying*.

● **Colour Scheme:** A film poster's colour scheme can make a dramatic impact and establish what kind of film is being promoted. A thriller or horror film may include lots of black, while a children's film may feature bright colours.

● **Key Words:** Some posters will include terms such as *terrifying*, *gripping*, *laugh out loud* or *tearjerker* to entice viewers to see the film.

● **Images:** Film posters try to grab viewers' attention by using striking images. These may feature a scene from the film or emphasise the performance of a celebrity actor.

● **Reviews or Award References:** Promotional posters may include positive reviews or mention awards that a film has received to help convince movie-goers that the film is worth seeing.

● **Reviewers' Comments and Awards:** It is very helpful for film-makers if a film has been positively reviewed or won an award. Film posters can be a great way of drawing attention to the positive reception a film has received by quoting a reviewer or listing any awards won, e.g. *Winner Cannes Film Festival* or ★★★★★ or *This is the best comedy to come out of Ireland in years*.

● **Target Audience:** Most mainstream films are aimed at a specific group or target audience. Film posters reflect this through the images and text used. The age classification of a film will help to define the target audience.

Reading for Meaning

1. (a) In which genre would you place each of the films advertised by the posters A-D on page 235?

   (b) How do the posters help to suggest which genre each film is?

2. (a) Write down the four taglines offered by the posters A-D.

   (b) Which tagline do you feel is the most successful in creating interest in the film?

3. Which of the four posters do you feel makes the greatest visual impact?

4. In the case of each poster, state the target audience and how the poster appeals to its target group. Consider the images, colour scheme, tagline etc.

5. From looking at the posters, which film would you most like to see? Explain your answer by referring to the posters (not the films themselves).

Writer's Workshop

Film Poster Design: Create a film poster for a movie of your choice. Find suitable images, choose a colour scheme and write a tagline for your poster. Keep in mind who your target audience is.

A

B

C

D

Cinematography

Cinematography is the art and technique of using a camera in filmmaking. It deals with all the visual elements of film, including the camera work, the lighting and the colouring of the film. It is usually the director and the cinematographer who plan how a camera will be used. Film-makers think about how a shot is framed, the distance of the camera and the camera angle. They also have to consider using lenses to colour the film and how to light scenes. These decisions affect how the story is told.

Camera Shots

Extreme Long Shot Extreme long shots require the camera to be placed very far away from the object that is being filmed. This type of shot is often used to establish the setting of the story. It may provide a bird's-eye view of a city or it may display the landscape from a distance.

Long Shot – A long shot shows a character visible from head to toe. It also provides information about the background.

Medium Shot – Medium shots present the viewer with an image of characters from the waist up. It is more intimate than the long shot.

Close-Up – Directors may want to stress a character's emotions or add a sense of intensity. This can be achieved by zooming in on a character's face in a close-up. This encourages the audience to think about a character's emotional or psychological state.

Extreme Close-Up – An extreme close-up adds even greater intensity to the screen. A director may choose to intensely focus on a part of a character's face. This is often done during a key moment in a film.

Point of View Shot – This is when the camera shows what a character is seeing. It allows the audience to see the world from the character's perspective. You might notice this type of shot being used in a thriller before a murderer attacks.

Depth of Field – This describes how much of the foreground, mid-ground and background appear in focus.

Camera Angles

Straight-On – This is the most common camera angle. It is focused at eye-level.

High-Angle – Directors may wish to make a character look smaller or more vulnerable. This can be achieved by placing the camera above the character's head so that the viewer is looking down on the subject.

Low-Angle – If a director wants to give the impression that a character is powerful, a low-angle shot may be used. This makes the viewer feel as if the character is towering above them.

Canted – To create a distorted feeling the camera can be tilted (or canted) to one side.

237

Camera Movement

- **Pan:** In this movement, the camera scans across the scene from one side to the other.

- **Tilt:** The camera can tilt up or down. This is like a panning shot except the camera moves up or down rather than side-to-side.

- **Tracking Shot (or Dolly Shot):** This is when the camera is mounted on a wheeled base known as a camera dolly. The dolly then moves along a small set of rails as the camera is filming. This camera movement is an excellent way of following a character as he/she moves across the screen.

- **Boom Shot:** A boom shot allows the director to give the viewers an aerial view. To achieve this, a crane is used to move a camera up or down above the action.

Lighting and Colour

How a film-maker chooses to light the film is very important. Lighting can add atmosphere to a scene. For example, a character who is partly shadowed may seem more mysterious or sinister.

Directors can change the colour of an image by using lenses and filters on the cameras. Colour can help to influence the emotions of the audience and communicate something about the characters and the setting. For example, a blue tint may add a coldness to the scene, yellow may add more positive emotions.

The three film stills below show how lighting and colour can help a director to tell a story and add emotion to a scene.

Cinematography Discussion: Watch a film with your class (feature length or short). Pause the film at various moments and discuss the use of cinematography. How is the camera telling the story? Which angles or cinematographic techniques are being used? What effect do they have?

Project: Film Report

Task

Write a report on a film you have studied independently.

Project Guidelines

Your report should contain all of the following information:

Cinematography: Write about the cinematography used in the film. Think about the camera angles, camera movement, lighting and colour.

Soundtrack: Write about the film's soundtrack. Was music used effectively in the film? Who wrote the music? Do you feel the soundtrack added to or detracted from your enjoyment of the film?

A Character Study: Choose one character from the film that you found interesting. Write about the character's personality, outlook on life, attitude, ability to deal with problems and the degree of success he/she achieves in the story.

Key Moments: Choose two important episodes or moments from the film. For each key moment, describe what happened and explain why you felt this scene was important. An episode may be important because it is a turning point in the plot, reveals something about the characters, contributes to your understanding of the theme or is exciting or entertaining.

Theme: Write about the theme of your film. Think about the message the director is trying to convey or the issue that is being explored.

Cultural Context / Social Setting: Describe the world of the film. Is it a place where characters enjoy freedom or are there obstacles in their way? What are the values of the society in the film? Is the world portrayed in a positive or negative light? You may want to consider some of the following ideas about society: gender roles, religion, wealth/poverty, power, freedom, race.

Film Review: Imagine you work for an online magazine. Write a review of the film to be published in next month's edition. See Chapter 2, page 73 for tips on writing a review.

Cartoons

Cartoons

A cartoon is an image that amuses or makes a point in a humorous way. Cartoons are a powerful form of visual communication because they make their point quickly and often without using many words.

Cartoonists use a variety of techniques in their work:

- **Caricature:** This is an exaggerated representation of a famous individual, often a politician. Cartoonists can use caricature to poke fun at somebody by exaggerating their facial features.
- **Satire:** This is when a cartoonist uses humour to expose the faults of a powerful individual or institution.
- **Caption:** Often cartoonists will use a short sentence or phrase to crystallise their ideas and compliment or explain the image.
- **Speech/Thought Bubbles:** These are used to represent the thoughts or words of characters in the cartoon frame. Like captions, bubbles help the cartoonist to make his/her point.
- **Wordplay:** Sometimes cartoonists will use wordplay such as puns in their work.

"It helps him realise I'm being serious."

Reading for Meaning

1. Explain what point is being made in this cartoon.
2. Do you agree with the point that is being made?
3. This cartoon is critical of the way teenagers live today. Do you think it is fair or unfair of the cartoonist to represent teenagers like this? Why / why not?

Paweł Kuczyński Cartoons

Paweł Kuczyński is a Polish cartoonist known for his use of satire, anti-war themes and original take on modern life. He has received numerous awards for his work.

Reading for Meaning

1. Explain the message behind Cartoon A. Refer directly to the cartoon in your answer.
2. Do you think Cartoon B raises any important issues about childhood? Explain your answer.
3. What point is being made in Cartoon C? Explain by referring to the cartoon.
4. Suggest an appropriate caption for Cartoon A. Explain why you chose this caption.
5. What title would you give Cartoon B? Justify your choice.
6. If you were to include a speech bubble for Cartoon C, what would it be?
7. In your view, are cartoons an effective way of making a point about the modern world? Why / why not?

Writer's Workshop

Discursive Essay: A discursive essay is one which offers an argument about a particular topic. Write a discursive essay inspired by the one of the cartoons on the previous page and above. Consider what point Paweł Kuczyński is making and argue in favour or against this.

Photography

Photography

Photography, just like other visual texts, has its own language. When we read a photograph, we have to reflect on how the meaning is communicated through the picture: What is emphasised? What is suggested? What is the atmosphere? Is a point being made? What emotions are being communicated?

The following terms will help you to discuss photographic images.

- **Composition:** How the visual elements of the image are arranged to make the whole photograph.

- **Intention:** The purpose of the photograph. What ideas are being explored by the photographer? What themes are present in the image?

- **Leading lines:** A photograph naturally draws the viewer's eye along lines (straight, diagonal, curvy etc.). The way a photograph is composed will affect the way we experience the image: pulling us into the picture, focusing our attention on a subject or bringing us on a journey.

- **Symmetry:** By balancing the objects in a picture, a photographer can create symmetry or a sense of harmony. However, sometimes the photographer may want the opposite effect and create an asymmetrical photograph.

- **Vantage point:** The vantage point is the position from which the photograph is taken. Much like in cinematography (see page 236) the angle between the subject and the photographer will create particular effects.

- **Light:** The way light works in an image is an important part of the composition. Think about which parts of the image are most lit. Are there shadows? Consider the quality of the light: natural or artificial, harsh or soft, reflected or direct, time of day?

- **Colour:** Photographers may use black-and-white film or try to capture the natural colour of a scene. Sometimes special coloured lenses are used to tint an image.

- **Contrast:** Sometimes an image can include strong differences between light and dark, the size of objects or the texture of elements. This use of contrast can make for a dramatic and striking image.

- **Focus:** Which areas of the photograph are the clearest and sharpest? Which are not? Why has the photographer focused on particular elements?

Migrant Mother

Dorothea Lange

Dorothea Lange was an American photo-journalist best known for documenting the Great Depression in America (1929–1939). Her work brought attention to the hardship experienced by the poor, many of whom were migrants travelling around America in search of work and a better life.

Migrant Mother (1936) is one of Lange's best-known images. Lange described the moment she captured this image: 'I saw and approached the hungry and desperate mother, as if drawn by a magnet. I do not remember how I explained my presence or my camera to her, but I do remember she asked me no questions…She told me her age, that she was 32. She said that they had been living on frozen vegetables from the surrounding fields, and birds that the children killed. She had just sold the tires from her car to buy food. There she sat in that lean-to tent with her children huddled around her, and seemed to know that my pictures might help her, and so she helped me. There was a sort of equality about it.'

Speaking and Listening

Discussion: In small groups, discuss the impact this photo has on you. What issues does it raise? How does it affect you emotionally?

Reading for Meaning

1. What is your initial reaction to this photo? What does it make you think and feel?
2. Two of the children are turned away from the camera in the image. How does this detail add to the power of the image?
3. Read Dorothea Lange's description on the previous page of the moment she took this photograph. Does this explanation add to the impact of this photograph?
4. What do you think was Lange's photographic intention (see page 243) when she took this shot?
5. '*Migrant Mother* shows a woman who is both helpless yet strong, poor but dignified.' Do you agree with this statement? Discuss this image in detail in your answer.

Writer's Workshop

Short Story: Write a short story inspired by the image above. Bring the situation to life using descriptive language and dialogue.

Links

This very famous photograph examines extreme poverty. In terms of its subject matter, this photograph can be linked to other texts in this book and elsewhere:

In this book: Sylvia Seymour Akin's tale, *Christmas Morning* (page 26)
Elsewhere: John Steinbeck's novel, *The Grapes of Wrath*

Seoul, South Korea

Steven Roe

Reading for Meaning

1. Comment on the following technical elements (see page 243) of this photograph:
   - (a) Colour
   - (c) Leading lines
   - (b) Light
   - (d) Contrast
2. The photograph is simply named after its location. What name would you give the photograph?
3. What is your impression of Seoul in South Korea from this photograph?

Writer's Workshop

Descriptive Composition: Write a descriptive composition inspired by this image. Use the descriptive devices listed in Chapter 4, on page 95 to capture the atmosphere of this scene.

A Normal Subway Ride

Josh Gordon

Reading for Meaning

1. What do you think is happening in this photograph?
2. What do you notice about the different ways the passengers are reacting to the man in the centre of the train carriage?
3. Do you find this image to be intriguing?
4. Comment on this photograph's (see page 243):
   (a) Leading lines
   (b) Light
   (c) Intention
5. Do you think, *A Normal Subway Ride*, is a good title for this photograph?

Writer's Workshop

Dialogue: Write a dialogue inspired by the image above. This can be a conversation between any of the individuals in the image. Consider what is going on in this picture and how the passengers and performers are feeling. Try to capture the energy and atmosphere of the scene.

Chapter 8:
No More Red Marks –
Punctuation and Mechanics

When your homework is returned do you find that it is covered in red pen – littered with circles, underlines and corrections? For many students there is confusion about how punctuation works and what its purpose is.

This chapter serves as an aid to students who need clarification on the mechanics of writing, particularly in regard to punctuation.

This chapter encourages you to consider the arguments about why punctuation is important. It also offers straightforward explanations and practice exercises so that you can eliminate all of those red circles from your corrected work.

"Yes, grammar rules do evolve over time,
but making up your own to 'stay ahead of
the curve' won't work in this English class!"

Punctuation

1. Punctuation Vigilante

Lynne Truss

Lynne Truss is a self-described 'punctuation vigilante'. The following extract is adapted from the introduction to her best-selling book *Eats, Shoots & Leaves*.

Either this will ring bells for you, or it won't. A printed banner has appeared on the concourse of a petrol station near to where I live. 'Come inside,' it says, 'for CD's, VIDEO's, DVD's, and BOOK's.'

If this satanic sprinkling of redundant apostrophes causes no little gasp of horror or quickening of the pulse, you should probably put down this book at once. By all means congratulate yourself that you are not a stickler; that you are happily equipped to live in a world of plummeting punctuation standards; but just don't bother to go any further. For any true stickler, you see, the sight of the plural word 'Book's' with an apostrophe in it will trigger a ghastly private emotional process similar to the stages of bereavement, though greatly accelerated. First there is shock. Within seconds, shock gives way to disbelief, disbelief to pain, and pain to anger. Finally (and this is where the analogy breaks down), anger gives way to a righteous urge to perpetrate an act of criminal damage with the aid of a permanent marker.

It's tough being a stickler for punctuation these days. One almost dare not get up in the mornings. True, one occasionally hears a marvellous punctuation-fan joke about a panda who 'eats, shoots and leaves', but in general the stickler's exquisite sensibilities are assaulted from all sides, causing feelings of panic and isolation. A sign at a health club will announce, 'I'ts party time, on Saturday 24th May we are have a disco/party night for free, it will be a ticket only evening.' Advertisements offer decorative services to 'wall's – ceiling's – door's ect'. Meanwhile a newspaper placard announces 'FAN'S FURY AT STADIUM INQUIRY', which sounds quite interesting until you look inside the paper and discover that the story concerns a quite large mob of fans, actually – not just the lone hopping-mad fan so promisingly indicated by the punctuation.

Everywhere one looks, there are signs of ignorance and indifference. What about that film Two Weeks Notice? Guaranteed to give sticklers a very nasty turn, that was – its posters slung along the sides of buses in letters four feet tall, with no apostrophe in sight. I remember, at the start of the Two Weeks Notice publicity campaign in the spring of 2003, emerging cheerfully from Victoria Station (was I whistling?) and stopping dead in my tracks with my fingers in my mouth. Where was the apostrophe? Surely there should be an apostrophe on that bus? If it were 'one month's notice' there would be an apostrophe (I reasoned); yes, and if it were 'one week's notice' there would be an apostrophe. Therefore 'two weeks' notice' requires an apostrophe! Buses that I should have caught (the 73; two 38s) sailed off up Buckingham Palace Road while I communed thus at length with my inner stickler, unable to move or, indeed, regain any sense of perspective.

Part of one's despair, of course, is that the world cares nothing for the little shocks endured by the sensitive stickler. While we look in horror at a badly punctuated sign, the world carries on around us, blind to our plight. We are like the little boy in *The Sixth Sense* who can see dead people, except that we can see dead punctuation. Whisper it in petrified little-boy tones: dead punctuation is invisible to everyone else – yet we see it all the time.

GLOSSARY

The Sixth Sense: a film in which the main character can see ghosts

2. The Case Against Rules

A.A. Gill

A.A. Gill was a celebrated social commentator for *The Sunday Times*. He also had a learning difficulty. Gill wrote, 'I am a dyslexic. A dyslexic who writes a lot – 1,500 words, give or take, a day . . . The spellchecker would say 1,000 are spelt wrongly. I am a grammar cripple, a functioning illiterate. Literally.' Gill's learning difficulty was so challenging that he had to dictate his articles to his secretary.

In the following extract, Gill describes visiting a school for children with learning difficulties.

I stood in front of this sea of blameless little faces, knowing that behind each of them there was already a room full of low esteem, full of catalogues of failure, a great weight of parental concern, and I wondered again at the horrible obstacle course we make of other people's childhoods.

And I caught sight of one student, and I felt the anger, the hot fury for the wasted, tearful, silently worried, failed years of school, and I had a Spartacus moment. I started talking, rather too loudly. I told them this was their language, this English, this most marvellous and expressive cloak of meaning and imagination. This great, exclamatory, illuminating song, it belonged to anyone who found it in their mouths. There was no wrong way to say it, or write it, the language couldn't be compelled or herded, it couldn't be tonsured or pruned, pollarded or plaited, it was as hard as oaths and as subtle as rhyme. It couldn't be forced or bullied or policed by academics; it wasn't owned by those with flat accents; nobody had the right to tell them how to use it or what to say. There are no rules and nobody speaks incorrectly, because there is no correctly: no high court of syntax. And while everyone can speak with the language, nobody speaks for the language. Not grammars, not dictionaries. They just run along behind, picking up discarded usages. This English doesn't belong to examiners or teachers. All of you already own the greatest gift, the highest degree this country can bestow. It's on the tip of your tongue.

And then I caught sight of myself, standing like a declamatory tick-tack man, bellowing like a costermonger, and I stopped and stared at the faces staring at me with expressions of utter incomprehension. From the back of the room, a teacher coughed.

GLOSSARY

Spartacus moment: a reference to the film Spartacus in which a group of slaves defies a powerful Roman general by each individually shouting 'I am Spartacus'

exclamatory: expressing protest or outcry

tonsured: shaved bare

pollarded: cut short / trimmed back. 'Pollard' usually refers to a tree stump or cut animal's horns

declamatory: using expressive or emotional language to protest

tick-tack man: a man that traditionally wore white gloves to communicate betting odds using hand signs

costermonger: a person who sells fruit and vegetables from a stall and often calls out to the crowd

Reading for Meaning

1. Outline Lynne Truss's argument regarding punctuation.
2. Outline A.A. Gill's view.
3. Do you find Truss's extract to be humorous? Why / why not?
4. Do you agree that A.A. Gill's language is rich and emotional? Explain your viewpoint.
5. Gill argues that for language there is 'no wrong way to say it, or write it' whereas Truss despairs about living in a world with 'plummeting punctuation standards'. Who do you agree with? Explain your answer.

Writer's Workshop

Debate Speech: Write a speech which supports or opposes the following motion:
'In the modern world it is more important than ever to maintain standards of spelling, punctuation and grammar.'

3. I Won't Hire People Who Use Poor Grammar. Here's Why.

Kyle Wiens

The following blog is adapted from the Harvard Business Review. It was written by Kyle Wiens, who is CEO of the largest online repair company, iFixit, and founder of Dozuki, a software company that helps manufacturers write and publish manuals.

Harvard Business Review

If you think an apostrophe was one of the twelve disciples of Jesus, you will never work for me. If you think a semicolon is a regular colon with an identity crisis, I will not hire you. If you scatter commas into a sentence with all the discrimination of a shotgun, you might make it to the foyer before we politely escort you from the building.

Some might call my approach to grammar extreme, but I prefer Lynne Truss's more cuddly phraseology: I am a grammar 'stickler'. And, like Truss – author of *Eats, Shoots & Leaves* – I have a 'zero tolerance approach' to grammar mistakes that make people look stupid.

Now, Truss and I disagree on what it means to have 'zero tolerance'. She thinks that people who mix up their itses 'deserve to be struck by lightning, hacked up on the spot and buried in an unmarked grave', while I just think they deserve to be passed over for a job – even if they are otherwise qualified for the position.

Everyone who applies for a position at either of my companies, iFixit or Dozuki, takes a mandatory grammar test. Extenuating circumstances aside (dyslexia, English language learners, etc.), if job hopefuls can't distinguish between 'to' and 'too', their applications go into the bin.

Of course, we write for a living. iFixit.com is the world's largest online repair manual, and Dozuki helps companies write their own technical documentation, like paperless work instructions and step-by-step user manuals. So, it makes sense that we've made a pre-emptive strike against groan-worthy grammar errors.

But grammar is relevant for all companies. Yes, language is constantly changing, but that doesn't make grammar unimportant. Good grammar is credibility, especially on the internet. In blog posts, on Facebook statuses, in e-mails and on company websites, your words are all you have. They are a projection of you in your physical absence. And, for better or worse, people judge you if you can't tell the difference between their, there and they're.

Good grammar makes good business sense – and not just when it comes to hiring writers. Writing isn't in the official job description of most people in our office. Still, we give our grammar test to everybody, including our salespeople, our operations staff, and our programmers.

On the face of it, my zero-tolerance approach to grammar errors might seem a little unfair. After all, grammar has nothing to do with job performance, or creativity, or intelligence, right?

Wrong. If it takes someone more than twenty years to notice how to properly use 'it's' then that's not a learning curve I'm comfortable with. So, even in this hyper-competitive market, I will pass on a great programmer who cannot write.

Grammar signifies more than just a person's ability to remember high school English. I've found that people who make fewer mistakes on a grammar test also make fewer mistakes when they are doing something completely unrelated to writing – like stocking shelves or labelling parts.

I hire people who care about details. Applicants who don't think writing is important are likely to think lots of other (important) things also aren't important. And I guarantee that even if other companies aren't issuing grammar tests, they pay attention to sloppy mistakes on résumés. After all, sloppy is as sloppy does.

That's why I grammar test people who walk in the door looking for a job. Grammar is my litmus test. All applicants say they're detail-oriented; I just make my employees prove it.

GLOSSARY
mandatory: compulsory
extenuating: excusing
résumé: a curriculum vitae (CV)
litmus test: a simple and accurate test

Reading for Meaning

1. Is Kyle Wiens successful in grabbing the reader's attention in the opening paragraph? Explain your answer.
2. (a) Why are grammar and punctuation important to Kyle Wiens?
   (b) Do you think he is justified in his position? Explain your answer
   (c) Do you think that all businesses should make job applicants take a grammar and punctuation test? Explain your answer

Writer's Workshop

Letter: Write a letter to Kyle Wiens in which you respond to the ideas expressed in this blog. Turn back to Chapter 3 for advice and examples of letter writing.

CAPITAL LETTERS AND COMMAS

Capital Letters

Capital letters should be used:

To begin a sentence

<u>W</u>hen the concert ended, the crowd roared in approval.

For proper nouns

Proper nouns refer to a specific person, place or thing: <u>E</u>mma, <u>C</u>ork, <u>S</u>ony. All proper nouns are given a capital letter. Proper nouns include:

- People's names: Una, Daniel, Doctor Murphy
- Days of the week: Monday, Wednesday, Saturday
- Months and holidays: June, October, Christmas, Easter (seasons are not given capital letters: spring, summer, autumn, winter)
- Place names: Galway, Australia, New York, Athenry
- Brands: Sony, Apple, Pepsi, Adidas
- Adjectives formed from proper nouns are also capitalised: Irish, American, Spanish

For initials

For many years, <u>A.J.</u> O'Neill had worked in counterintelligence for the <u>C.I.A.</u>

For all the main words of titles of books, films, songs, etc.

'<u>T</u>he <u>O</u>ld <u>M</u>an and the <u>S</u>ea', '<u>H</u>arry <u>P</u>otter and the <u>D</u>eathly <u>H</u>allows'

For the first word of direct speech

The farmer roared, '<u>G</u>et off my property!'

For 'I' as the first person singular

That was the first time since the storm that <u>I</u> had seen the ruined house.

Practising capital letters

Rewrite the following passage, inserting capital letters in the correct places.

i remember that christmas like it was yesterday, particularly the cold weather: the way my breath seemed to freeze instantly in the air. the biting wind seemed as if it could cut through my eleven-year-old bones and my mother insisted on wrapping me in layers of clothing before i could even consider leaving the house. that was also the winter when i learnt the true meaning of fear, the winter when i first met master khan.

master khan was an illusionist. i was never sure where he was from. i suspected china but if somebody had told me korea, america or alaska, i wouldn't have been the least bit surprised. he seemed to exude a kind of worldliness, the sense that he was from another place or another time.

the first time i saw him, master khan's eyes seemed to bore into my soul, like he was looking at me, through me and inside me, all at the same time. i'd bumped into him on station road, quite by accident, just outside the local burger king. having just read dickens's oliver twist, i was reminded of the character of fagin.

'come here boy,' he said as one of his long, bony fingers beckoned me to approach. he grinned at me like some kind of devil. his stern voice made me feel like an iceberg had eclipsed the sun, blocking out the meagre winter light. as he did his best impression of a smile, his lips seemed to peel back from his mouth revealing a frightening set of pointed yellow teeth. he spoke in a low, threatening voice, 'do you want me to ask you again boy?'

Commas

Commas are used:

- **To separate items in a list**
  He bought flour, eggs, milk, butter and a lemon.

- **To divide up sentences, making them easier to understand**
  The stuntman, despite the fact he was injured, still decided to jump from the burning building.

- **To break up large numbers**
  Lucy had just won €740,000 in the lottery.

- **When opening and closing letters**
  Dear Frank, . . . Yours sincerely, Eva

- **In direct speech**
  'Let's get out of here,' whimpered the terrified mouse.

Practising capital letters and commas

Rewrite the following passage, inserting capital letters, commas and full stops in the correct places. Remember that full stops are placed at the end of a sentence.

the kitchen was squalid dark and hidden from the view of the street by thick black curtains tony stared around him and felt the cold creep into his bones the only source of light or heat was a sputtering candle that appeared dangerously close to being blown out by a cold draught panic rose up in his throat as he realised he was locked in

feeling tired and hungry tony resigned himself to sitting on the stone tiles as he was thirsty he fished out the half empty bottle of pepsi from his bag the sugar seemed to sharpen his senses and gave him the energy to search the room for something to help him escape after rifling through the grimy drawers and cabinets he placed his acquisitions on the table: a bread knife a can opener the flex from a kettle and a box of matches it didn't seem promising

above him he could hear the floorboards creak as his captors paced around upstairs 'how long will they keep me here?' he whispered aloud suddenly as if in response a key turned sharply in the lock behind him

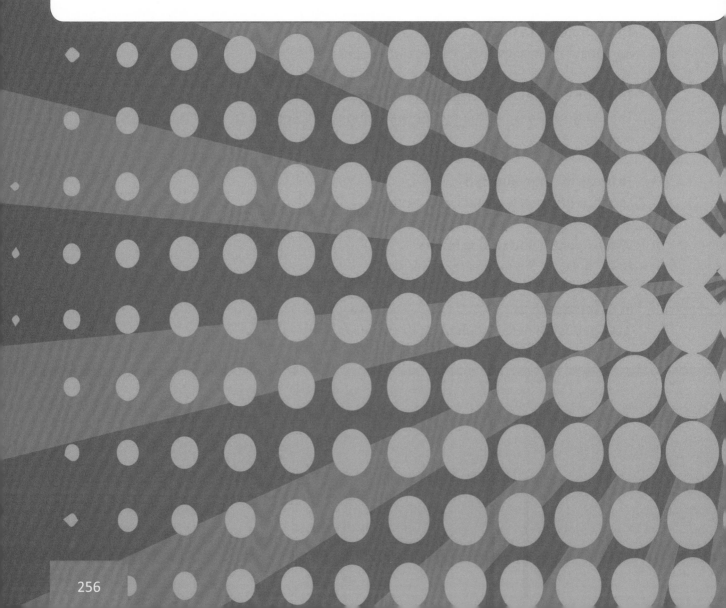

EXCLAMATION MARKS AND QUESTION MARKS

Exclamation Marks

The exclamation mark is used to show strong emotions such as surprise, anger or excitement. It also indicates loudness. For example:

I can't believe it!	→	Surprise
Bang! The gun exploded in the alleyway.	→	Loudness
'Help! Somebody help me!' shouted the frantic child.	→	Urgency
That's it! I can't take this anymore!	→	Anger

Overuse of the exclamation mark takes away its power and meaning, therefore it should be used sparingly. As the writer F. Scott Fitzgerald commented: 'Cut out all those exclamation points. An exclamation point is like laughing at your own jokes.' One exclamation mark is enough. Avoid doing the following:

The boy shouted, 'Wow!!! What an incredible car!!! I have to get one!!!!!!'

Question Marks

A question mark is placed at the end of a question.

Direct speech

Both exclamation marks and question marks are placed inside inverted commas in direct speech:

'Stop!' shouted the man.
'How much does it cost?' asked the woman.

Practising exclamation marks and question marks

Rewrite the sentences below using exclamation marks and question marks. For some of these sentences, either punctuation mark will fit. Remove commas and full stops where necessary.

1. 'Would you like a cup of tea,' the woman gently enquired.
2. 'The lotto. I just won €5,000,000 in the lotto,' shrieked the man.
3. 'If I ever see your face around here again, you're dead. Do you hear me. Dead.'
4. 'Where have you been,' the irritated boss snapped.
5. How many soldiers have the enemy sent.
6. 'Now. Push the eject button now. This plane is going down.'
7. That's incredible.
8. 'Is everyone alright down there,' the rescue worker shouted.
9. Crash. The entire building collapsed in a cloud of dust.
10. 'I can't believe it. You won. That's fantastic. '

HOMOPHONES

Homophones

Homophones are words that sound similar but have very different meanings. The following ten homophones commonly cause confusion.

- We're / Were
  We're = we are.
  Were is the past tense of **are**.

- Ensure / Insure
  Ensure means to make sure.
  Insure is what an insurance company does.

- Who's / Whose
  Who's = who is.
  Whose is concerned with ownership: Whose football is this?

- Threw / Through
  Threw is the past tense of **throw**. It is a verb.
  Through is used in every other case.

- Weather / Whether
  Weather refers to the climate: raining, windy, humid, etc.
  Whether is used to indicate alternatives: Do you know whether or not he is coming?

- Past / Passed
  Passed is the past tense of **pass**.
  Past refers to a period of time that has already happened.

- Principal / Principle
  Principal is an adjective meaning the most important or main person, as in a school principal.
  Principle is a noun meaning law, rule or standard: He was an idealistic person with unshakable principles.

- Their / They're / There
  Their is used to indicate possession: their house.
  They're = they are.
  There is used to indicate a place or is used with the verb to be: The house is over there. There are too many people in this car.

- Too / To
  Too means also or excessively: Can I come too? The cake was far too sweet.
  To is used in all other cases.

- Your / You're
  Your indicates possession: 'Say goodbye to your gold,' smiled the pirate.
  You're = you are

- Practise / Practice
  Practice is a noun: We have to go to band practice tomorrow.
  Practise is a verb: We practise with our band every week.
  To help you remember the difference, think of adv<u>ic</u>e (noun) and adv<u>is</u>e (verb)

Practising homophones

Rewrite the following sentences inserting the correct homophones.

1. '_____ lost,' complained the irritable husband. (We're/Were)
2. 'Please _____ you keep your heads inside the windows,' ordered the bus driver. (Ensure/Insure)
3. He was the kind of man _____ eyes were bigger than his stomach. (Who's/Whose)
4. The child _____ the rock with incredible force _____ the double-glazed window. (Threw/Through)
5. The _____ forecast was unclear. The fishermen were uncertain _____ to go out to sea or not. (Weather/Whether)
6. The mother hoped that her son had _____ his exams. He hadn't been hugely successful in the _____. (Past/Passed)
7. The student's parents explained to the _____ why their son would not be returning to school. (Principal/Principle)
8. Their _____ reason for emigrating was the country's high unemployment rate. (Principal/Principle)
9. _____ car broke down just over _____. I think _____ going to walk. (Their/They're/There)
10. I'm driving _____ Galway today; you can come _____ if you like. (To/Too)
11. Ciara, the classroom is no place for Rover. Will you please bring _____ dog back to _____ house or _____ going to be expelled from this school. (Your/You're)
12. The show was the next day; Robert really needed to _____ his dance routine. (Practice/Practise)

INVERTED COMMAS

Inverted Commas

Inverted commas are also called quotation marks. They are used:

- in direct speech
- for quotations
- for titles of poems, articles etc.
- to emphasise a word

Inverted commas may be single: 'Good morning' or double: "Good morning". Both styles are acceptable, but you must remain consistent.

Direct speech

When a character speaks out loud, inverted commas are placed around the words spoken. This separates the character's words from the narrator's. For example: 'You had better give me that back,' he threatened, 'I won't tell you again.'

Punctuation such as question marks, exclamation marks, commas and full stops are placed inside the inverted commas: 'Is anybody there?' asked the terrified man.

If more than one person is speaking, a new line is started for each speaker.
'Did you do your homework?' asked Rachael.
'Of course I did,' replied Sarah. 'Didn't you?'

Quotations

When quoting somebody, you should use inverted commas to indicate that the words are not your own. For example:

Homer Simpson reminds the audience of his stupidity when he tells Lisa, 'Vampires are make-believe, like elves, gremlins and Eskimos.'

Single inverted commas have been used in the example above. For a quote within a quote, double inverted commas should be used:

'Dad said, "Vampires are make-believe,"' recalled Lisa.

Titles

To avoid confusion, you should place titles inside inverted commas. The following examples show how inverted commas can change the meaning of a sentence. The first example is about the play 'Hamlet', the second is about the character of Hamlet.

'Hamlet' radically changed my outlook on life.
Hamlet radically changed my outlook on life.

When typing, titles of books and films may be italicised or underlined instead of using inverted commas: *Hamlet, The Great Gatsby, Game of Thrones*

Emphasis

Look at how inverted commas change the meaning of the following sentence:
She served me her food with a grin.
She served me her 'food' with a grin.

Most people would rather eat the food in the first example. The inverted commas radically change the meaning of the sentence.

Look at the following sentence:
The teacher shared his wisdom about life with the class.
The teacher shared his 'wisdom' about life with the class.

Most people would rather not listen to the teacher in the second example.

Practising inverted commas

Rewrite the following sentences using inverted commas.

1. Where do the inverted commas go? asked the student.
2. We're over here! shouted the stranded climbers.
3. My favourite book of all time has to be Oliver Twist.
4. Stop that man, the hysterical woman shrieked, he's stolen my purse!
5. Albert Einstein celebrated innovative thinkers when he said, Anyone who has never made a mistake has never tried anything new.
6. Children really brighten a home, stated the father. They never turn the lights off.
7. It was Pádraig Pearse who proclaimed, Ireland unfree shall never be at peace.
8. Although released a few years ago, Game of Thrones has remained thrilling to watch.
9. As Marie Antoinette was led to the guillotine, her last words were: Pardon me, sir. I did not do it on purpose. She had accidently stepped on the executioner's foot.
10. I went to a bookstore and asked the saleswoman, Where's the self-help section? She replied, If I tell you, that would defeat the purpose. (George Carlin)

COLONS AND SEMICOLONS

Colons

Like commas and full stops, colons encourage the reader to pause. They are also used to introduce the next part of a sentence.

Colons are used to:

- **Announce the next part of a sentence**
  This much was obvious: the woman was completely insane.

- **Introduce a list**
  He loved only three things in this world: his wife, his child and when they both went out for the day.

- **Introduce a quote**
  As Dylan Thomas writes: 'Old age should burn and rave at close of day.'

- **Introduce an explanation, definition or a qualification.**
  Space: the final frontier.
  Z: the last letter in the alphabet.

- **Divide a main title from a subtitle**
  Barking Mad: Man Imitates Dog During Court Case

- **Separate characters' names from dialogue in a drama script.**
  MACBETH: Is this a dagger which I see before me...?

Practising colons

Rewrite these sentences inserting colons in the correct places.

1. Despite her bad temper and ill patience, she had one good quality her generosity.
2. Oscar Wilde's dying words still amuse today 'Either that wallpaper goes, or I do.'
3. Capricorn the sign of the goat.
4. Poetry A Packsack of Invisible Keepsakes
5. Juliet O Romeo, Romeo, Wherefore art thou Romeo?
6. There are four things one should never forget when going to the airport passport, tickets, money and more money.
7. His reason for robbing the bank was quite straightforward he wanted the money.
8. Have some sympathy for the most commonly misused and abused punctuation marks colons, semicolons, apostrophes and exclamations marks.

Semicolons

Like colons, semicolons indicate a pause in a sentence. Semicolons can often be replaced by a full stop or a comma. However, semicolons can help to make a piece of writing clearer and avoid confusion.

Semicolons are used:

- **Instead of a full stop.** This occurs when two sentences are closely related.

  I remember when he used to eat six hamburgers a day; now he's running marathons and drinking smoothies.

  Here a full stop could be used instead of a semicolon:

  I remember when he used to eat six hamburgers a day. Now he's running marathons and drinking smoothies.

  However, because the two ideas are closely related, a semicolon works better.
  In the following examples, we can see how the relationship between two ideas is stronger using a semicolon rather than a full stop.

  I told my boss I was quitting. I hope he knows I was joking.
  I told my boss I was quitting; I hope he knows I was joking.

- **To separate phrases in a list.** When writing lists, semicolons sometimes prove more useful than commas. Look at how the following list is confusing without semicolons.

  He tried to contact his girlfriend in every possible way: on Twitter, the microblogging site, by messaging her on Snapchat, by texting her, using his new iPhone, by calling her landline, and even (shock horror) by visiting her home. After a week, he started to get the feeling that she was avoiding him.

  The meaning becomes much clearer when semicolons are introduced:

  He tried to contact his girlfriend in every possible way: on Twitter, the microblogging site; by messaging her on Snapchat; by texting her, using his new iPhone; by calling her landline; and even (shock horror) by visiting her home. After a week, he started to get the feeling that she was avoiding him.

Practising semicolons

1. Join these pairs of sentences together by replacing the full stops with semicolons.
   (a) She had tried bungy jumping, skydiving and white-water rafting. Now she was planning to take up base jumping.
   (b) Emma didn't want to be parted from the new puppy. That night the dog slept at the foot of the little girl's bed.
   (c) The roof had collapsed in the storm. The plaster on the walls was swollen with rain water, and ducks quacked in the living room.
2. Rewrite this sentence, replacing commas with semicolons to clarify the meaning.

   They had toured the world: Japan, where they got food poisoning, New York, where they were mugged, Bali, where they ran out of money, and even found themselves in Dublin, where it rained the entire time.

APOSTROPHES

Apostrophes

Apostrophes are used in two instances: to replace missing letters and to indicate possession.

Missing letters

Some words are formed by joining two words together and replacing the omitted letters with an apostrophe.

For example: could + not = couldn't. In this example the apostrophe has taken the place of the missing o.

It + is = It's. Here, the apostrophe has replaced the missing i.

Possession

Apostrophes are also used to show possession. A misplaced apostrophe can radically change the meaning of the sentence. Look at the following example:

The cakes over there are my sister's.   The cakes belong to my sister.

The cakes over there are my sisters'.   The cakes belong to several of my sisters.

The cakes over there are my sisters.   The cakes are my sisters.

Putting the apostrophe in the wrong place here could leave this family fighting over the cakes; leaving it out may raise some eyebrows!

Singular possession

When the noun is singular (one owner) add 's to indicate possession:
Brian's computer, the woman's child, the bird's beak.

Plural possession

For plural nouns ending in s, add an apostrophe after the s:
The ladies' meeting, the boys' school, the cats' meals, the witches' brooms

If the plural form of the noun does not end in s, add 's:
The children's father, the men's wages, the women's club

Names ending in s

For modern names ending in s, add 's:
James's bicycle, Mr Jones's house, Agnes's best friend

For classical names ending in s, just add an apostrophe:
Socrates' pupil, Pythagoras' theorem

Its / It's

It's means **it is**. The apostrophe has replaced the missing i.
Its indicates possession. For example: The cat licked its fur.

Double possession

When more than one person owns something, the last person's name is given the apostrophe. If both names are given apostrophes, this indicates separate objects.

Jack and Jill's hill	→ The hill of Jack and Jill
Noah and Barry's contracts	→ The shared contracts of Noah and Barry
Noah's and Barry's contracts	→ The separate contracts of Noah and Barry

Practising apostrophes

1. **Missing letters**

   Use apostrophes to form new words from the following:

   (a) do + not =

   (b) should + not =

   (c) I + am =

   (d) could + have =

   (e) is + not =

   (f) you + are =

   (g) they + will =

   (h) she + is =

2. **Its / It's**

   Rewrite the following sentences using its or it's.

   (a) The dog dropped _____ bone.

   (b) _____ been too long since we last saw you.

   (c) Cuba is in the Caribbean; _____ capital is Havana.

   (d) '_____ just around the corner,' said the man, 'but _____ closed for renovations.'

   (e) The birdwatcher stared as the eagle gripped _____ prey in _____ claws. 'Looks like _____ lunchtime,' said the birdwatcher darkly.

3. Rewrite the following passage adding an apostrophe or 's where appropriate.

   The childrens toys littered the floor. Douglas picked his way through the mess and flopped onto the couch. He heard the boys shouting outside. 'I dont want to deal with this now,' he thought, 'I just cant.' The boys shouts got louder and Douglas conscience forced him up from the couchs soft comfort. 'I couldnt even get a moments peace could I?' he thought to himself.

   'Whats going on out here?' he yelled as he swung open the backdoor. The suns bright rays blinded him momentarily but his eyes soon adjusted to the light. 'Where are you guys?' he shouted, sounding a little less angry as he couldnt see his boys anywhere. 'Lads? Michael? John? Are you out here?'

   Douglas ears picked up a whimpering from the bushes. He rushed to the sounds source. On the ground he found Michael with tears in his eyes; blood dripped from a cut on his leg. 'He pushed me, Dad. John pushed me.'

Douglas youngest son, John, stood close by. Johns eyes shone with a fierce determination. 'Thats what you get when you dont share.'

On the ground Michael and Johns go-kart lay smashed against the foot of the tree. Two of its wheels were strewn on the grass. 'Thats what you get,' John repeated, 'when you dont share.' Douglas stared at his youngest son in disbelief.

Notes

Notes

Notes

Notes

Notes

Notes